Praise for *Brand Bewitchery*

"A must-read for everyone in communications, marketing, or sales, *Brand Bewitchery* will completely change the way you think about your story and how to tell it."
—**Jay Baer**, founder of Convince & Convert and co-author of *Talk Triggers*

"*Brand Bewitchery* is an enchanting tried and true magical learning adventure for anyone daring to uncover Park Howell's spellbinding universe of story learning, story crafting, and storytelling. A levitation charm for any organization and leader seeking to elevate their brand, Howell's brilliant Story Cycle sorcery will have you smiling, engaged, and unbinding the true business of story for ultimate success."
—**Miri Rodriguez**, storyteller and global head of internships at Microsoft

"The story about your business IS your business. Park's book is a must read for people who want to use the power of story to design and dominate their own market category."
—**Christopher Lochhead**, #1 Apple podcaster, #1 Amazon author

"This is the most important guide to marketing of our times. Park's Story Cycle ensured that Airloom Supplement was able to forge a meaningful connection with customers while building an authentic brand that upheld our true values."
—**Avni and Dr. Shyam Shridharani**, creators of Airloom® Supplement

"Park Howell is a gifted storyteller AND is host of the best podcast for story in the business world, BUT he knows you need to dig deeper and understand the bewitchery of story itself, THEREFORE he has written this excellent book that will enable you to start drawing on the true power of story for all your communications."
—**Randy Olson**, scientist-turned-filmmaker, author of *Houston, We Have A Narrative*, and Harvard PhD

"I love the guidebook approach for *Brand Bewitchery*. Each of the Story Cycle System's 10 steps is explained in a manner allowing you to craft and communicate your brand's compelling story. We just sold our business, and I can tell you first hand your story and

storytelling is critically important to grow your business and add value. Park helped me lay this framework for our business a few years ago. We determined what made us unique and wrapped our story around it. Implement these steps and it will change your business — for the better."
— **Arnie Kuenn**, founder and CEO of Vertical Measures (retired)

"Recruiting young executives who understand their personal brand story ensures a significantly higher success in the recruiting process. I recommend *Brand Bewitchery* as a must-read for career-focused young executives."
— **Bill Franquemont**, partner, DHR International

"Park Howell was tending the flames of business storytelling long before most self-proclaimed experts were looking for a match. His *Business of Story* podcast continues to advance our craft by fueling those flames. If business stories are kindling, it only takes one Park to start a great fire."
— **Ron Ploof**, StoryHow.com

"I have had the pleasure of watching from near and far Park's journey. His up and downs and most of the times trying to find the humor in this crazy mixed-up world. We have collaborated, we have dreamed, but all in all what I admire the most is his life lesson coming out in print for all to see. It is never easy to expose your soul, but I see there are many aspects of this book when used will make a huge difference. Park has a wonderful way of writing that makes you feel you are just out for a stroll and shooting the breeze. It's an easy read, smooth swing right down the middle."
— **Mike Martin**, vice president of Brokk Inc and host of the *Brokkology* podcast

"Park's counsel is real, relevant, and immediately applicable. If you want to unlock your true potential, this is the read for you."
— **Jennifer Russo**, director of corporate communications, Banner Health

"*Brand Bewitchery* unlocks the magic of storytelling to craft a potent brand brew. With Park as your guide, you are learning from one of the best, and his wit, humor, and great stories make it a page-turner. I'll be sure to have it at arm's reach in my office."
— **Shawn Callahan**, founder, Anecdote International

The Story Cycle System helped us craft our brand story so clearly that it has become the bible for everything we do at Pret Auto Partez. There is gold in these pages! Plus a lot of fun stories that illustrate the impact of this powerful brand-story-crafting process. Read it and see if your story is all it could be."
— **Andre Martin-Hobbs**, founder, Pret Auto Partez

"For those of us challenged with articulating a brand narrative in order to advance our mission, Park Howell makes it intuitive and helps you gain some discipline by guiding you through his Story Cycle System. The case scenarios are relatable giving you the confidence to draw parallels, ample workbook space to delve deep into key questions, and the benefit of a personalized playbook before you go live with your own Business of Story."
— **Avein Saaty-Tafoya**, healthcare growth professional

"If you want to confidently share your personal brand story to grow your influence and your career, read this book. Thank you so much, Park, for helping me capture my story, own it, and most importantly, to be comfortable sharing my story in the right way."
— **Anjella Crowe**, director of partner management, Silverline

"As a business development consultant I know the power of story-telling for new business. I've found Park Howell's new book, *Brand Bewitchery*, to be a great resource. It provides an easy system to help craft your story that will differentiate your brand from your competitors and create an emotional appeal with your audience that leads to action. This is an interactive workbook that equips you through specific step-by-step instructions. It is filled with personal examples and case studies from Park's extensive research and years of experience. He is a story telling mastermind. I've been enriched by the content and I know you will be as well."
— **Michael Gass**, founder, Fuel Lines

"I advise clients on how to effectively solve complex social problems. But inspiring others to take action is even tougher. Without stories it's impossible. Park Howell's guidance in *Brand Bewitchery* empowers social change agents to build trust, connect with their audiences and literally change the world. I know, because it's worked for me."
— **Russell Goldstein**,CFP®,CAP®,CSRIC™, BoardSource Certified Governance Trainer, Bank of America

Brand Bewitchery

How to Wield the Story Cycle System™ to Craft Spellbinding Stories for Your Brand

Park Howell

HAPPY H
PRESS

Phoenix

To Michele, Corbin, Parker, and Caedon, whose creativity, wit and wisdom have inspired my storytelling.

Contents

Preface

In March 2019, I sniffed into an old claustrophobic bookstore in Queenscliff, Australia, like a mouse searching for cheese. You know how people sometimes look like their dogs? Well, Pete, the proprietor, resembled his store: rather disheveled, with a somewhat bedeviling manner of answering my questions with questions that coaxed me in deeper. You got the sense he was daring you to judge him by his cover, which apparently I was.

The labyrinth of For Pete's Sake bookshop on Hesse Street feels like the clogged arteries of a chain reader. And I swear that the nine-foot musty walls of sagging bookshelves and piles of tomes were going to cave in on me at any moment. But there they had stood, for what appears decades: a swollen fruit cellar of stories preserved in time, radiating an alluring energy, quaking with inquisitiveness.

"Where do you find all these books?" I asked Pete.

"Oh, I don't find them, they find me."

THE ATTRACTION OF STORY

Stories have a way of summoning forces, especially the stories we tell ourselves. Perhaps, as a leader of a purpose-driven brand, you have created one or several of the following personal narratives? And could that explain why this book has attracted you?

"We're growing, but we're not differentiated from our competition—and that scares the hell out of me."

"We're adding lots of team members, but we can't get them all pulling in the same direction for lack of a story they can buy into and align with."

"I was so embarrassed the other day when an investor asked me what our story was, and I had to tell him I didn't have one."

"I want my lifestyle business to have a greater impact in the world, but I need to find a way to stand out."

"I've had a successful career, but now I want to make it significant by developing my personal/professional brand story."

One thing is certain: Life is chaotic. Storytelling is the remedy that we seek to create meaning out of the madness of being alive. I have found, as you will too, that when you craft and tell your compelling brand story you will increase your influence as a leader, grow your organization and your people, and evolve a successful career into a significant one. But you have to understand the magic to cast the spell. That's what drives me to share with you what I've learned about the applied science and bewitchery of storytelling.

It has taken me nearly a decade to write, edit, test, toss, capture, and share the proven Story Cycle System™ in this guidebook,* and I can promise you one thing: It *works*. I will show you how this 10-step brand story strategy framework provides the solution and way forward to any and all of the personal narratives above that you may be telling yourself, as well as any others I didn't list. I don't call it a "proven" system for no reason; this book is chock-full of case studies that demonstrate in detail how others have successfully activated the Story Cycle System. And you'll be able to do the same. Plus, as a useful bonus, when you apply each of the 10 steps of the Story Cycle System you will develop your storytelling skills and grow as a confident and compelling communicator. You will not only dial in your brand story, but you will grow from an intuitive to a masterful and intentional storyteller.

MY 100 PERCENT HAPPINESS GUARANTEE

I guarantee that the Story Cycle System will clarify your brand story, amplify your impact, and simplify your life. If it doesn't deliver, you can keep this how-to book *and* I'll refund all your money. How can I make this 100 percent happiness guarantee? Because time and time again I've witnessed the game-changing, life-altering,

---

*If you want all the gory details about how the Story Cycle System came to be, feel free to jump to Appendix Two: My Origin Story.

world-improving impact of the right story told on purpose. I've witnessed it with companies and their brands, and I've seen it with individuals who sought to develop a compelling, "high-resolution" personal story to share with the world. My aim is to do exactly that for you.

This is not so much a storytelling guide as it is an instruction manual on how to realize the influence and impact that is pent up within your brand, just waiting to be released through the stories you conjure. You will use these storytelling spells to become a formidable leader who can nudge the world in any direction you choose — so choose wisely.

Plus, this book is designed to reignite within you the one true superpower we all possess — storytelling — by teaching you captivating narrative frameworks to enchant your audiences. Soon, you'll find that storytelling is your most valuable and yet underutilized business asset. You'll realize a whole new competitive edge to dramatically increase revenues, summon the focused forces of your team, and excel through the stories you tell.

So, I'm curious: Did you find this book, or did it find you?

How to Wield
This Guidebook

"You have to understand the magic to cast the spell.

— Me

There's magic in these pages. But nobody seems to like to read anymore, except for you. Welcome. I've written this quick introduction to help you navigate this guidebook at your preferred pace and in your preferred order. But I'll warn you, every shortcut I've ever taken in business has just led me to disaster faster — and I imagine you know just what I'm talking about.

You see, this is more than a how-to book with information to learn and spaces for you to fill out. It's a communications cookbook, brimming with enchanting stories, crafty anecdotes, and potent storytelling exercises to get your brand story straight as you personally grow as a storyteller. I will take you by the hand and together we'll work to elevate the humanity within your personal, professional, and organizational brand story. And this I promise: My one goal for you, following an industrious 15 years of exploring, activating, and coaching the applied science and bewitchery of storytelling, is to help you excel through the stories you tell.

You will learn how to clarify your brand story using the proven Story Cycle System. You will amplify your impact as you grow as a storyteller using the three proven and time-tested narrative frameworks found in these pages that will make your communications not only compelling, but irresistible. Your focused story will also help you simplify your life. Because when you are on the journey to your true North, you will learn to say yes to those things that honor your story. But more important, you'll have the courage to say no to those seemingly friendly forces that are out to intentionally or inadvertently thwart your progress.

But, you must first understand the magic to cast the spell. This is where you begin.

THERE ARE A FEW WAYS FOR YOU TO NAVIGATE THIS GUIDEBOOK

If, like me, you have the attention span of a first-grader and the untamed urgency of a spastic colon, then you don't have to digest this entire book in one sitting. Just leap to the first exercise in Chapter 1 to determine your brand's position in the marketplace. This is your first determined step out of the primordial muck of commoditization, and it provides a taste of what's ahead for you. If you do nothing more than this first exercise, at least you'll be clear on how your brand is positioned — meaning you'll understand what you do differently, and therefore better, than your competitors.

Or are you a skimmer? Do you have a hard time getting through *any* book? Then you might try just completing the first three exercises in Chapters 1 through 3, which will help you to define your backstory, prioritize your heroes (audiences), and determine what's at stake in their life and journey. I dub this Act I of your brand storytelling process.

Each step in the Story Cycle System provides tremendous value and builds on the previous activity and outcome. You'll experi-

CLARIFY YOUR BRAND STORY TO AMPLIFY YOUR IMPACT

How the Story Cycle System creates emotional meaning for your brand to create bewitching engagement and loyalty with your customers.

ence a compounding effect as your brand narrative becomes clear and meaningful. Here, I've even created a graph for you that shows how a well-defined brand story clarifies meaning for your customers, which in turn ensures customer engagement because they now understand what you stand for. It differentiates you in the market, making you more valuable to those who need your product or service. And you don't need me to tell you about how value leads to higher revenue and increased margins. Plus, your completely refined brand story connects with all your audiences on a primal level. It will enhance customer loyalty, generate repeat sales, and encourage word-of-mouth marketing.

So, if you want to be more than just a brand storyteller's apprentice, then I encourage you to explore and apply all 10 steps of the cycle, in order. If you do this, I have no doubt your innate storytelling sorcerer will appear, as it has for me.

If you're the curious type and are intrigued about how the Story Cycle System materialized in the first place, you'd probably enjoy reading its (and my) backstory. I've tucked my origin story into the back of your book as Appendix Two. After writing this appendix, I realized that the Story Cycle System found me more than I discovered it! As you'll learn, stories have a way of summoning mighty forces.

A QUICK OVERVIEW OF YOUR JOURNEY AHEAD WITH THE STORY CYCLE SYSTEM

I think it's important for you to understand the origins of the Story Cycle System so you can appreciate the magic (madness?) behind the method that makes the system work so well.

In 2006, after 25 years in the branding arts realm and a decade running my own agency, Park&Co, I realized that advertising as we knew it had stopped working. While brands used to own the influence of mass media, technology leveled the playing field. The masses had become the media. They took control of our brand stories and now they own them. So I went in search of an answer. I found an anecdote was the antidote. Brands had to become story makers by giving their customers the opportunity to become storytellers.

In his 2012 predictions for the tech industry, pundit Mark Anderson, CEO of Strategic News Service, said, "Steve Jobs didn't really invent anything at all. But he was great at integrating things into a product."

He argued that most of the technology that created the Mac, iPod, NeXT cube, etc. was already available. Jobs was simply able to see things others couldn't in combining disparate technology advancements to create new products. Apple's innovation was not so much a product of invention, but observation and integration.

I've found the same concept of invention-via-integration to work in business communications, too. Specifically with brand storytelling.

When people ask me how the proven Story Cycle System came together, I share these essential ingredients:

> **"The Story Cycle is distilled from the timeless narrative structure of the ancients, inspired by the story artists of Hollywood, influenced by masters of persuasion, guided by trend spotters, and informed by how the human mind grapples for meaning."**

So let's unpack this statement.

DISTILLED FROM THE TIMELESS NARRATIVE STRUCTURE OF THE ANCIENTS

This phrase is the result of my mentorship by Joseph Campbell, America's foremost mythologist. Sure, he had been dead for 20 years before I really got to know his work, but his storytelling legacy lives on today.

Campbell unearthed a primal map of storytelling that he called the monomyth, or Hero's Journey. The Hero's Journey is a 19-step pattern to telling stories that has been around since the beginning of storytelling time. You can find it in the first recorded story of Gilgamesh right up to *The Wizard of Oz* to *Star Wars* to today's Lego movies. Pixar has animated an empire based on using the Hero's Journey framework to tell its stories.

I first learned about the Hero's Journey when our son Parker was studying film at Chapman University in Orange, California. Its universal structure resonated with me immediately, perhaps because it parallels many of the concepts I learned while earning a degree in music composition and theory from Washington State University.

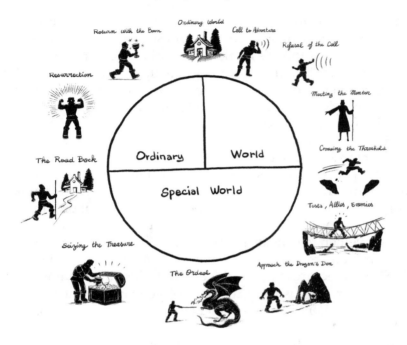

Joseph Campbell's Hero's Journey narrative framework

So when I say the Story Cycle System is distilled from the "timeless narrative structure of the ancients," I'm crediting Campbell's Hero's Journey as the blueprint for our brand story strategy system. His framework is an example of the applied science of storytelling that leads to its bewitchery.

INSPIRED BY THE STORY ARTISTS OF HOLLYWOOD

The Story Cycle System is inspired by the story artists of Hollywood because they use the Hero's Journey every day in innumerable ways to produce the movies we love. Hollywood story consultant Christopher Vogler dissects the Hero's Journey for communicators in his seminal book, *The Writer's Journey*. In it, he outlines how screenwriters and authors can use this universal template to craft their stories.

"The Hero's Journey is not an invention, but an observation. It is a recognition of a beautiful design, a set of principles that govern the conduct of life and the world of storytelling the way physics and chemistry govern the physical world," writes Vogler.

That's when I realized that if the Hero's Journey is to philosophy what physics and chemistry are to the physical world, then I believe the elements of Campbell's monomyth could function as the essential framework for brand story strategy creation and activation. This idea was further underscored for me when Vogler wrote: "Every storyteller bends the mythic pattern to his or her own purpose or the needs of a particular culture."

I decided to bend it to my purpose of creating more authentic and powerful brand narratives.

So I mapped the Hero's Journey to business. I sensed that by using this narrative framework, you could create a more humanized organization that is in better sync with the natural progression of life. I also thought that since the art of storytelling had evolved us from cavemen to consumers, it would help you and me connect with our customers on a more primal, subconscious level. The Story Cycle System requires you, as the brand, to become the mentor to your customer, who is truly the hero of your brand journey. It is indeed your audience and customers who are at the center of your brand story.

I learned yet another permutation of the Hero's Journey, Blake Snyder's 15-beats story structure, in his best-selling book, *Save the Cat*. Snyder was Hollywood's top screenwriter in the 1980s, selling more family-genre scripts than anyone else. You can overlay Snyder's 15 beats onto the Hero's Journey and see the parallels of structure.

While Snyder boiled down Campbell's 19 steps of the Hero's Journey to 15 story beats, and Vogler pared the framework down to 12 elements, I refined the story structure to 10 steps, each specifically mapped to the realities of modern business. The Story Cycle System is the chassis for brand story creation, business communications, and leadership development.

As I built my Story Cycle System, the architectural blueprint for the narrative arc for your brand story, I found two simple but sturdy story structures that function like the support beams and guy-wires of your overarching story. These include the And, But & Therefore foundational narrative framework, which you will learn and use starting in Chapter 4, and the five primal elements of a short story to create big impact, which we'll cover in Chapter 7.

INFLUENCED BY MASTERS OF PERSUASION

While the Story Cycle is distilled from the timeless narrative structure of the ancients and inspired by the story artists of Hollywood, it is also influenced by masters of persuasion. One of my chief influencers is Dr. Robert Cialdini, author of *Influence: The Psychology of Persuasion*. In this book he covers the six principles of persuasion, which I found not only aligned with storytelling but are activated by story. These principles are:

Reciprocity: Give first to get something in return

Commitment: People want to act consistently with their beliefs and values

Social proof: We like to feel validated based on what others are doing

Authority: Building your influence through vulnerability, authenticity, and integrity

Liking: The more you like someone, the more likely you'll be persuaded by them

Scarcity: When something appears to be in short supply, you want it more

I tested Cialdini's six principles of persuasion as my wife, Michele, and I subjected ourselves to a Hawaiian timeshare pitch on the Big Island, just to see how those denizens of sales events used these techniques. The experience was fundamental in my development as a brand storyteller. I marveled as they told story after story to create a connection, build rapport, promote scarcity, and aggressively ask for the sale. (But ours was a discovery session on the elements of persuasion, so we went in with our deflector shields up and, fortunately, left without buying a timeshare!)

GUIDED BY TREND SPOTTERS

There are countless storytelling "gurus" who will *tell* you about the importance of storytelling in your business. But few actually *show* you how to do it.

I've learned that when you teach the Story Cycle System to your clients and their leadership, staff, and salespeople, you will begin to build a powerful storytelling culture that drives performance.

That's why I say the Story Cycle System is guided by trend spotters. When you follow the brands that are either ahead of the trends or creating movements, you'll notice they are built upon status-quo-tipping narratives. You know these brands. They include Nike and its *Just Do It!* narrative; Apple and its *Think Different* slogan; the marvelous brand showman Sir Richard Branson and his Virgin Atlantic. Airbnb. Audi. Patagonia. Lady Gaga. Muhammad Ali. Bud Light.

> **"The most powerful person in the world is the storyteller. The storyteller sets the vision, values, and agenda of an entire generation that is to come."**
> —Steve Jobs

You can learn much from these brands precisely because they have marvelous narrative intuition and have mastered brand storytelling. Look closely at their brand stories, and you will also see elements of Campbell's monomyth permeating everything they do.

INFORMED BY HOW THE HUMAN MIND GRAPPLES FOR MEANING

Finally, I validated my Hero's Journey/Story Cycle System hypothesis using as much brain science as I could wrap my head around. I've studied the work of one of the foremost psychologists, Dr. Daniel Kahneman, Nobel Prize-winning economist and author of *Thinking Fast and Slow*. I've interviewed Dr. Paul Zak, author of *The Moral Molecule*, on how you build trust through storytelling (stories trigger oxytocin in our brain). I've explored the brain science of storytelling with Kendall Haven, author of *Story Smart*, and I've chatted with Lisa Cron, author of *Wired for Story: The Writer's Guide to Brain Science to Hook Readers from the Very First Sentence*.

But I've also witnessed how our brain automatically makes up stories in an attempt to understand obscure and obfuscated messages, which is generally the description of most business PowerPoints. Jonathan Gottschall, in his book *The Storytelling Animal: Why Stories Make Us Human,* introduced me to the Heider Simmel study, which started in 1946. Watch the old black-and-white video at the core of their research on perception and behavior and pay attention to what's going on between your ears. You'll see how your brain automatically fashions a fiction to make sense of meaningless data. It demonstrates that your audience will not get the story you intended unless you intentionally tell them a story.

All told—and you've probably heard this a million times—our *Homo sapiens* brain is hardwired for storytelling. A well-told story is the single most powerful organizing force for our species. Yuval Noah Harari, in his book *Sapiens: A Brief History of Humankind,* details how our ability to tell stories to create imagined realities we call fictions is exactly why we became the most aggressive, invasive species in the universe as we know it. He writes, "Much of history revolves around this question: How does one convince millions of people to believe particular stories about gods, or nations, or limited liability companies? Yet when it succeeds, it gives *sapiens* immense power, because it enables millions of strangers to cooperate and work toward common goals."

Your brand is a fiction, an imagined reality. And it is only through the stories you tell that you will humanize it and bring it to life.

Legendary screenwriting coach Robert McKee told me in his four-day course on story writing, as well as later on my podcast, that stories are what we use to make meaning out of the madness of being human. I heard this same sentiment underscored during the Landmark Forum personal improvement seminar I went through when they repeatedly stated that we are meaning-making machines. From my personal revelation gained in 2015 through Landmark, I have committed myself to helping people live into their most powerful stories.

10 STEPS TO YOUR BRAND STORY AND BECOMING A MORE SUCCESSFUL COMMUNICATOR

I mentioned above that the Story Cycle System consists of 10 steps. The entire rest of this book is devoted to explaining those steps so you can successfully craft and communicate your brand's compelling narrative. But I want to give you a quick overview of the 10 steps so you can get an idea of the road ahead:

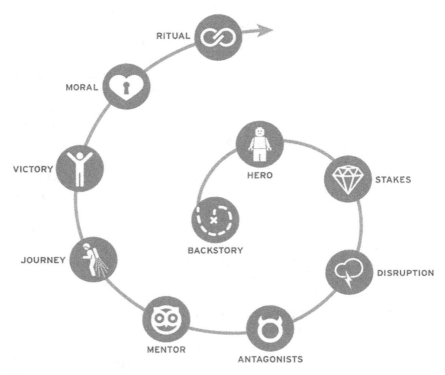

Use the applied science of the proven Story Cycle System™ to craft your bewitching brand narrative, which will reveal compelling stories for you to capture along your journey.

1. In your BACKSTORY you will clarify your brand position statement to differentiate what you functionally do in the market to outperform your competitors.

2. Then you will prioritize your HEROES, the customers and audiences who are the central figures in your brand story and who are instrumental to your organization's success.

3. You will determine what the STAKES are for them: what they wish for and want from you to help them achieve their personal vision of success.

4. You will embrace the DISRUPTION in the marketplace that your brand is responding to, making your offering timelier and relevant as captured in your unique value proposition.

5. But ANTAGONISTS will attempt to thwart your progress. Therefore you need to identify and exploit these obstacles to make your offering all the more irresistible.

6. You, as the MENTOR to your customer's hero, will determine your nine brand descriptors while defining your brand's emotional promise, intrinsic gift, and unique personality — all which sync together to express the human character at the core of your organization.

7. In the JOURNEY you will learn how to use the nine brand descriptors you've created earlier in the Story Cycle System as story themes to attract your ideal customers and invite them into your brand story.

8. And you will set key VICTORY milestones to celebrate customer engagement wins along their journey of brand awareness, adoption, and appreciation.

9. The MORAL of your brand story will be revealed as you declare your brand purpose: why you exist and how you elevate the people you serve to further amplify your impact.

10. Finally, you will strategize the RITUAL use of your product or service to grow your internal people, attract customers, build repeat business, and generate word-of-mouth marketing to scale your story and your organization.

LIVE INTO YOUR MOST POWERFUL STORY

At this point, you may be wondering that if stories are so powerful and effective, why don't we use more storytelling to grow our brands, businesses, and people? Quite simply, it's because our education system and corporate cultures are just beginning to understand the importance of business storytelling but don't know how to incorporate it into our professional lives. We are taught to think and speak from a logical perspective. To try to look smart. Be Logical. Rational. Reasonable.

But try as we might to be those things, emotion wins the day. We buy with our hearts and justify our purchases with our heads. Another of Robert McKee's insightful quips is this: "Our conscious mind is the P.R. department for our subconscious mind, where all the real decisions are being made."

Stories hack through the noise to hook the heart. So let's start building yours.

For added guidance and value, I've included in each chapter case studies demonstrating how the Story Cycle System has helped brands grow by as much as 600 percent. I know, that sounds unreal. But it's true. Plus, I show you how this timeless narrative structure has been instrumental in the creation of both my personal brand and the Business of Story's (my company's) brand. Skip these sections at your own peril, for without this knowledge you will not fully realize your innate storytelling powers.

Finally, since you're truly committed to completing the Story Cycle System for the good of your purpose-driven brand and the people who support you, I challenge you to declare a date when you will finish your journey. Some readers have completed their story in a week or two. But they're unicorns. Plan on four to six weeks for your thoughtful and inspiring exploration. It's worth it beyond your wildest imagination.

I,_____, will complete my Story Cycle System guidebook to clarify my story, amplify my impact, and simplify my life by this date: _____.

Think about it: All protagonists in every epic adventure are whisked along by a looming date with destiny. You have literally just cracked the book on yours.

Story on, my friend!

— Park

1

Backstory

How to Clarify Your Brand Story for Deliberate Growth

"When one has taken root, one puts out branches."

—Jules Verne

CELEBRATE YOUR DIFFERENCES

Take a moment right now and consider your origin story. Where you came from. Where you are now. And where you're headed. This is your backstory, the foundation for everything to come.

You and I came into this world as a commodity until we defined our personalities. As we grew we became known for special abilities that made us different from our siblings and unique to our friends. We became the go-to guy or gal in the schoolyard for our special ability. We learned that the things that make us different are the things that make us stand out. That was our first lesson in branding: It's a survival instinct.

In Campbell's Hero's Journey, we're introduced to the main characters in their ordinary world. This is often where we get their backstory to set the stage for everything to come. I used this plot point as the backstory in the Story Cycle System. This is where you describe what you have built as a product or service offering and how its superiority is defined by its functional uniqueness.

My own personal branding backstory began in the ordinary world of Woodinville, Washington. Our mom and dad, Keith and Pat Howell, got married in 1954. They were 28 and 29 years old respectively, which was kind of late in the getting-married process for their generation. So they wasted no time—cranked out seven kids in nine years. I was number five.

Our dad had one rule for our brood at the dinner table: You had to "keep one foot on the floor." Everything else was free-market

Figure 1.1 Howells pictured from left to right: Dan, Chris, Steve, Park, Tom, Mike and Melody

dining. This was simply a reflection of what he thought about life. "You have to take care of yourself, because no one else will," he coached us. I'm sure this sentiment was a product of his depression-era upbringing in Sheldon, North Dakota.

My mom and dad gave our childhood home, a 12-acre spread in Woodinville, nestled among the rain-slicked evergreens and dewy blackberry vines, a brand name. Fifty years later it is still known as the "Happy H," an enduring brand that represents what they stand for, finding and promoting happiness in the lives of everyone they came to know and love. "Happy" was the North Star that guided everything they did and how they raised us. This sentiment remains at the heart of our ever-growing extended families.

One time, when we were all piled in the Town & Country station wagon, off on another adventure, my younger brother Chris asked Dad if we were rich. Without hesitation he answered, "We sure are. Seven kids rich." That's just the way they rolled.

Keith loved the Seven Dwarfs because they reminded him of us kids. What I find interesting about this Disney comparison is that each dwarf had his own distinct brand: Happy, Sleepy, Dopey,

Bashful, Sneezy, Doc, and Grumpy. And each used their unique brand position to win the affections of Snow White. I realized at an early age the importance of standing out in a crowded, competitive market, especially if I was going to get my fair share in the hungry Howell household.

I liked to express my creativity. I started taking piano lessons in the third grade, wrote songs through high school, and earned a degree in music composition and theory in college. As a kid I wore a ridiculous milkman's hat everywhere. It was distinct because it had the same blocky color design as the Partridge Family's bus

Figure 1.2 Me in my Partridge Family-inspired milkman's hat. We went everywhere together.

(look it up). I'm not sure if my brand actually curried favor with my parents, but, like my name, it made me distinct from Dan, Melody, Tom, Steve, Chris, and Mike (who were a construction manager, Arabian horse trainer, construction manager, physical therapist, farrier, and equine veterinarian, respectively), each finding their own unique brand voice.

While getting my music degree, I learned the power of a focused brand during a popular marketing course in the Edward R. Murrow School of Communication at Washington State University. Figuring I probably wouldn't achieve fame and fortune as a composer, I hedged my bet with a degree in communications, too. Now, continuing a 35-year career in the branding arts, I combine all these attributes to help leaders of purpose-driven brands excel through the stories they tell, and I'm enjoying every minute of it.

What are the curiosities and passions that drive your success? Which dwarf are you? Tap into these core attributes as you work through the Story Cycle System. When you do, you will win the affections of your customers. Your employees. Your shareholders and stakeholders. Even your vendors.

COMPETING IN A LAND OF ABUNDANCE

Capitalism and market dynamics are based on the law of scarcity. But we live in a time of abundance. Your customers and my customers have myriad choices for practically every product and service we seek. So how do we make our offerings stand out to become *the* choice to an overwhelmed world?

Wikipedia lists 160 brands of shoes, and that doesn't include their subbrands. In the US alone, 164 car brands compete for your attention. But you probably only know Ford, Chrysler, General Motors, Jeep, and Tesla. And among the big three are 10 subbrands.

In the realm of American professional services, there are around 42,000 CPA firms, around 50,000 law firms, and — *gasp* — 1.34 million lawyers. If you're an MBA, welcome to the crowd. US universities graduate approximately 200,000 MBAs every year. Some experts argue that the ubiquity of the master's degree has diluted its appeal in business. It's no longer a differentiator unless you are in a specialized field.

I experienced the need to define a personal brand even in the context of the market for master's degrees. In 2013 I began a five-year stint creating and teaching the Story Cycle System at Arizona State University for its Executive Master of Sustainability Leadership (EMSL) program. EMSL is a 12-month master's program that elevates middle managers into high-level positions in their organizations and industries by focusing their business expertise on sustainability. Executives for such global brands as Cummins, American Express and Bayer use our course to clarify their personal sustainability leadership stories to amplify the stories' impact on their careers and in the world.

I was one of four professors. My job was to turn executives into Chief Storytelling Officers to help them advance their social initiatives further and faster through the power of the focused story. Plus, the EMSL degree differentiates our graduates from all other MBAs because it instills in them a personalized purpose-driven focus. My goal was to help each graduate stand out by clearly communicating what they stand for.

YOUR BRAND POINT OF VIEW

The first step in truly understanding what you stand for is to articulate your backstory by defining your functional position in the marketplace. In her book *Fascinate: How to Make Your Brand Impossible to Resist*, international brander Sally Hogshead says you define your brand position by asking yourself this question: "What do you do differently, and therefore better, than anyone else?"

In my estimation, *Fascinate* is one of the three most important books on finding your brand's place in the world that you should include in your library. Another is the marketing classic that defined positioning: *Positioning: The Battle for Your Mind: How to be Seen and Heard in the Overcrowded Marketplace*, by Jack Trout and Al Ries. The third book is what I believe is the modern version of Positioning, a book titled *Play Bigger: How Pirates, Dreamers and Innovators Create and Dominate Markets*, coauthored by Christopher Lochhead, one of my *Business of Story* podcast guests.

In *Play Bigger*, Lochhead and company describe how to create a point of view (POV) for your brand. When I read their example of a brand POV, I intuitively recognized its power to focus a brand story and saw how it was a natural outcome of defining your backstory in the Story Cycle System . As you determine your #1 position in the market, you are establishing your brand's point of view. And a really strong and differentiated position will act to design a whole new market category where you're the king or queen. The best way to demonstrate the POV is to show it to you in how we positioned a new all-natural allergy product that we launched in the spring of 2018 called Airloom®. Think about the POV of your brand as you read through Airloom's origin story and brand POV story.

YOUR BRAND ORIGIN STORY DEFINES YOUR MARKET CATEGORY

The creator of Airloom came home following another day of performing delicate spinal surgeries to find his young wife collapsed on the living room floor of their Washington, DC, condominium.

For five years she had battled allergies. They had seen top medical specialists who put her on several medications including steroids and antihistamines. Even injections. These helped, but also caused harsh side effects. She suffered from weight gain, fatigue, irritability, sleeplessness, dry eyes, and decreased daytime alertness.

He kneeled next to her and asked what was wrong.

Figure 1.3 Airloom's launch website captures the all-natural approach
to allergy relief.

"I took all of my meds, but I think they are making me sicker,"
she told him. "You're so brilliant and help everyone else. Please
find a way to help me," she pleaded.

Using the same rigor of study that had him graduate at the top
of his classes in leading medical schools and surgical training
programs, he began researching all-natural remedies that didn't
promote the side effects common with Big Pharma meds.

He discovered five plant-based flavonoids/phytonutrients that
had proved effective in combating allergies by naturally supporting
healthy respiratory and immune systems. But he couldn't find them
in one supplement. So he formulated his own remedy.

She tried it and found relief from her allergies in just 48 hours.
Friends and family marveled at her transformation and asked to try
the formula themselves. His trial group grew over five years until
one day they realized they had to make their all-natural allergy
remedy known to the world.

We were lucky. Avein Tafoya, the mindfully indomitable CEO of
Adelante Healthcare, referred her friends who created the allergy
supplement and asked to us to help them craft the brand story
for their new allergy product. Avein had already experienced the
power of the Story Cycle System brand strategy process when we

helped her rebrand the community healthcare center she runs in Arizona. The rebranding was a tremendous success, sparking 600 percent growth in the ensuing years that turned the center into one of the nation's leaders in sustainable healthcare.

DEFINE YOUR #1 POSITION IN THE MARKETPLACE

The first step in the Story Cycle System is to define your defendable, differentiated brand position in the marketplace. You accomplish this by considering the backstory of your offering and articulating how you functionally stand out in the market. In other words, how are you different and therefore better than your competitors? Don't worry if your brand differentiation isn't made clear immediately to you, especially if you are competing in a highly commoditized industry. The Story Cycle System will help you ferret out your differentiator as you pursue your narrative journey throughout the process. For now, craft your brand position statement to where it feels like you're in the ballpark. You'll hit it out of the stadium later.

One way to define your #1 position in the market is to use Lochhead's POV exercise. I like it because its natural narrative structure makes you consider all the market dynamics your brand is up against and think about how to turn numerous obstacles into opportunities. As you hone your story, your market category emerges. You carefully consider your positions of strength within your category and ultimately arrive at your #1 specialty as captured in your position statement (I've provided an exercise at the end of this chapter to help you claim your #1 position in the market). A super-focused position statement will define a whole new market category that you can lead and dominate because you created the category.

With the first argument in his book *Hit Makers: The Science of Popularity in an Age of Distraction*, Derek Thompson posits that hits like movies, songs and books are the product of something familiar contorted with a surprising twist. "Most consumers are simultaneously *neophiliac* — curious to discover new things — and deeply *neophobic* — afraid of anything that's too new. The best hit makers are gifted at creating moments of meaning by marrying new and old, anxiety and understanding. They are architects of familiar surprises."

I believe this is an excellent way to think about your position statement. You want to communicate the familiar market category you service to connect with your customer's thirst for meaning. But to stand out and create curiosity, you must be novel. The Mini Cooper is more than a sports car. The brand's marketers crafted a new, more exhilarating market category: *motoring*. To separate itself from all other customer relationship management platforms, Hubspot coined the term "inbound marketing" and designed its new category to lead this market segment. Elvis didn't set out to disrupt the existing category of jazz. He created a new one vamping off the familiarity of rhythm and blues to become the King of Rock n' Roll.

HOW WE OVERCAME THE CONGESTED MARKET OF ALL-NATURAL ALLERGY SUPPLEMENTS

I mentioned above that in 2018 we worked with a company called Airloom, which we thought was well positioned to own the all-natural allergy supplement category. But when we Googled "all-natural allergy supplement" we found more than 20 million hits (*cough*). So we checked Amazon. It delivered us more than 36 pages of products with the same search! (*hack!*)

To craft Airloom's position statement, one that would leverage the familiar market segment of all-natural allergy supplements but in a novel way, we deployed Lochhead's POV narrative exercise. Here is the script we crafted to develop and launch their new category:

How many times do you breathe each day?

About 20,000 inhales and exhales.

And that's not always easy if you suffer from airborne allergens.

Some 50 million Americans do.

75 percent of whom still rely on over-the-counter medications.

But they don't realize that these drugs are often ineffective and . . .

could be making them even sicker.

WebMD lists 34 side effects to common allergy meds,

including dry mouth, drowsiness, itching, irritability, and nightmares.

But they don't mention what other studies have found.

That prescription and OTC allergy drugs can lead to cognitive impairment.

Including a lowered IQ and potential increases in dementia and Alzheimer's.

When it comes to understanding the true impacts of allergy meds, Americans are suffering from a severe case of . . .

. . . mental mucus.

UNTIL NOW!

Introducing Airloom for "Conscious Allergy Relief"

Airloom is the smartest, all-natural support for allergy season,

with the most potent herbal supplement formulation designed for people mindful toward their mind and body.

It's small-batch, fresh allergy relief centered on clearing the air about the environmental and Big Pharma impacts of allergy season on you.

So you can . . .

inhale a healthy dose of life again.

THE "CONSCIOUS SEASONAL WELLNESS" BRAND STORY
We had the ideal category designed to carve out our niche in the congested all-natural allergy supplement industry: "Conscious Allergy Relief." Our target customers were found in the yoga and mindfulness communities, two growing practices that both begin

Figure 1.4 Airloom® Conscious Seasonal Wellness

with breath. When allergies restrict your breathing, your experience is diminished.

Our strategy was to help people "own their breath" with Airloom.

This target audience was already thinking about natural health and wellness. And when they discovered something that works, Airloom, they become the ultimate "sneezers." They talked about the product with their friends and happily built our word-of-mouth marketing to help us grow into the larger consumer market.

But the problem is the Food and Drug Administration (FDA) wouldn't allow us to say, "allergy relief," even though numerous studies from around the world have documented the efficacy of Airloom's five botanical ingredients: grapeseed extract, quercetin, bromelain, butterbur extract, and turmeric. We couldn't say "allergy relief" because the couple who created Airloom, and who have brought it to market entirely with their own money, couldn't afford (like most natural supplement creators) the millions of dollars in studies the FDA requires to make such claims.

It's not surprising that the FDA wields so much power over natural supplement marketers. These marketers compete with Big Pharma, the top lobbying industry in Washington, DC. Big Pharma invested $269 million dollars in lobbying efforts in 2017 outspending its nearest competitor, the insurance industry, by 57 percent in 2017, according to Statista, which tracks lobbying expenditures.

So, as brand storytellers for Airloom, we had to use what FDA attorneys label "mere puffery" to describe how this all-natural supplement works. We prefer to call it "enthusiastic euphemisms." These are constructed using metaphors, which actually make for more compelling brand storytelling because metaphors allow audiences to connect the dots. They become an active participant in the story.

Enthusiastic euphemisms include thoughts like these:

> **Airloom's ingredients read more like a shopping list for your local farmer's market than something you'd find in a drugstore.**

> **Encouraging healthy histamine levels without the mind-numbing side effects of Big Pharma.**

> **Airloom helps keep your immune system in chill mode by supporting a healthy immune response to seasonal stress.**

So we changed conscious allergy relief to "conscious seasonal wellness." But the market position we designed and our target audience strategy remained intact.

The goal of Airloom is not just to provide relief from seasonal airborne irritants, but to awaken the masses to the side effects of prescription drugs and OTC medications when nature provides what you need for better health. We would phrase it like this for customers: "If you want to be mindful of the environmental and Big Pharma impacts on you and your loved ones due to airborne allergens, then try Airloom. It's your conscious seasonal wellness supplement that supports a healthy respiratory and immune system so you can inhale a healthy dose of life."

Which leads us to our FDA-approved disclaimer: "These statements have not been evaluated by the Food and Drug Administration. This product is not intended to diagnose, treat, cure, or prevent any disease."

To summarize, the couple who created Airloom began by solving a problem and fulfilling a need for their customers. Then they took the time to understand the market environment they would be competing in by articulating the brand's POV. Once they clarified their position in the marketplace, they articulated it by crafting a position statement claiming their #1 position, which they would define and defend against the competition. These efforts created meaning for their customers about what Airloom stood for: "Conscious Seasonal Wellness."

I hope this brand story has cleared up your mental mucus, too.

By the way, notice the strategic use of the word *but* in Airloom's POV story. You'll learn the immense power of that little word in all of your brand storytelling in Chapter 4.

NOW IT'S YOUR TURN TO DESIGN YOUR MARKET CATEGORY USING THE STORY CYCLE SYSTEM

Let me do a quick bit of table setting here, just so you fully know how to get the most out of this book. Each chapter that details a part of the 10-step Story Cycle System will be presented in three steps:

Step 1. I'll provide you the example of how I have used the concepts in the chapter to create my own Business of Story brand story (plus, I'll usually include third-party case studies, such as Airloom's story, above).

Step 2. I'll demonstrate how to use the brand story-crafting worksheet to summon the unique narrative elements that will reveal your brand story.

Step 3. You'll work the exercise to cast the particular spell for your brand story.

Plus, at the end of each chapter, I'll connect you with key insights provided by international story artists who have shared their expertise with my listeners on the *Business of Story* podcast. Listen in! I promise it will be worth it. Also, you can start building your own business storytelling library with the additional written and video resources we'll provide.

I'll even throw in a few extracurricular activities to help you and your people build your storytelling muscles outside of the office. These aren't mandatory, but they are fun. The story quests will evolve you from an intuitive storyteller to an intentional one activating in you the most underutilized but powerful skills in business. You'll soon learn that you can use stories to nudge the world in any direction you choose.

DECLARE YOUR #1 POSITION IN THE MARKETPLACE

I have been in advertising and branding for nearly 35 years, and I have helped hundreds of organizations grow through the influence of mass media.

But the Internet has shifted the balance of power, allowing the masses to become the media. They can and will control your brand story, if they're even listening to you at all.

Therefore, in 2016, I founded the Business of Story® to consult, teach, coach, and speak on the applied science and bewitchery of storytelling — to help leaders of purpose-driven brands clarify their stories, amplify their impact, and simplify their lives.

The three paragraphs above are a super-concise three-act summary of my backstory — setup / problem / resolution — to set the stage for my brand story. This simplified and focused version of the Business of Story backstory was distilled by parsing my own much longer origin story or backstory. (By the way, if you are intrigued about the genesis of the Business of Story and our proven Story Cycle System, then please read my personal origin story in Appendix Two. It will provide you a deeper understanding of how the Story Cycle System developed into what it is now, and why it works so well.)

You can do the same thing. Consider where you have been, where you are now, and where you are going. Write your back-story so that it captures the origins of your brand and why you do what you do and share it with others. Then simplify your backstory to make it as concise and specific as possible. For example, I wrote the first paragraph of this section (the backstory summary) from what follows:

WHERE WE HAVE BEEN

I have been in the advertising, marketing, and branding industry for 35 years, ran my own ad agency called Park&Co for 20 years, and have been steeped in brand storytelling for the past 15-plus years. Our agency helped hundreds of brands and the thousands of people who support them grow through traditional advertising and public relations. We were experts at growing purpose-driven brands that focused on the environment, education, and social causes.

But, in 2006, the advertising paradigm shifted. Technology and the Internet began leveling the communications playing field. While brands used to own the influence of mass media, the masses were becoming the media. External and internal communications have undergone a tectonic shift as our audiences are now floating in a sea of blogs, tweets, YouTube videos, Snapchats, emails, and texts, all of which combine to drown out our messages. People who thought the Internet promised greater connection found themselves increasingly disconnected by virtue of a screen versus a scene: the actual human connection of one-on-one, in-person communication.

I learned that the primal power of story is the answer to overcoming the cacophony of communication created by our technological prowess. An anecdote is the antidote.

WHERE WE ARE NOW

As of 2016, I pivoted Park&Co away from operating as a full-service advertising agency to an internationally acclaimed business storytelling consultancy for purpose-driven brands. Our Business of Story offering includes brand story strategy creation and consulting, teaching an eight-week story mastery program for teams, coaching storytelling for leaders and salespeople, and keynote speaking on the power of story in all personal and professional pursuits.

Brands that rely on the Business of Story programs include global enterprises like the United States Air Force, Cummins, American Express, Wynn Resorts, Hilton, McCormick's, and Forever Living Products International. We also assist academic institutions such as Emory University, Arizona State, Washington State, and Nova Southeastern University, as well as emerging mom-and-pop companies.

We also help individual executives seeking to sharpen the contours and grow the influence of their personal brands. Executives access the Story Cycle System through books, online training, our popular weekly podcast, DIY brand development, full-brand consulting, storytelling workshops, and speaking engagements.

WHERE WE ARE GOING

As of this writing, the Business of Story is three years old, although I've been learning, consulting, and teaching on brand storytelling since 2006. Like all industries, and given the interest in business storytelling today, there are innumerable self-proclaimed story gurus to choose from. Most tell you that storytelling is important in your business and present opinions, assertions, and generalizations about how you're supposed to use narrative.

The Business of Story is different. Like the writing axiom "Don't tell, show," we reveal to you the applied science and bewitchery of storytelling so that you can apply it immediately in your life. We believe you must understand the magic to cast the spell. So we teach you how to tell stories on purpose.

There are storytelling coaches who focus on personal development, innovation, diversity and inclusion, and branding for startups, small companies, technology, healthcare—you name it. The Business of Story focuses on helping individuals clarify their stories, amplify their impact, and simplify their lives, whether they are enhancing the influence of their personal brand or growing their enterprises and their people. We will scale the Business of Story platform to be a leading international story consultancy with physical workbooks, online training, and immersive workshops and master classes. We will measure our impact by the number of people served—as well as the financial ROI attributed to storytelling our clients share with us—developing a company that will be valued at a minimum of 4X revenue by 2025.

When you write down your backstory, as I have done above, you begin to see your brand's unique point of view in the world. As your POV becomes clearer, your #1 position in the marketplace starts to reveal itself. Define a strong enough market position and you will essentially create a new market category for your offering that your brand will own.

NOW IT'S YOUR TURN

Please share your backstory—the more detailed, the better. A rule of narrative is that the story is found in the specifics. Be specific!

WHERE WE HAVE BEEN:

_____

_____

_____

_____

_____

WHERE WE ARE NOW:

_____

_____

_____

_____

_____

WHERE WE ARE GOING:

_____

_____

_____

_____

_____

From your backstory, dial in your #1 position in the marketplace. I learned this exercise from a book I read back in the late 1990s. I wish I could recall the title and its author(s), but I'm telling you now in case they come across this guidebook and say, "WTF? This guy's using our positioning method." I share it because it works. Here's how I've used it for the Business of Story platform:

INDUSTRY: Communications

CATEGORY: Advertising, marketing, and sales

SPECIALTY: Strategic brand storytelling

#1 SPECIALTY

The Business of Story is the #1 resource for leaders of purpose-driven brands to align their people, engage their customers, and build trust for their offering using the proven power of the Story Cycle System.

We exclusively offer the proprietary Story Cycle System process, which enables us to design a new market category of brand story strategy creation with intention. The category we designed is _Purpose-Driven Brand Storytelling_. A more fun way to say it is "telling stories on purpose." And our efforts manifest themselves in leaders of purpose-driven brands who evolve from innate storytellers to intentional ones, helping them excel through the stories they tell.

This is the first step out of the primordial muck of commoditization. Here is where you define what you functionally do differently, and therefore better, than your competitors. Claim your #1 position

Your Position Statement	
Industry	
Category	
Specialty	
#1 Specialty	

Worksheet 1.1 Define your #1 position in the market

in the marketplace that you can own and defend, and consider how you can design a new market category around it:

How does your position statement (#1 Specialty) compare with mine, above? Is it unique to you, relevant to your customers, and defendable from encroaching competitors?

The anatomy of a declarative position statement is fluid. But here is a simple way to write yours. Again, I'll use my own brand as an example.

Name your brand: The Business of Story

Identify your audience: For leaders of purpose-driven brands

Declare what you solve: who want to clarify their stories, amplify their impact, and simplify their lives

Announce your unique offering: The proven power of the Story Cycle System (which they can't get from any other provider).

What market position can you own?: The Business of Story is the #1 resource for leaders of purpose-driven brands to align their people, engage customers, and build trust in their offering using the proven power of the Story Cycle System.

With my example in mind, craft your own position statement and see if you can define a new market category that is familiar but novel.

FINAL THOUGHTS

Congratulations—you've taken that first step to clarifying your brand story. You considered your backstory about the origin of your brand and declared your #1 position in the marketplace. If your new market category is not immediately apparent to you, no worries. It will reveal itself as you complete the rest of the book. Then you can return to your backstory, clarifying your position statement even more.

This backstory/market position exercise is the only activity in the Story Cycle System that focuses on the function of your offering. It's enormously important to determine what you do differently, and therefore better, than your competition to make you stand out.

But now, there's another thing to consider: What do you stand for? From here on, you will begin to humanize your brand, illuminating it with every step of this purpose-driven storytelling system. So when you're ready, turn to Chapter 2 and say hello to the true heroes in your brand journey—your audiences.

ADDITIONAL RESOURCES:

If you would like a deeper dive into creating your position statement and designing your category, visit businessofstory.com/backstory for these great resources:

- Read Vol. I of the *Business of Story* online magazine: "Backstory: Determining Your Brand Position"

- Listen to Christopher Lochhead on the *Business of Story* podcast: "How to Play Bigger and Dominate a Category"

- Watch my quick explanation on how to claim your #1 position in the marketplace: bit.ly/StoryCycle-Backstory

- Download your DIY Brand Story-Crafting Guide

STORY ON ACTIVITY

Your first extracurricular activity is an easy one. Find three brands — large, medium, and small — that you think do a good job of owning and defending their #1 position in the marketplace. Ask yourself why their story works for you.

My examples are:

- Apple, which actually encourages you to "Think different"

- Man Crates, which uses brand storytelling for one purpose only: to send cool sh!t to men

- Santa Rick, Atlanta's premier real-bearded Santa, available year-round for private parties, corporate events, and print/radio/TV advertisements. Santas are as ubiquitous as Elvis impersonators, but Santa Rick's specific brand position is jollier than most.

Figure 1.5 Santa Rick's jolly brand position proves that you don't have to be a Fortune 100 brand to define your place in the world.

And I have one more favorite brand example: It's called "The Happy H," the home I grew up in in Woodinville, Washington.

2

Heroes

How to Understand Your Customers to Build a Tribe

"I always like to think of the audience when I'm directing, because I am the audience."

—Steven Spielberg

WHO ARE YOU FOR?

Narcissus was a brave hunter and unabashedly handsome. One day he was walking in the forest when the mountain nymph Echo saw him and fell deeply in love with him.

Narcissus felt the presence of Echo and called out, "Who's there?" Echo, in hiding, repeated, "Who's there?" This exchange went on for days, which intrigued and, as you might imagine, slightly annoyed Narcissus. Then one day the shy Echo revealed herself and expressed her love for him. But Narcissus rejected her outright. She fled, embarrassed and heartbroken, spending the rest of her life in lonely glens until nothing but a distant echo remained of her.

Nemesis, the goddess of revenge, learned of Echo's slight and set out to punish Narcissus for his callousness. Nemesis lured him to a pool, where he was greeted by his magnificent reflection. Transfixed by his image, Narcissus sat by the pool for days, staring at himself. When he realized his love could never be achieved, he committed suicide.

The lesson found in the story of Narcissus is this: Don't fall prey to your ego. Selfies, for instance, can be fun and are often intoxicating. But they can reflect poorly on you, too. Your Nemesis might turn your unflattering pic on you, making it viral, echoing forever through the glens of the Internet.

This is not so much a cautionary tale for self-centered social media use as it is a reminder that you and your brand are not the focus of your story. Your audiences are.

When brands are too self-absorbed, gazing at their own presumed beauty instead of empathizing with and appreciating the humanity of their audiences, the goddess of revenge takes her toll. Morale sags. Customer engagement vanishes. People care less about your self-absorbed brand. Harsh, huh?

Look in the mirror and ask yourself: How transfixed are you on your customers? Think about it a bit, and then answer this question: I am for _____.

What did your answer reveal? You may be like most readers and arrived at a number of different audiences. It's normal to feel like you want to be all things to all people. It seems safe. But it's dangerous. Because if you try to be all things to all people you become meaningless to most. Just as in Chapter 1, when you declared your #1 position in the marketplace to begin clarifying your story, you now need to be singularly focused on your #1 audience. Once you've identified them, the rest of your audiences become more focused because they all share a similar wish and want that you and your brand fulfill.

It's worth repeating here that this book uses the terms *customer(s)* and *audience(s)* interchangeably. Because if you're sharing a story, you're selling something (your wit, experience, insight, product, service, internal initiative, getting your kid to eat their peas, etc.). So every audience is a customer and every customer is an audience. And here's the most important part of audiences and customers: *They* are at the center of your brand story. Not you or your brand. It's just like the Hero's Journey. Every story built on its framework has a central character with a sidekick who helps them achieve what they want on their journey. You, my friend, are the Obi-Wan Kenobi to their Luke Skywalker, or the Glinda the Good Witch of the North to their Dorothy.

So, how do *I* answer the question above? At the Business of Story, we are for *you* if you appreciate the power of storytelling to enroll your people in a common mission, align them with a focused vision, inspire their contributions, and build trust in a journey they can all live into and prosper from. By "live into" I mean a narrative you can embrace with all your heart and soul, that is true to you and your journey in life.

You, our customer, are the storytelling herald within your organization, but you must overcome the threshold guardians of doubt, indecision, and indifference to propel your people and your career forward. Therefore, we teach the applied science and bewitchery of storytelling to help you nudge the world in any direction you choose.

To make your story work, you as the storyteller must possess an unwavering understanding of and empathy for your customers. Your power comes from telling your stories from your audience's perspective, helping them make your story their story. But you first must overcome your own navel gazing to make this story transmutation work.

Spoiler Alert: Nine out of 10 times when I ask an executive who is the hero of their brand story, they will say the brand is the hero. It's not. At the heart of every brand story are your audiences of customers, employees, shareholders and stakeholders, vendors, the community you serve, etc., depending on who your story is for. They are the heroes of the brand story you are crafting for them. Your brand is the beneficiary of this process — it is not the hero. However, you play a vastly more important role as mentor or guide, which we'll explore in Chapter 6, "Mentor."

Let's take a look at how Coca-Cola used the Story Cycle System to double its fleet's fuel efficiency by focusing on the true heroes of their SmartDriver eco-driving initiative.

ONE GOAL, MANY AUDIENCES

Ecodriving Solutions, a Phoenix-based provider of eco-driving training programs, was launching its national brand story that we crafted with the Story Cycle System™. Impressively, the first customer for its online and classroom training curriculum for fleet truck drivers was Coca-Cola and its 60,000-plus fleet of drivers. Coca-Cola hired Ecodriving Solutions as the content experts for its internally branded SmartDriver program, and Ecodriving Solutions hired us to design the story strategy for its launch in the Coca-Cola fleet.

Our challenge was to sell a planet-friendly driver training program to road-worn truck drivers who were focused on meeting demanding delivery schedules and keeping their vehicles up and running. Given the divisiveness of ecological issues—from callous attitudes about carbon emissions, to what some call the "uncertain science" behind global warming, to controversial images such as dog-paddling polar bears—we knew it might be difficult to get truck drivers, by nature an independent-minded lot, behind a program that they could view as just another sorry attempt to save the planet. We knew that to make this work we had to craft and tell the initiative's brand story from behind their steering wheels, not from our passenger seat. We had to place the truck drivers at the center of the story and make them the heroes.

If you visit the Ecodriving Solutions website, you won't find images of fluffy bunny rabbits, green grass, blue skies, or leafy logos. Instead, we built a brand archetype that speaks directly to the typical fleet owner's interest in growing revenue, reducing risk, and enhancing their brand. We've learned that selling sustainability is not about the environmental outcomes but the business outcomes. Saving our planet and therefore our collective ass is simply added value.

With Coca-Cola, we absolutely had to connect with the sentiments of their truck drivers, the heroes of Coca-Cola's SmartDrive story. Their primary interest was efficiency, safety, and a little competition.

We used the Story Cycle System customer persona guide (you'll read about this powerful technique later in the chapter) as an interview template to get to know our audiences. What we found from our research is that Coca-Cola's fleet of drivers had four primary motivators:

1. They were committed to helping their company, Coca-Cola, tune up its operations.

2. Their independent nature inspired them to be the best and safest drivers they could be.

3. Since each driver was part of a regional team, they exhibited a competitive spirit to outperform other company fleet divisions, not to mention their fellow drivers.

4. They expressed a sense of national pride to do their part to help America reduce its reliance on foreign oil.

Figure 2.1 The Ecodriving Solutions website is designed from the fleet driver's point of view, connecting their story to Ecodriving Solution's brand narrative.

We captured the insights we gleaned about Coca-Cola's fleet drivers and drafted a customer persona we called Chuck. Here is the profile we wrote to describe him:

Chuck is proud to have been driving for his company for nearly 10 years. He's thirty-four years old, and his Midwest upbringing helps him appreciate what it means to work for a solid company. He's not the "rah-rah" cheerleader type. Chuck is just extremely happy to be contributing to his team in his own personal way, and he knows the company appreciates his efforts.

Chuck believes in fairness, honesty, and an America that his father always said was the finest country in the world. He's indifferent to climate change because he's not really certain of who to believe. He finds global warming to be a political subject, rather than a real one.

Chuck is saddened at America's involvement in the Middle East but figures we have to protect our interests and abdicates to the men and women in leadership who are "smarter than he is" for such decisions.

Although Chuck, the fleet driver, was the primary audience (who the SmartDriver program was ultimately for), we identified eight other internal audiences who needed to buy into the program and pinpointed what each uniquely cared about relative to the SmartDriver initiative. And then we told the story from their perspective, which now placed them at the center of the story. Here's what we found, which is pretty standard across all corporate entities:

- Fleet managers want to reduce fuel and maintenance costs.

- Chief training officers want to implement a proven turnkey training program without tying up their own IT and training resources.

- Human resource directors want a new platform that engages employees and builds camaraderie.

- Directors of risk management want to sleep better at night because the eco-driving training results in safer drivers.

- Corporate sustainability officers want a measurable sustainability program they can promote to stakeholders that delivers real numbers on the company's reduced impact on the community and the planet.

- Chief marketing officers want to use the results of eco-driving training as a powerful way to strengthen their company's corporate social responsibility story.

- Chief financial officers want an immediate return on their investment in the forms of reduced fuel and maintenance costs.

- Chief executive officers want to be proud of the leadership role in their industry inherent in a program that positively impacts people, planet, and profits.

It's worth repeating that Coca-Cola *doubled* its SmartDriver goals in the first few months of launching the initiative in 2010 because they presented a story that their fleet could buy into and prosper from. Coke focused on culture rather than compliance to make their SmartDriver program a hit.

THE STORY CYCLE SYSTEM OVERVIEW OF COCA-COLA'S SMARTDRIVER PROGRAM

Here's a quick look at the road ahead for you and the Story Cycle System. This is how it mapped out for Coca-Cola. You'll cover each of these steps at length in the chapters of this book.

1. BACKSTORY: Coca-Cola launched an eco-driving training program called SmartDriver to reduce the carbon emissions of its fleet by 3 percent

2. HEROES: Dedicated Coca-Cola fleet drivers and their staff with secondary audiences in leadership, as described above

3. STAKES: Drivers wish to help their company, community, and country and want an effective driving program to reduce their fuel consumption and ecological impact

4. DISRUPTION: Introducing a new internal initiative that is going to require them to drive differently

5. ANTAGONISTS: Old habits die hard, and the potential sentiment that the program seems like an intrusive backseat driver

6. MENTOR: Ecodriving Solutions and Coca-Cola's new SmartDriver program

7. JOURNEY: Proven classroom and online Ecodriving Solutions training

8. SUCCESS: Coca-Cola doubled its fuel savings and reduced its carbon emissions in just the first few months of the program

9. THE MORAL: Pride in knowing how to make a positive impact in your job every day

10. RITUAL: Daily dedication to driving responsibly and being rewarded for it, even when they're at home with their families

IDENTIFYING YOUR TARGET AUDIENCES: WHO YOU ARE FOR

Are we in agreement? You and your brand are *not* the heroes of this journey. Your audiences are, as the Coca-Cola case study demonstrates. They are at the center of your brand stories. You are the story maker. They are your brand storytellers. You surprise and delight them by delivering on the promises you make in your brand stories. Then they become your most vocal advocates, sharing your story with their world. But that all begins by viewing them as the heroes. So make sure you understand, appreciate, and empathize with the journeys they're on and how they see the world and your brand's place in it.

It's important because when you truly connect with your audiences you can craft irresistible brand stories that turn engagement into enthusiasm into evangelism (making your story their story).

For instance, I've learned over the decade-plus of using and teaching the Story Cycle System that I'm for you if you're a leader of a purpose-driven brand — whether it's your personal/professional brand to grow your influence, or your organizational brand to grow your enterprise and your people. Although many different kinds of people rely on the Business of Story, I focus my brand storytelling to attract the following three hero archetypes. They all have one thing in common: They possess at least a cursory knowledge of storytelling and appreciate its power to connect their brand on a primal human level with their customers. Each of these audiences now seeks a proven way to excel through the stories they tell.

1. FOUNDER/CEO OF AN EMERGING ENTERPRISE

You have founded a purpose-driven organization that has a proven business model generating up to 10 million dollars in annual revenue. But your competition has taken notice and is encroaching on your business, causing confusion in the marketplace because you have not declared your clear brand differentiator. Regardless, you are still growing and urgently need to express your focused mission with your expanding workforce, something that will inspire them to pull together for a common cause. And perhaps most embarrassing (I've heard this a lot!), your banker or investor recently asked you what your story is, and you didn't have one. Sigh.

2. DIRECTOR OF BRANDING, MARKETING, SALES, OR HUMAN RESOURCES

You are either a chief branding officer, director of marketing and sales, or human resources executive (which, incidentally, may be the toughest storytelling position of all if you have to sell your people on embracing diversity and inclusion). You want your people and their teams to buy into your brand of leadership and grow your external sales and marketing programs or internal employee initiatives. These are emerging enterprises within your organization, and the same approach to brand story strategy will work for you as well as it does for someone growing a brand per our first audience, above.

3. ASPIRING EXECUTIVE

You are a middle-management or C-level executive who has garnered success in your 20+ years in your industry, and you want to grow your influence and results in the second stage of your career, either in your current position or with a new job. But you realize that you are up against stiff competition from colleagues and executives who have an equal or better curriculum vitae. Plus, you may have felt like you haven't even hit your stride yet, due to your lack of a focused story. You turn to Business of Story's resources to help you clarify your personal/professional brand story to amplify your impact and simplify your life.

So, as you can see, I am for leaders of purpose-driven brands who believe in the power of storytelling to help them nudge the world in any direction they choose. I am for those who tell stories with purpose. They are my heroes.

I encourage you to craft simple definitions of your top three audiences as I have, above. Jack Handey, my favorite motivational guru from *Saturday Night Live* (yep, you read that right), said it best: "Before you criticize someone, walk a mile in their shoes. That way, you'll be a mile from them and have their shoes."

Actually, you're not criticizing but characterizing. Who are your customers and what do they want from you?

CREATING CUSTOMER PERSONAS USING THE STORY CYCLE SYSTEM

The Story Cycle System, like the Hero's Journey, is totally meta. It's self-referential in that the same narrative framework is found on many levels. For instance, you're using it now to craft the foundational elements of your brand story. You can also use the Story Cycle System to guide your communications plan. You will even use it as a framework to create your individual story assets, including TV commercials, blog posts, videos, presentations, white papers, etc.

The Story Cycle System is also a powerful guide to knowing and understanding your audiences by defining their characteristics. By using its 10-step system to craft their personas, you gain an appreciation for the journey your audience is on, the stories they are telling themselves about your brand, your competition, and maybe even your industry. The goal is to align your story with their story.

Use the following outline (which should be getting more familiar to you now!) to understand, appreciate, and empathize with your customer and the journey they are on relative to your brand offering. Then you will align your customer's journey points with the proper brand stories to communicate your value proposition and connect your shared values.

STEP 1: BACKSTORY

Explain where your customer has been, where they are now, and where they want to go.

STEP 2: HEROES

Describe the demographic and psychographic attributes of your customer.

STEP 3: STAKES

Determine what is important to them, both personally and professionally, and consider how your offering will help them achieve what they want. Consider where your audience is along the Adoptive Curve Scale developed by the tech industry: Innovator, Early Adopter, Early Majority, Late Majority, or Laggard.

STEP 4: DISRUPTION

Detail what has changed or is going to change in your customer's environment to turn their ordinary world upside down and make your offering more relevant than ever.

STEP 5: ANTAGONISTS

Identify who and what stands in their way—including their own internal demons—of adopting, using, and evangelizing your offering.

STEP 6: MENTOR

Outline how your brand's position, promise, personality, and purpose will help your customers achieve what they want.

STEP 7: JOURNEY

Portray how you anticipate the journey will unfold for your audience, how they will overcome their obstacles, what short-term success looks like, and how they will be empowered by your offering.

STEP 8: VICTORY

Describe what initial success (meaning the adoption of your offering) looks like through the eyes of your customer.

STEP 9: THE MORAL

Define what your customer values and how they will connect with the shared values of your brand.

STEP 10: RITUAL

Describe how, through ritual and evangelism, your customer will interact with your offering now and in the future to create a lasting brand bond.

BUSINESS OF STORY AUDIENCE PERSONA: FOUNDER/ CEO OF AN EMERGING ENTERPRISE

Let me provide you a concrete example from my own business of how to use the steps above to craft a customer/audience persona. I encourage you to work with what you know now about your customer, but it's OK to even make some assumptions about their circumstances and behaviors that you will test late in the Story Cycle System. You can always hone these personas later as your brand story becomes clearer to you.

We were working with the founder of an emerging enterprise, who needed us to help him in the following ways:

BACKSTORY: Sam is the founder and CEO of a seven-year-old healthcare technology firm that he started in a coworking space. The company has grown to 30 employees and is now headquartered in his own 10,000-square-foot building. Business has been brisk because they have done a good job focusing on expert delivery of both their product and customer service. But as they emerge as a mid-market tech company, Sam knows that the organization has neglected to define its brand story and align it with its employees and customers. Therefore, he feels urgency to create a brand narrative to spur the next level of growth for his organization.

HEROES: Sam is 47 years old, married, and the father of two kids active in sports who also have reluctant piano lessons scheduled in, "because the arts are important, too." In fact, Sam believes computer coding is a blend of art and science that can unlock the potential of users. He is a driven entrepreneur who analyzes every business move and requires a lot of data and proof in his decision-making. He runs four times a week, meditates occasionally, and eats healthy food, because he knows it's good for him and he feels it's important to model healthy behavior throughout his organization and industry — as well as to his children.

STAKES: While a focus on outstanding product delivery and fastidious customer service has led to growing sales, Sam feels the company is falling short because it has not clarified its brand story. Although an innovator on the Adoptive Curve Scale in some areas of his operations, as well as in his personal buying habits, Sam is more of a late Early Adopter/Early Majority person when investing in professional services for his company. For instance, he has just implemented leadership coaching after considering it for two years. He wishes to feel smart and optimistic and wants a powerful brand story that will align his team and create trust with his customers.

DISRUPTION: Sam knows international growth necessitates his company being more professional through all its advertising, marketing, and sales, but everyone in his organization seems to be telling their own story about the brand and its offerings. While nose-to-the-grindstone growth has been the norm for Sam and his company, he intuitively knows he needs to disrupt this routine by taking the time to unify the organization around a central brand story that everybody can buy into and prosper from. And it must be accurately and powerfully reflected through all of the company's advertising, inbound marketing, sales, and customer service.

ANTAGONISTS: As an analyzer, Sam has difficulty getting out of his own way to make a decision. He needs proof and recommendations from others before he will invest. He is also concerned about the resources required to get his brand story straight, but he is starting to appreciate the importance of making the investment of time and money.

MENTOR: Demonstrating to Sam the epic growth clients have achieved through the Story Cycle System will be a critical factor for his decision to proceed. The systematic approach of the 10-step process — with deliverables in each step demonstrating tangible progress — will be important points of influence to his analytical mind. Plus, the combination of Hollywood storytelling coupled with brand marketing plays to his art sensibilities. Oh, and the ROI of storytelling is hugely important to him.

JOURNEY: Sam's learned about the Business of Story platform from a referral. He will adopt the program by first doing a one-on-one session to vet the Story Cycle System, which may mean attending a one-day workshop. He may also use some of the platform's free online storytelling tools to test the quality of the materials. He will then invite his leadership team into the process to develop the overall brand story, because building consensus in his organization is profoundly important to Sam. Appreciation for the Story Cycle System will come following the workshop, and he will be evangelized once his overall brand story is created.

VICTORY: Sam will be inspired by the workshop and will look forward to getting his team involved in an outside process that he discovered and vetted for the company. We will celebrate the creation of their brand story by rolling it out to the organization with great fanfare. Our goal is to make Sam a vocal ambassador of the Business of Story platform and the Story Cycle process, which he will happily share with his peers and colleagues.

THE MORAL: Sam values a proven, intentional process that is an enchanting combination of art, science, and sales — a process that aligns his leadership, brand, employee, and customer stories to deliver real results for his organization and people in a timely fashion.

RITUAL: We will arm Sam with the story plans and tools to embed storytelling throughout his organization to assist in the growth of his people and enterprise, while also providing the online portal of businessofstory.com for rich content around storytelling.

NOW IT'S YOUR TURN

Although you are for one kind of professional, you should prioritize your top three audiences and consider what they have in common. I know you probably have more than three important audiences to communicate with, but to make life simpler, please select your top three for this exercise. I've found that what you learn by exploring these three audiences will be effective in connecting with the rest of the communities you serve.

Now craft your customer personas for each audience as described above, using the Story Cycle System to help you empathize with their wishes and wants. Strive to understand where they are on their journeys and identify how to connect with them in a meaningful way.

Target Audiences	
Audience #1	
Want	
Audience #2	
Want	
Audience #3	
Want	

Worksheet 2.1 Prioritize your top three audiences and briefly describe what they want

FINAL THOUGHTS

Is your brand story already becoming a bit clearer? In Chapter 1 you declared your #1 position in the marketplace. In Campbell's Hero's Journey, this is your ordinary world. You took your first decisive step out of being a commodity to your customers. And now, in Chapter 2, you've identified who cares about your #1 position by defining who you are for: the central characters at the heart of your brand story. Next, in Chapter 3, you explore what's at stake for your audiences: what they emotionally wish for and physically want to invest in to fulfill that wish. It's only when you understand and appreciate what they wish and want that you can trigger their will to act through the stories you tell, which we'll cover in Chapter 4.

So, when you're ready, let's figure out the wishes you'll be granting.

ADDITIONAL RESOURCES

If you would like a deeper dive into creating customer/audience personas, visit businessofstory.com/hero for these additional resources:

- Read Vol. II of the *Business of Story* online magazine: "Who's the Hero in Your Brand Story?"

- Listen to Ardath Albee on the *Business of Story* podcast: "Who's Your Hero?: Creating Customer Personas for Your B2B Marketing"

- Watch my quick explanation on how to claim your #1 position in the marketplace: bit.ly/StoryCycle-Hero

STORY ON ACTIVITY

Do you want to get in tune with your audiences? This exercise will make you hyper-focused on them. Just fill out the following abridged Story Cycle System (I told you it was meta) with one-sentence answers and see how your offering and the people you are for come into clearer focus. For even greater insight, ask each of your team members to fill out this quick form so you can locate the trends and gaps in your collective interpretation of your brand story and audiences.

1. BACKSTORY: What do you do differently, and therefore better, than anyone else?

_____

_____

_____

2. HEROES: Who cares about your brand and story?

_____

_____

_____

3. STAKES: What do _they_ want relative to your offering?

_____

_____

_____

4. DISRUPTION: Why do they want it?

_____

_____

_____

5. ANTAGONISTS: Why don't they already have it?

_____

_____

_____

6. MENTOR: How are you equipped to help them get it?

_____

_____

_____

7. JOURNEY: What are you going to do for them?

_____

_____

_____

8. VICTORY: What does success look like for them?

_____

_____

_____

9. THE MORAL: What does success feel like for them?

_____

_____

_____

10. RITUAL: How will you keep them coming back for more?

_____

_____

_____

3

Stakes

How to Connect with
the Wishes and Wants of Your Customers

**"When a person really desires something, all the universe
conspires to help that person to realize his dream.**

— Paulo Coelho

ANSWER ME THESE QUESTIONS THREE

You are investing valuable time and money to clarify your brand
story. What's at stake is the power that comes from a focused narrative. In this chapter, you'll learn what's at stake for your customers.
It's important because knowing what motivates them informs what
brand story you tell to trigger their will to act.

But as with all hero journeys, there's a threshold guardian in the
form of doubt that appears at this point to test your resolve. The
threshold guardians that appear in the stories we love are metaphors for the forces of life that punch us in the nose whenever we
want something, just to test us on how badly we want it.

Think of Miracle Max in one of my favorite movies, *The Princess
Bride*. Billy Crystal plays the threshold guardian who tests Ingo
Montoya on his quest to avenge his father's death. The wizard in
The Wizard of Oz who tests Dorothy's mettle is another threshold
guardian. And who can forget the guardian of the Bridge of Death
in *Monty Python and the Holy Grail*: "Stop! Who approaches the
Bridge of Death must answer me these questions three."

The questions three at this stage of the Story Cycle System™ that
help define the emotional and material stakes for your heroes —
their quest — are:

1. How do your customers wish to feel?

2. What do they want to purchase to fulfill their wish?

3.   Which stories trigger their will to take action?

The best way to understand the wishes and wants of your customers is to first try these questions on yourself. I will play the threshold guardian and ask you to answer these three questions before you can proceed.

HOW DO YOU WISH TO FEEL?

Think of your wish in question one as what you seek emotionally — how something will make you feel. Philosophically, what do you want out of a relationship with your brand? With your brand storytelling, do you wish to:

- Feel understood and accepted?
- Realize peace of mind as an entrepreneur?
- Experience the exhilaration of fast growth?
- Be confident you're on the right journey heading in the right direction?
- Be attractive to the best talent?
- Elevate your purpose by engaging others?
- Build trust among all those you serve?
- Be appreciated for your beliefs and values?
- Look smart? (Don't discount this last one.)

Your wish is what sets every story into motion. Just ask Disney. Disney created a ubiquitous brand that fulfills wishes. Sing with me, "When you wish upon a staaaaar . . ."

WHAT DO YOU WANT?

Think of your want (question two) as the physical product, service, or experience that will fulfill your wish.

Unlike your internal wishes, wants are the external measures defined as both a course of action to achieve a particular purpose and how you quantify your success. For example, you may wish to feel the exhilaration of driving a sporty car, so you want a red Tesla. Coke may appeal to your wish for the momentary happiness of a sweet fizzy jolt, which makes you want their cola. E-Trade targets customers who wish to feel in control of their investing and therefore want its online service.

I wish to look smart and be insightful about the power of story-telling in branding, but many logic-driven executives push back, discounting story's impact on their business. Therefore, I want to show them the return on investment (ROI) of our proven story-telling framework to engage their people in a brand-driven story-telling enterprise. When they witness the ROI of storytelling, they'll think, "Hey, he's pretty smart." My wish is fulfilled, as is theirs, which is to perhaps be viewed as innovative, or bold, or wise.

You may wish to be the storytelling wizard in your workplace, but you want to demonstrate your success through a demonstrable ROI. So before we can grant the wish, we need to look at the want to help ourselves overcome the threshold guardian of doubt.

WHICH STORIES TRIGGER YOUR WILL TO ACT?

The third question to consider after identifying your prospect's wish and want is which stories you will tell to trigger their will to act. I've learned with the Business of Story that some of my most effective stories focus on the ROI of storytelling. When I can illustrate a significant return on investment for my prospect's work with business storytelling, it incites them to act. We will talk about "will triggers" in greater detail in Chapter 4, "Disruption."

So in this journey to clarify your brand story, how do you wish to feel, what do you want to achieve from this book, and what will motivate you to continue moving forward even when some of the exercises feel like they're pushing back on you? Perhaps your motivating force is the return you will earn on the investment of your time in the Story Cycle System?

THE ROI OF STORYTELLING VERSUS THE THRESHOLD GUARDIAN OF DOUBT

On September 20, 2018, I was at the lectern in the Phoenix Art Museum addressing more than 400 local business leaders on behalf of Goodwill of Central and Northern Arizona (GCNA) for its fourth annual Empower Breakfast. GCNA sought to increase its donations at the fundraiser by 30 percent from the previous year. So they designed the event with storytelling at its core. I was the final speaker, following empowering stories by its leadership. My job was to make "the ask."

So I shared a simple anecdote with the audience. When I was 12 years old, I told them, I was digging fence posts with my brothers on the 12-acre home where we grew up in the Pacific Northwest. (Like you, the audience was probably thinking, Where in the hell is this going?) My dad, a civil engineer and president of Constructors PAMCO, a heavy construction company in Seattle, swung into the driveway on a drizzly Wednesday afternoon. When he got out of his car, I whined about having to build this cedar fence. He simply looked at me and made a memorable point about outworking the competition: "A guy might want to pick up that shovel, or someone else will." Then he turned and walked away. It was the wisdom of a man who grew up in North Dakota during the Depression as the son of a lumberyard operator.

"That was the moment I understood the importance of a strong work ethic," I told the audience.

Knowing smiles lit up the faces of these alpha executives. They, too, appreciated what a meaningful job can do for a soul. And that is exactly what GCNA provides through the workforce development programs we were asking the audience to invest in.

What was at stake for Goodwill that morning was a fundraising goal of $200,000 to help put Arizonans back to work. But it actually raised $348,000, 75 percent above its goal. And that was $207,000 more than what they had raised during the same event before (more or less) the same audience at the same place the year prior. Tim O'Neal, CEO of Goodwill of Central and Northern Arizona, credited the organization's intentional approach to brand storytelling for the fundraiser's success in generating an ROI 260 percent above the previous year. Wish fulfilled 10 times over.

Did you feel it? Your threshold guardian of doubt just flinched.

The emotion of brand storytelling might work in fundraising, but what about actual brand development? In a minute I'll show you how it helped GCNA grow its annual revenue by more than 400 percent. But let's first take a look at how brand storytelling can make the most insignificant products sell for more than 28 times their worth (talk about ROI!).

Remember that you and I live in the land of abundance. Our products and services are all mere commodities unless we clarify our brand stories to make them stand out and mean more in the hearts and minds of our customers. A terrific example of brand storytelling ROI is found in the Significant Objects project.

In July 2009, Joshua Glenn, a cultural and brand semiotician (I had to look it up, but *semiotician* essentially means a sign guy), and Rob Walker, a journalist who writes on material culture, launched the Significant Objects project. They wished to understand buying behavior relative to storytelling, and wanted to publish a "literary and anthropological experiment" to objectively measure the effect of narrative on an object's subjective value. They purchased 100 tchotchkes, knickknacks you can find in thrift stores like Goodwill, for an average of $1.25 apiece. Then they hired creative writers to attach a fictional story to each object and sold the items at auction on eBay.

For example, they purchased this acrylic-encased globe for $1.49. Guess what it sold for because of its story? $197.50!

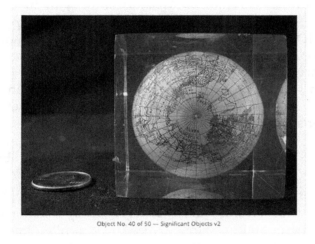

Object No. 40 of 50 — Significant Objects v2

Figure 3.1 Significant Objects globe paperweight
with story by Debbie Millman

The Significant Objects project tested the power of story to create meaning and money out of the mundane. Glenn and Walker invested a total of $128.74 for the first collection of baubles, sold that collection for a combined $3,612.51, and created an ROI of 2,800 percent.

"Stories are such a powerful driver of emotional value that their effect on any given object's subjective value can actually be measured objectively."

—Joshua Glenn and Rob Walker

Their stories fulfilled the **wishes** of their customers to be moved emotionally, which created their **want** for the objects at what you might consider relatively obscene amounts of money. Yet the price was still so insignificant that it didn't take much to trigger the will to act.

I, like millions of people around the world, fall for a story every day. I wish to express my individuality and creativity; therefore I want an Apple computer to help fulfill this inner need to "think different." I have to muster the will to part with the money, but that usually just takes some internal coaxing, perhaps in the form of one or two well-honed stories: What I stand to gain by making the investment, or perhaps what I stand to lose by remaining in status quo (FOMO—the Fearing of Missing Out), is a huge motivator to lots of people. I know, it seems shallow. But that's life as a socially driven storytelling monkey called *homo sapiens*.

If brand storytelling can bring a significant return on insignificant items, imagine what it will do for you and your exceptional product or service?

THE COST OF *NOT* DEVELOPING YOUR STORYTELLING CULTURE

Let's talk for a moment about the growth of your own people. What's at stake for them philosophically and physically? Are the wishes of your leadership, staff, and employees being fulfilled by living into your brand story? What happens when they haven't bought in yet due to confusion about your vision and mission, which have been weakened and distorted by a convoluted narrative? What are the threshold guardians of doubt your people are confronting?

While not every story will be as bullish as the stories I described above, you still cannot afford to ignore investing in storytelling within your organization.

Susan Heathfield, a sought-after human resource expert by entities such as the *New York Times*, the *Washington Post*, and NPR, is a top management and organization development consultant and co-owner of TechSmith Corporate, a software development firm with more than 280 employees. According to her, among the top concerns employees have is their relationship with their boss and colleagues, a consequence of the lack of interpersonal communication inherent in large companies.

But what does that mean? I went to the 2017 Employee Engagement and Retention Statistics report by Access Perks and pulled some of the startling findings. (By the way, this is one of the few times in the book I'll pepper you with bulleted NUMBers, but only because I've set their context first through telling you stories. I'm a big believer that PowerPoints riddled with bullets kill presentations. The same is true with books. Oh, and I'm going to give you the barrage of bullets all at once just to get it over. Lucky you.)

- 51 percent of the US workforce is not fully engaged in their work, which means their employer is not fully realizing their potential contributions to productivity, culture, revenue, and profits (Gallup)

- Disengaged workers cause massive losses in productivity — between $450 and $500 billion a year (Mental Health America)

- Only 16 percent of employees said they felt "connected and engaged" by employers (EmployeeChannel)

- 56 percent of workers are planning to look for a new job in the next 6 months (PayScale)

- 78 percent of employees who say their company encourages creativity and innovation are committed to their employer (ReportLinker)

Employees are an appreciating asset, meaning they produce compounding value for the organization over time. So losing them is costly. Josh Bersin, of Bersin by Deloitte, in an article on employee retention, outlined the following factors a business should consider in calculating the real cost of losing an employee:

- The cost of hiring a new employee, including advertising, interviewing, screening, and hiring is expensive

- The cost of onboarding, training, and management time is expensive

- Lost productivity: It can take a new employee up to 24 months to reach the productivity of an existing person

- Lost engagement: Fellow employees who see high turnover often disengage and lose productivity

- Customer service issues: New employees take longer to assist customers, are often less adept at solving problems, and tend to make more errors

- Training cost: A business likely invests 10 to 20 percent of an employee's salary or more in training over their first two to three years

- Cultural impact: Whenever someone leaves, others wonder why, which distracts them from their job at hand

- Wisdom withdrawal: Long-term employees who decide to leave the company take loads of historical knowledge with them, creating an insight and expertise void for the new employees

WHAT IS BUSINESS STORYTELLING WORTH TO YOU?

Airbnb CEO Brian Chesky said, "People remember the magic of an experience." Stories are always about experiences, those moments of surprise that lead to clarity and understanding. Your people love business points that are illustrated through drama, not data. By the way, Airbnb is worth more than $24 billion.

Tony Hsieh, founder of the online shoe company ZAPPOS, which sold to Amazon for north of $900 million, said, "A great brand is a story that never stops unfolding." ZAPPOS hosts a special website (zapposinsights.com) where their employees share stories that power their culture. As the company grows, so do their stories.

Legendary entrepreneur Sir Richard Branson of Virgin fame said, "The Virgin story — its ups, downs, opportunities, and challenges — is what attracts people to its products and services, as well as attracting employees to join the Virgin family. We would be nothing without our story."

What kind of stories will you share to connect with what's at stake for your internal audiences — their wishes and wants? Here are a few good ones to consider:

- Your **Origin Story**: Share the moments that have informed who you are today and why your brand does what it does in the world to enroll your people in a crystal-clear vision.

- Your **Quest Story**: Align your people with your focused mission.

- Your **Transformation Story**: Share when a significant change in strategy is afoot.

- Your **In a Hole**: Talk about something unanticipated that has happened and how you plan to climb out of the "hole."

- Your **They're Just Like Me Story**: Share a case study of someone who wished for and wanted the same thing as your audience; detail what triggered their will to act and the resulting outcome.

These stories are not long-winded epic adventures, but short stories that deliver a big impact. They use the five primal elements of an anecdote that we will discuss in Chapter 7: Journey.

Suffice it to say, at the core of brand leadership training is communication through storytelling. A story clarifies a situation, illuminates the way forward, and connects with the primal wishes and wants of your audience, triggering their will to act. What other business asset can you count on for a 10+ percent return on your investment?

So far in this chapter we've demonstrated a 100 percent ROI on storytelling in fundraising, and 10+ percent return on employee retention and motivation. But how about brand building? This guidebook is filled with examples of how brands have achieved exponential growth by clarifying their stories. Let's take Goodwill of Central and Northern Arizona again for another example.

BRANDS ARE IN THE WISH-GRANTING BUSINESS

Understanding what's at stake for your audience — what they wish for and want — is critical for you to get them to buy into your brand story.

In 2003, when I was running my agency, Park&Co, Goodwill of Central and Northern Arizona asked our team to help freshen their eighty-year-old brand in metropolitan Phoenix. The organization was generating $17 million in annual revenue through 24 thrift stores. That revenue funds workforce development programs that help Phoenicians find jobs. When we began rewriting its brand story, Goodwill had trained more than 4,000 people that year and placed 885 individuals in jobs throughout metropolitan Phoenix. But the most critical first step we had to take, after understanding their unique brand position in the marketplace, was to understand and appreciate the wishes and wants of their core audience: Goodwill shoppers.

We studied the customer persona of their shoppers and found a fascinating group whose story would be fun to tell. We called them the "Soccer Mom Closet Shoppers."

These are women who love to unearth retail treasures but are reluctant to reveal their thrift store loot. We learned that they are typically very social moms with household incomes of $50,000-plus, and they share a fear of what their friends (who frequent swankier stores) might think of their secondhand shopping habits.

I know this closet shopping woman well. She's my wife, Michele. One night, while I was working on Goodwill's initial brand story strategy, Michele sprang into our living room clutching a Goodwill bag and sat down close to me. It was just the two of us. She slipped a beautiful robin's-egg-blue blouse out of the bag and in a secretive voice said, "You can't believe it. But I just bought this $150 Nanette Lepore blouse at Goodwill for $6."

I replied, "That's great, honey, but why are you whispering?"

She shrugged and giggled at her score. But I knew why. Michele is our target audience. Shoppers like Michele wish to express their unique creativity by displaying unexpected and unusual finds in their home and on themselves. They want these items to be one-of-a-kind totems of their individuality. Price and savings are not the drivers, but the bonus. However, the fear of these shoppers is appearing cheap, so they go about their thrift-store adventures quietly.

Her unfounded fear of being branded with the scarlet letter of "thrift-store shopper" is based on the obstacles the thrift industry itself perpetually has to overcome. Those antagonistic threshold guardians include the perception of dirty stores, messy aisles, tattered clothing, and what some might regard as questionable patrons without much money.

But these closet shoppers are responsible for a good deal of thrift retailers' income, as compared to that derived from needier shoppers. That's why this is an important market to empathize with and tap into.

I know that positive sentiment for "thrifting" has grown over the past 16 years, but back in 2003 it was still considered gauche by many consumers. So before our team could craft a new brand story, we asked GCNA to begin living it by cleaning up their stores. They fixed light fixtures, painted walls, tidied aisles, and expanded their inventory so more treasures could be discovered. In some stores, we even suggested moving the coffeemaker to the front to help mask that exotic scent-of-thrift.

Then we created a 30-second TV commercial that featured our hero — the closet shopping soccer mom — stealthily flowing through the aisles, collecting her treasures. But then she runs into her friend at the front of the store. Neither of the ladies wants to admit they're shopping at Goodwill, so our leading lady says she's just dropping off donations as she places her newly purchased items in the donation bin. Her friend also pretends she's just dropped something off, and once they say their goodbyes she slips back into the store to shop. When the coast is clear, our first mom darts back in to collect her purchased items she pretended to donate and dashes out of the Goodwill store with a big smile. We close with the title card: "Good Stuff. Good Work. Goodwill."

We "outed" the soccer mom, and in doing so we connected with this shopper on her terms, demonstrating understanding and empathy for her wishes. GCNA was concerned that the commercial would look like they were making fun of their shoppers, especially the shy ones. In fact, GCNA told us that if this didn't work, we'd be fired. This had the makings of a short love story. But we felt in our heart of hearts that this tale of the treasure hunter's journey would resonate with their customers.

It took courage from everyone to tell a story that underscored the basic truth of these unique value shoppers: "Be proud of who you are." This approach to customer-centric storytelling came in many forms over the subsequent years, leading to GCNA's 400 percent growth. By 2017, GCNA had grown beyond 90 stores and generated more than $162 million in total annual revenue to power their mission of providing quality services and programs. They served more than 105,000 people and placed more than 45,000 individuals in jobs throughout the Phoenix community.

Nationally, the Goodwill narrative has changed over the years from one of a secondhand industry to a story about celebrating the thrift-store phenomenon. That's what authentic, well-lived, and well-told storytelling can do for the character arc of a brand. But first you must understand and empathize with the wishes and wants of your customer so you can overcome their threshold guardians and trigger them to act.

THE WISHES AND WANTS OF YOUR BRAND

Before you consider the wishes and wants of your audiences, I want you to first consider what's at stake for your brand. What do you *wish* for and what measures do you *want* to make happen to grow your organization, your people, and the communities you serve?

Then consider the same goals for the three audiences you developed in the previous chapter. What do they *wish* for that makes them *want* your product or service? For instance, my *wish* for the Business of Story is to feel vital. To feel vital means that you, as one of our customers, understand that storytelling engages people. You recognize the usefulness of Business of Story's proven frameworks to get your people on board with your clear mission. You appreciate how a well-crafted narrative will build your personal brand, your business, and your team. And you've discerned how our deliberate practice program can create more effective and empathetic communicators. Plus, you seek an impressive ROI with performance-driven outcomes that include growing your personal influence, enrolling your people in a common mission, aligning priorities, and building trust in a journey that your people can buy into and prosper from.

To fulfill my wish of being vital, I want you to invest in our eight-week deliberate practice program. Plus, I want you to invite me to speak at your events and work with your people to connect them to the power of story. I want you to appreciate how you will experience the measurable value of enhanced creativity, more persuasiveness, increased collaboration, greater adaptability to people, problems, and opportunities, and even improved time management skills.

I wanted you to buy this guidebook, and you did. Thank you! Now I wish to hear about the value you have received as you clarify your brand story to amplify your impact and simplify your life with the Story Cycle System. Why? Because then I'll feel smart. Actually, it's more than that. I will feel fulfilled that you have benefitted from the applied science and bewitchery of storytelling, as I and thousands of leaders have.

Let me further illustrate this in terms of Business of Story's three main audiences. The table on the next page shows what I've come to learn that our audiences wish for and want from their brand storytelling development and what triggers their will to go for it.

Target Audiences for the Business of Story	
Audience #1	**Founder/CEO of an Emerging Enterprise**
Want	You *wish* to feel confident and optimistic in the growth and direction of your organization and not be frustrated by its lack of focus. You *want* a proven brand story strategy system to help you clarify your narrative with metrics you can measure. Your *will* to act comes from your need to combat increasing competition that is taxing your organization's competency and survival at every level.
Audience #2	**Directors of Marketing, Sales, or Human Resources**
Want	You *wish* to feel trusted as a high performing leader by getting your team to buy into a common purpose-driven brand narrative. You *want* a proven, measurable storytelling curriculum that will grow your team as confident and productive communicators. Your *will* to act comes from your need to overcome your competition that is using storytelling to gain a competitive edge over you and your organization.
Audience #3	**The Industrious Executive**
Want	You *wish* to feel more respected and influential for the experience you have earned through a productive career. You *want* a proven way to capture and articulate your unique personal brand story to differentiate you from your competition. Your *will* to act comes from the fact that you don't have time for anything other than a career move that supports your core purpose as a professional and amplifies your impact.

Table 3.1 Business of Story audience example

WHAT'S AT STAKE FOR YOUR BRAND AND YOUR AUDIENCES?

As you craft your brand story strategy, you not only want to detail your audience's measurable short, medium, and long-term gains, but what their will is to actually fulfill their wish. By will I mean the reason, the driving force that motivates them to act. In the Hero's Journey, Campbell called this the "Call to Adventure," so I will, too. We'll cover how you can trigger their will to act in the next chapter. But for now, think about a story that they can buy into that nudges them to purchase your product or service. There are two kinds of stories you will tell to accomplish this, depending on how well you understand what makes your customer tick:

1. What will they gain by buying into your offering?

2. What will they lose by remaining in status quo, doing nothing?

I know what you're thinking: My product or service is so great and it's going to help them so much that I need to communicate how much better off they'll be just by using it. And that may be true for some audiences, especially those with a mind-set of abundance and natural optimism. But it's been proven time and again that we *homo sapiens* are beset with a negativity bias, an internal mechanism that runs on autopilot to help ensure our survival. Studies have shown that we will work harder to not lose $100 than to gain $100. So you might consider telling stories on what your audience will lose if they don't buy into your offering. As mentioned earlier, FOMO is a huge motivator. Is it FOMO that has driven you this far to clarify your brand story and increase your storytelling capabilities? Or do you just naturally see the world through an empowering narrative lens, and you want to build on that perspective?

Connecting people through storytelling is hard work. So what fuels my will to invest an enormous amount of time, money, and energy into building the Business of Story platform around the world? Quite simply, it's boredom. Boredom is my nemesis. When was the last time you were bored into buying anything? An innovative product or service, an important social initiative like diversity and inclusion, a critical sustainability mission, a forward-thinking vision?

Never!

If I can't excite and inspire people about how to make a positive impact in their world through the stories they tell, then status quo and boredom win out. I simply can't have that. Boredom goes against every fiber in my being and runs counter to what turns out to be my personal archetype—the Fool. (No, that's a good thing. I'll explain this in Chapter 6, "Mentor.")

NOW IT'S YOUR TURN

First, fill out the wishes and wants of your brand.

Your Brand	Wish	Want	Will
Gain			
Loss			

Worksheet 3.1 Consider what you wish for and want to make happen for your brand and what you stand to gain by accomplishing your desires and what you will lose by doing nothing.

Then determine what customer you are selling to. How are you communicating your offering to increase their want of it? And what brand stories will ignite their will to act? How are you going to measure your ROI through short, medium, and long-term goals? Remember, while you wish to feel the confidence and influence that comes with wielding your storytelling capabilities, you want to measure the impact of the applied science and bewitchery of story on your business to demonstrate real ROI. This encourages your will to proceed. You sell to the wish by communicating your offering in a way that increases your customers' want. How? Through a story that stirs their will to act.

Answer the wish, want, and will questions for yourself and brush aside your threshold guardian of doubt as you chart a clear course venturing into the next chapter.

Audience #1	Wish	Want	Will
Gain			
Loss			
Audience #2	Wish	Want	Will
Gain			
Loss			
Audience #3	Wish	Want	Will
Gain			
Loss			

Worksheet 3.2 Fill out what your audiences emotionally wish for, physically want to make happen to fulfill their wish and what triggers their will to act (we'll cover triggering their will in the next chapter, but it's worth considering now).

THE ROI OF YOUR STORYTELLING

What will be the return on investment for your brand storytelling? You must set your short, medium and long-term goals so that you can measure your outcomes. I mean, even your purpose-driven brand is in the business of making money.

Goals	Short Term	Medium Term	Long Term
Business of Story	Host a minimum of four workshops, master classes, or speaking engagements per month	Coach 10,000 people annually in immersive workshops, master classes, and speaking engagements	Have the flexibility to scale the Business of Story platform by selling it at 4× earnings by December 31, 2025
Founder/CEO of an Emerging Enterprise	Clarify and align the brand strategy in three months to create new possibilities for growth and prosperity	Assemble a guiding coalition among staff and employees in six months to create internal buy-in and alignment with the brand story to prepare for an external launch	Launch the new brand story to external audiences within 12 months to differentiate the offering in the market
Director of Marketing, Sales, or HR	Craft a brand story platform / culture in three months for more consistent and resonant communications	Craft #___ brand marketing stories and activate through #___ channels in six months	Increase brand awareness, adoption, and appreciation by ___% in 12 months
The Industrious Executive	Create a personal brand story platform in three months for focus, confidence, and influence	Apply the new refined brand story for measurable impact within an internal team or in a career search within six months	Celebrate demonstrable results of increased leadership influence by 12 months

Table 3.2 The ROI of storytelling for the Business of Story

Consider how you will measure the impact of your purpose-driven brand for you and each of your audiences.

Goals	Short Term	Medium Term	Long Term
Your Brand			
Audience #1			
Audience #2			
Audience #3			

Worksheet 3.3 Your ROI of brand storytelling

FINAL THOUGHTS

You are at the turning point between the first and second acts of the Story Cycle System. You've defined your #1 position in the marketplace to declare how you are functionally different from your competition, and therefore superior to them. You have prioritized your top three audiences. And now you've determined what's at stake for those audiences: what do they wish for and want to have to fulfill their wish. You have set the context for your brand story.

Now, in the next chapter, you will cause or embrace disruption in the world to become the most urgent and relevant offering for your customers. You will determine what will trigger their will to act and capture that sentiment in your unique value proposition.

Ready to shake things up?

ADDITIONAL RESOURCES

If you would like a deeper dive into determining what's at stake for you and your audiences, then visit businessofstory.com/stakes for these additional resources:

- Read Vol. III of the *Business of Story* online magazine: "What's at Stake?"
- Listen to TV producer Chapman Downes on the *Business of Story* podcast: "How HBO's Real Sports Tells Stories on Purpose"
- Watch my quick explanation on how to determine your short, medium, and long-term goals: bit.ly/StoryCycle-Stakes

STORY ON ACTIVITY

Ask your spouse, partner, friend, or colleague what they truly wish for themselves in a specific area of their life. Then ask what they want to make happen to fulfill their wish. Is it the purchase of an item, service, or an experience? How does this purchase help them achieve their wish? Then consider something you wish for. What item, service, or experience do you purchase to uplift yourself, express your personality, and fulfill your wish?

ADDENDUM FOR THIS CHAPTER

Here's a list of adjectives that describe emotions, from A to Z. Use them to determine what you and your audiences wish for.

A
Affectionate, Awed, Amazed, Astonished, Amused, Absorbed, Able, Admired, Admirable, Affable, Agreeable, Alluring, Animated

B
Brave, Blissful, Buoyant, Bold, Bewitching, Beautiful, Boundless

C
Cheerful, Cooperative, Confident, Calm, Curious, Content, Considerate, Carefree, Composed, Capable, Caring, Careful, Charitable, Crushed, Cantankerous, Critical, Crucial, Complete, Convincing, Consummate, Conclusive

D
Delighted, Determined, Daring, Devoted, Dynamic, Decisive, Direct

E
Elated, Enthusiastic, Embarrassed, Edgy, Excited, Envious, Eager, Exuberant, Euphoric, Extravagant, Ecstatic, Emboldened, Essential

F
Funny, Fair, Forgiving, Fulfilled, Fantastic, Fresh, Fundamental, Factual

G
Generous, Grateful, Gleeful, Glad, Gracious

H
Happy, Heartfelt, Hardy

I
Interested, Inspired, Inspiring, Inquisitive, Indefatigable, Industrious, Integral, Important, Influential, Irrefutable

J
Joyful, Joyous, Jocular

K
Kind, Keen, Key

L
Loving, Lively

M
Marvelous, Moved

N
Nice, Needed

O
Overjoyed, Optimistic, Open, Open-minded

P
Peaceful, Playful, Powerful, Pleased, Proud, Prideful, Potent, Peppy, Paramount

Q
Quirky, Qualified, Quivery, Quiet

R
Relieved, Relaxed, Refreshed, Rational, Reasonable, Reasoned, Rebellious, Reassured, Rejuvenated, Real

S
Surprised, Silly, Serious, Satisfied, Sensitive, Safe, Secure, Serene, Sociable, Sympathetic, Sincere, Strong, Spirited, Spry, Standout, Significant

T
Thankful, Thoughtful, Trusted, Trusting, Trustworthy, Tickled, Touched, Tender, Tranquil, Thorough

U
Unruffled, Unafraid, Useful, Uplifted, Unequivocal, Unmistakable

V
Vivacious, Vain, Vibrant, Valued, Valuable, Vital, Victorious

W
Wistful, Wishful, Willful, Willing, Whimsical, Warm, Witty, Worldly

Y
Youthful, Yielding, Yearning

Z
Zany, Zealous, Zestful, Zippy

4

Disruption

How Your UVP Will Win the Day

"We're here to put a dent in the universe. Otherwise, why else even be here?"

—Steve Jobs

TO LAUNCH A BRAND STORY YOU MUST BE DISRUPTIVE

We climbed out of our bunk beds hours before Sunday mass, toasted blueberry Pop-tarts®, and scrambled to the TV in our pajamas.

I was eight years old. My brother Tom was 11. At precisely 6:32 a.m. Pacific Daylight Time, time stopped. I sat mesmerized, watching the grainy black-and-white video from space that dispelled our last bits of sleepiness. We stared as the audio beeped and crackled, watching the spaceman descend from his craft. On cue, he said, "That's one small step for man, one giant leap for mankind." On July 20, 1969, 50 years ago as of this writing, American astronaut Neil Armstrong left an enduring footprint on the surface of the moon and made an indelible stamp on our world.

All because of a story that disrupted the status quo . . .

Eight years earlier, on May 25, 1961, President John F. Kennedy delivered his historic "Moon Shot" speech to Congress, wherein he told the country of his wish to demonstrate America's superiority in space by putting a man on the moon and returning him safely home.

Kennedy knew he had to marshal the will of the American people to achieve such an audacious feat, so he didn't simply announce that we were going to the moon and leave it at that. Instead, he authored a science-fiction fantasy harnessing the gravitational pull of story on our collective imaginations to enroll the country in a monumental quest:

"I believe that this nation should commit itself to achieving the goal, before this decade is out, of landing a man on the moon and returning him safely to the Earth. No single space project in this period will be more impressive to mankind, or more important for the long-range exploration of space, and none will be so difficult or expensive to accomplish.

"We propose to accelerate the development of the appropriate lunar spacecraft. We propose to develop alternate liquid and solid fuel boosters, much larger than any now being developed, until it is certain which is superior. We propose additional funds for other engine development and for unmanned explorations — explorations which are particularly important for one purpose which this nation will never overlook: the survival of the man who first makes this daring flight.

"But in a very real sense, it will not be one man going to the moon — if we make this judgment affirmatively, it will be an entire nation. For all of us must work to put him there."

To make sure America did not lose its will to land a man on the moon, in the following year JFK advanced the story in his "Moon Speech" at Rice University in Houston on September 12, 1962:

"We choose to go to the moon in this decade and do the other things, not because they are easy, but because they are hard . . .

" . . . [if] we shall send to the moon, 240,000 miles away from the control station in Houston, a giant rocket more than 300 feet tall, the length of this football field, made of new metal alloys, some of which have not yet been invented, capable of withstanding heat and stresses several times more than have ever been experienced, fitted together with a precision better than the finest watch, carrying all the equipment needed for propulsion, guidance, control, communications, food, and survival, on an untried mission, to an unknown celestial body, and then return it safely to Earth, reentering the atmosphere at speeds of over 25,000 miles per hour, causing heat about half that of the temperature of the sun — almost as hot as it is here today — and do all this, and do it right, and do it first before this decade is out — then we must be bold.

"And, therefore, as we set sail we ask God's blessing on the most hazardous and dangerous and greatest adventure on which man has ever embarked."

Five decades later, America remains the leader in space exploration because of JFK's disruptive call to adventure.

HOW TO DISRUPT YOUR AUDIENCE AND TRIGGER THEIR WILL TO ACT

Although you and your purpose-driven brand may not be exploring the outer reaches of our universe to save and advance humankind, you are on this earth to propel those you serve to a bit of peace and prosperity, which is no small feat. But to stir your audience's will to act, you must first get them to buy into your quest. You must first ignite their curiosity about you and your offering.

In Chapter 3, "Stakes," we explored what your audiences wish emotionally to have for themselves, and what they want physically to help make it happen. But where does their will to accomplish their goal come from?

We all seek opportunities to make our lives better while mitigating the risk inherent in that effort. But it's hard to shake ourselves out of the safety of the status quo. So we want what we believe are foolproof ways to achieve our wishes that provide us with the will to move forward. We want the singular provider in our pursuit — the brand — to offer exactly what we need and be the best at what the brand provides.

This is where your Unique Value Proposition (UVP) comes in. Your UVP defines what makes you the most timely, relevant, and urgent offering for your customers. It explicitly states what you do and how you're different, separating you from the surly bonds of your marketplace competition. Think of your UVP as your own personal space race. Your goal is to land your "brand module" not on the moon, but in the correct space in your customers' minds that will ignite their will to act. Your competitors, with their own UVPs, are racing you toward that spot.

The secret about your brand story and UVP is that they are *not* about what you make, but what you make *happen* in your customer's life. Your UVP is the spark that ignites the humanity in your brand story.

Here are a few UVPs that I think do a great job of articulating each brand's moon shot:

Airbnb = Belong anywhere

Mailchimp = Send better email

Dollar Shave Club = A great shave for a few bucks a month

Apple = Think different

FreshBooks = Small business accounting software designed for you, the non-accountant

Evernote = Remember everything

ClassPass = The most flexible fitness membership ever

Lyft = Ride in minutes

Uber = Get there: Your day belongs to you

Target = Expect more, pay less

NASA = Explore. Discover. Understand. (NASA could probably use a new UVP.)

Creating a compelling UVP that everyone can buy into and prosper from is the fourth step of the Story Cycle System™. The UVP is your brand's declaration about how you help your audiences respond to disruption (or avoid it) in their lives. Remember, a well-crafted UVP makes your offering the most urgent and relevant to help your customers get what they want out of life. Here's an example of how it worked for a community health center that needed to invigorate its brand story.

THE UVP THAT GREW ADELANTE HEALTHCARE
BY 600 PERCENT

In 2009, Clinica Adelante was a Federally Qualified Health Center in Maricopa County, Arizona, having received its first federal grant in 1979. However, the community health center had been founded years earlier as a free farmworker clinic. Clinica Adelante's mission was to "improve the health of our communities by providing quality, comprehensive primary healthcare, regardless of a patient's ability to pay."

But Arizona immigration laws, urban sprawl, increased competition in the healthcare market, and the Great Recession threatened the organization's survival.

Therefore, we guided Clinica Adelante through the Story Cycle System to author a refreshed brand story that celebrated the organization's legacy, while creating an aspirational narrative of "sustainable healthcare for all." The clinic's new purpose-driven brand story was supported by three brand pillars of operating as a financial, cultural, and environmentally sustainable organization.

The business results have been off the charts. By 2019, Adelante had quadrupled in size and scope, with 550+ employees, over $80 million annual revenue, 75,000 unique patients (from newborns to centenarians), and nine health center locations providing over 252,000 encounters per year.

As an expression of its "sustainable healthcare for all" UVP, Adelante opened the nation's first and currently only LEED Platinum–certified Community Health Center in Mesa, Arizona. Plus, Adelante now has two LEED Gold–certified centers in Peoria and Goodyear, Arizona.

By using the Story Cycle System to guide Adelante Healthcare's new brand story, the organization secured its own sustainability as a business, while becoming a national leader in providing sustainable healthcare for all. Let's explore exactly how this was accomplished.

"The Story Cycle was instrumental in defining our new and aspirational story, based on our legacy, that created an inspiring market position that our organization could live into: providing sustainable healthcare for all.

— Avein Tafoya, former CEO, Adelante Healthcare

HOW THE STORY CYCLE SYSTEM DEFINED ADELANTE'S BRAND STORY ELEMENTS

Let me walk you through the Adelante Healthcare story using the 10 steps of the Story Cycle System. You can use it as a guide to create your own healthy brand story and UVP.

BACKSTORY: Clinica Adelante was a 33-year-old community health center founded to treat the healthcare concerns of, primarily, the migrant farm population in western Maricopa County near Phoenix, Arizona. We rebranded the organization in 2010 as Adelante Healthcare.

HEROES: At the center of the Clinica Adelante story are three primary audiences:

1. The uninsured or underinsured patient

2. The insured patient

3. Premiere providers (doctors, nurses, and staff)

STAKES: Clinica Adelante had two important things at stake that were polar opposites. Avein was first concerned with the survival of the organization. Once she got it healthy again, her goal was to become a national leader in sustainable healthcare, and time was of the essence to carve out that brand position. To become a sustainable healthcare leader they delivered on what was at stake for their patients: access to comprehensive care regardless of their ability to pay. Operationally, the stakes were high with providers who wanted to practice world-class care in a sustainable, healthy environment.

DISRUPTION: Clinica Adelante's disruptive call to adventure was the critical need to refresh its brand to become more relevant to the population it wished to serve, and to reverse its declining patient rolls. Once they reframed their brand story, the organization became Adelante Healthcare with a UVP of "Sustaining Healthcare for All Arizonans."

ANTAGONISTS: The changing healthcare landscape was due in part to new, more restrictive Arizona immigration law, urban sprawl that replaced farms with houses, increased competition from for-profit healthcare providers, and the Great Recession.

Additionally — and even though their hearts were in the right place — the board of directors of Clinica Adelante initially posed an obstacle for progress as they held tight to the legacy of the organization and exhibited a natural reluctance to seek a new direction.

MENTOR: Adelante Healthcare has become the go-to provider in Arizona for sustainable healthcare for patients through its practice to the public. They operate 12 clinics, half of them LEED Certified, and operate all their centers through a lens of sustainability while maintaining the availability of quality healthcare for all.

JOURNEY: Adelante Healthcare supported its brand position and unique value proposition with three brand declarations:

1. We will sustain the health of each individual patient.

2. We will sustain the availability of healthcare for all.

3. We will sustain the environmental health of the communities we serve.

VICTORY: Adelante Healthcare has enjoyed approximately 600 percent growth in the past decade, while becoming a thought leader in sustainable healthcare nationwide.

THE MORAL: Adelante Healthcare's success shows that we can honor the past while not letting it constrict what's possible for a healthy future.

RITUAL: In addition to becoming the family physician for a growing number of patients, and building and staffing more LEED-certified centers, Adelante is now a national go-to resource for healthcare sustainability across the enterprise.

CRAFTING YOUR UVP WITH THE ABT

When you are creating your UVP, you first consider what's at stake for your brand, as I described above with Adelante Healthcare. Then you look outward to understand what's at stake for your external audiences. Your goal is to create a UVP that bridges these two worlds by being aspirational to your people and actionable to your customers.

Once you've determined what's at stake for your brand, define the disruption that is happening in your customers' world. Then, describe how you are their answer to this disruption, making your brand the most timely, relevant, and urgent offering to help them get what they want and wish for. I'm about to introduce a great tool to help you craft your UVP, but first let's take another quick look at JFK's space exploration story:

> On October 4, 1957, the Russians disrupted the free world by beating America to space with their satellite called Sputnik, and later by launching the first man into orbit, Yuri Gagarin. But to keep from being bested by the Ruskies during the Cold War, Americans had to muster the will in response to JFK's daring call to adventure to land a man on the moon and return him safely to Earth. This disruption in the space race was exactly what the nation needed to trigger its will to compete and win by investing north of $25 billion dollars for the Apollo program.

Did you feel the tension in the paragraph above? Did it draw you in? That tension is created by a small but powerful narrative framework called the And, But & Therefore (ABT). I learned it from Dr. Randy Olson, the Harvard evolutionary-biologist-turned-USC-filmmaker and author who teaches scientists how to use storytelling to secure grants and clarify their lofty thinking for us commoners.

Dr. Olson, author of *Houston, We Have a Narrative: Why Science Needs Story*, states that the ABT framework is the "nucleus of narrative." I call it the DNA of story because it uses the narrative structure of agreement | contradiction | consequence that our monkey brains love. To bring the ABT down to earth, Olson wrote a new book for business leaders titled *Narrative Is Everything: The ABT Framework and Narrative Evolution*.

I think of it even more simply as setup | problem | resolution. MBAs would call it situation | conflict | resolution. Jerry Seinfeld would describe it as setup | twist | punch line. The bottom line is that the ABT is a perfect three-act structure. Your mind loves it because it specifies what you're solving for. This is important for you because, while your brand is in the wish-granting business, it's the problem you solve for your customer that fulfills their emotional wish. The clearer you are on stating the problem, the easier it is for your audiences to buy into your story. Isn't that what you want to grant your wish?

You make a statement of agreement AND raise the stakes. BUT then you inflict conflict or contradiction. THEREFORE, you provide the answer to the question "What next?" This propels your story forward while establishing the problem your brand is solving for. Here's a simple way of working through this fundamental narrative structure:

Set the stage AND Raise the stakes

BUT State the problem

THEREFORE Reveal your solution.

Think of the ABT as your brain's fundamental operating code that instantly processes all of life events: Where am I? What's changing? How must I react? The AND sets the stage for what is. The BUT upends or disrupts the status quo — it's the contradiction to a paradigm, the complication that you must overcome. The greater the contrast between your setup with the AND part of your ABT and the BUT element, the more relevant your offering becomes, which is resolved with the THEREFORE statement.

If you're going to trigger your customer's will to go after what they wish for and want, you must accentuate their need or reason to do so. Otherwise, their wish and want will go unfulfilled and you'll be without a sale.

Trevor Hill, CEO of Global Water and a client whose brand story we crafted, said to me, "In sales, all you do is find the hurt, amplify the pain, and heal the wound." Now that is a concise ABT!

An ABT I've been using lately is:

Most executives communicate AND care BUT don't connect. THEREFORE, use the fundamental narrative framework of the ABT to make people care.

Here's the ABT for the Business of Story:

You have an important purpose-driven brand story to tell AND you wish it was being heard to create exponential growth for your business, your people, and the communities you serve.

BUT, like your myriad competitors, you're toiling in a crowded, noisy, and distracted world that commoditizes your product or service unless you find a way to stand out.

THEREFORE, use the primal power of storytelling to hack through the noise and hook the hearts of your audience, align your people, engage your customers, and build trust in your offering that everyone can buy into and prosper from.

This ABT helped me clarify the need for the Story Cycle System to help purpose-driven leaders clarify their stories to amplify their impact and simplify their lives. It's time for you to create an ABT that will lead to your UVP. By the way, I think of the ABT as your storytelling dumbbell, because becoming a good storyteller takes practice and exercise to build your narrative muscles.

Use the ABT in all your communications. I've had my Arizona State University executive master's students tell me that using the ABT has shortened their email writing by as much as two-thirds, AND their colleagues thank them for being much more concise and understandable. BUT, the ABT takes practice. THEREFORE, use it every day in every way, starting right now for your UVP.

NOW IT'S YOUR TURN
WHAT'S YOUR ABT?

AND _____

_____

BUT _____

_____

THEREFORE _____

_____

Now that you have clarified the need for your offering and identified what market dynamics you're responding to that amp up your customers' will to act, let's bring these first four chapters of the Story Cycle System together to craft your unique value proposition. Here's how it works for the Business of Story:

BACKSTORY: The Business of Story is the #1 resource for leaders of purpose-driven brands to align your people, engage your customers, and build trust for your offering using the proven power of the Story Cycle System.

HEROES: We're for you if you're a founder of an emerging business, a C-suite executive, or an entrepreneur who . . .

STAKES: . . . wishes to experience exponential growth for your organization, your people, and the communities you serve, and who wants a measurable approach to communications to stand out in a crowded market, to be heard, and to move people to action.

BUT we are unlike traditional ad agencies and typical digital marketing firms that provide standard branding services without an intentional focus on a narrative that hacks through the noise, hooks human emotion, and humanizes your offering.

CALL TO ADVENTURE: The Business of Story conjures compelling brand stories through the applied science and bewitchery of storytelling in a 10-step system that is distilled from the timeless narrative structure of the ancients, inspired by the story artists of Hollywood, influenced by masters of persuasion, guided by trend spotters, and informed by how the human mind grapples for meaning.

THE BUSINESS OF STORY UVP: *Excel through the stories you tell.*

Now it's time for you to capture the following elements of your brand story and ultimately craft your UVP:

Crafting Your Unique Value Proposition	
Audiences	For _____ _____ _____ _____
Stakes	Who wish for_____ _____ _____ and want_____ _____ _____
Competitors	But_____ _____ _____
Offering	Therefore,_____ _____ _____

Worksheet 4.1 Use this framework to set up
your unique buying proposition.

Craft Your Unique Value Proposition
_____

Worksheet 4.2 Now craft your succinct and compelling
unique value proposition.

FINAL THOUGHTS

The first three steps of the Story Cycle System focused on how you are functionally different from your competition and who you are for, relative to your audiences and what's at stake in their journeys. Now you are beginning to humanize your brand by declaring your unique value proposition. Plus, you've earned the added bonus of learning the And, But & Therefore (ABT) narrative framework, which will be invaluable in clarifying all your communication to amplify your impact and simplify your life.

Remember Trevor Hill's sales wisdom about finding the hurt, amplifying the pain, and healing the wound? Well, in Chapter 5, "Antagonists," you will learn how to amplify the pain and capitalize on market tension for an even more compelling brand story. Let's go meet your villains, peer through the fog, and bridge the crevasses in your story.

ADDITIONAL RESOURCES

For a deeper dive into creating your unique value proposition, visit businessofstory.com/disruption for these additional resources:

- Read Vol. IV of the *Business of Story* online magazine: "Disruption: Creating Your Unique Value Proposition"

- Listen to Jennifer Russo on the *Business of Story* podcast to learn how she clarified her personal brand story to land the director of communications role for Banner Health: "How to Bring Clarity and Energy to Your Brand Story."

- Watch my quick explanation on how to create your UVP: bit. ly/StoryCycle-Disruption

STORY ON ACTIVITY

Find three brands you admire and see if you can determine their UVP. Is it clear and compelling? Subtle? Does it need clarifying, or is it perhaps even nonexistent?

5

Antagonists

How to Capitalize on Competitive Forces

"Story = Character + Predicament + Attempted Extrication"

—Jonathan Gottschall, author of *The Storytelling Animal:
How Stories Make Us Human*

EMBRACE YOUR ANTAGONISTS

You have the wish to clarify your brand story. You want a proven system to improve your odds of fulfilling your wish, so you're working through the Story Cycle System™. Your will to progress is fueled by market events that are impacting your brand. You must position yourself against growing competition. You need to engage employees to get them all pulling in the same direction. Recruiting and retaining top talent is paramount to your success. And you want to answer decisively when someone asks you, "What's your story?"

But the universe is testing you. It throws all kinds of obstacles and antagonists in your path just to see how badly you really want it. These threshold guardians are many and varied. They include aggressive competitors; internal confusion about what you stand for; ghastly gaps in your performance. In addition to all the hurdles you experience when reaching out to your customers to buy your product or service. You're competing for their attention, their mindshare and their money. Maybe they don't understand your offering. Or perhaps you haven't bridged the gap between their wish and want, so consequently they don't have the will to proceed with you.

In this chapter, we'll explore the three categories of story tension you will want to embrace and exploit in your brand story to make your offering more urgent than your competition's. Because story tension is actually a good thing. It provides the mystery, surprise, and delight in your stories that your audiences relish. There's a reason why the oldest story in the world is "A man falls into a hole." Life is about conflict, resolution, and the growth that results. So instead of pushing your antagonists away, embrace them to capitalize on their power.

For your brand storytelling purposes, I've broken these antagonists down into three primary categories: villains, fog, and crevasses.

Villains are defined by internal and external competitive forces, including competitors undercutting you, resource scarcity (e.g., time, money, staff), and your internal demons that summon fear and self-doubt to demoralize and detour you. Fear is often our greatest foil.

Fog is your blind spots: what you don't know you don't know. But to your credit, even though you're not totally sure yet that you're on the right path with your brand story, at least this book has equipped you with a proven field guide to help you navigate the jungle and clear the air.

Crevasses are the gaps between your mental plans and your operational execution. You think and say one thing, but you're doing something else. I'm not throwing you under the bus here—we all do this. But you must mind the gap because your new brand story will be making big, wish-fulfilling promises to your audiences and you'll need to deliver on those promises.

The jujitsu trick is not to combat these forces, but to use them to your advantage to further power your will and catapult your offering. Plus, when you examine the villains, fog, and crevasses that confront your customers, and you can help them overcome these obstacles and antagonists, you become the go-to brand. You play the important role of mentor in their life, which we will cover in the next chapter.

FIND THE HURT, AMPLIFY THE PAIN, HEAL THE WOUND

I was sitting in founder and CEO Trevor Hill's office at Global Water when he told me his jarring definition of sales that I related in Chapter 4: "In sales, all you do is find the hurt, amplify the pain, and heal the wound." Global Water is a local water utility that has become an international leader in the reclamation and reuse of water in arid communities. Trevor learned his brand of water management as a water resource officer on aircraft carriers in the

Royal Canadian Navy. So it made sense that he was now in the desert, where conservation is at a premium, building a company that ensured the provision of clean and safe water.

The chief villain in the Global Water brand story is wasting water. We designed a customized market category for Global Water within the water utility industry that defined their position as experts at "resource scarcity management," Conscientious water management and delivery is what they "make." Protecting this crucial resource for generations to come is what they make happen. And without the focused mission of combating water waste, Global Water would be just another utility.

So why did they call us in to help? Because Trevor wished to differentiate his company from the typical utilities that just delivered water. He wanted to demonstrate water conservation at the service level to encourage customers to do the same. Plus, Global Water's brand of water utility made solid business sense, too. Instead of delivering water, handling the sewage, treating the effluence, dumping it back into the ground as state regulations required for additional filtering (and water loss, by the way), and then pumping it back out again and starting the cycle over, it made much more financial sense to treat it at the source and return it to customers. Technology had advanced to the point that this was a healthy, viable approach to water management—but old mind-sets die hard.

To become successful in the early 2000s at their innovative approach to reclaiming and reusing water in our communities, Global Water needed to sell regulators on the importance of reuse. They had to help regulators overcome their primary **villain**, which was their belief that recycled water was not "clean" water. To defeat this villain, Global Water demonstrated the latest highly effective water purification technology and told stories about how European communities are using this technology to save millions of gallons of water and tons of money.

But villains weren't the only antagonists at play. Trevor and his team had to clear up the **fog** around the tremendous waste associated with current water management practices of delivery, sewage, treatment, pumping back into and then out of the ground, retreatment, and redelivery. They opened regulators' eyes to the technology through facility tours and informational meetings. And they built a community educational center to help residents and businesses understand the new way to use and reuse water, thereby increasing their conservation ethos.

Finally, there was an enormous **crevasse** between what public officials were saying in their publicity campaigns about the need for everyone to responsibly conserve water and what they were actually doing in municipal water management.

While Global Water was a forward thinking utility, it was not telling their brand story because they hadn't yet captured it. By going through the Story Cycle System, they clearly understood how to use the villains, fog, and crevasses to their advantage. Trevor built one of the fastest growing purpose-driven water utilities in the country.

You might think Trevor's definition of sales is a bit on the dark side. But it makes sense, especially given our natural negativity bias in service to our survival. His definition is in a perfect three-act story structure, too. Find the hurt = setup. Amplify the pain = problem. Heal the wound = resolution. To me, this is just another example of how our minds are wired for the setup / problem / resolution framework, because processing knowledge in this fashion is how our primal storytelling apparatus ensures our survival as a species.

So in the first four chapters of this guidebook, you were finding the hurt: What problem do you solve better than anyone else? Who cares? What do they (your customers) want solved? Why do they want it solved?

WHAT DOESN'T KILL YOU . . .

In this chapter, you are learning how to amplify the pain to make your brand story even more compelling. You do this by asking how you can help your customers overcome their internal and external barriers to heal their wound. By articulating for them the various obstacles and antagonists they face, you are also demonstrating that you understand what they're up against. This creates connection and empathy. They feel you are like them and have their back. This is when trust is built. Stories reveal a truth that creates trust. They start to feel that your story is their story. This leads to brand adoption and appreciation, which in turn equals sales and money for you.

In the mythic structure of Campbell's Hero's Journey, this portion of the story is called "Tests, Allies, and Enemies." The stakes are being raised and the pressure is mounting for the central character.

That's why this is a natural juncture for your villains, fog, and crevasses to surface. First determine what obstacles and antagonists are out to thwart the growth of your brand — it's kind of like a story SWOT analysis* — and then identify the oppositional forces that your customers must overcome to buy into your brand story.

For instance, if you're not battling the nasty villain of obfuscation to create meaning for your brand, then the service Business of Story offers wouldn't be relevant to your journey. Obfuscation runs with the crusty henchman of confusion, who's out to muddle your messaging. Oh, and don't forget boredom. He's always just sitting there dragging his big toe through the dirt in the shadows. He's subtly sadistic, because when was the last time you were bored into buying anything?

So you're leveraging the Story Cycle System to overcome these antagonists. The win comes in creating clarity to align your people with a focused vision. But the clearing of the fog reveals more obstacles in the way — gaps in performance that you must close. By tackling these challenges you add even greater significance to your mission for your people as they rally against a common foe. Without these competitive market forces and adverse operational dynamics, you would remain motionless in status quo. You simply would have no reason to do anything but sit there.

But, do you know what's the most hideous example of a villain that damages the performance of a brand? It's the worst kind of adversary. It's shiny and alluring. But this bully clouds the ego with false praise while it widens the performance gap between perception and reality, setting up the recipient for a fall.

This villain is called the participation trophy. You know those insidious totems of childhood. They are presented without merit to any kid anywhere who happens to show up, even occasionally, in a uniform, even on the crappiest team in the league. I believe that participating should be encouraged but not rewarded. The prize comes in the form of positive outcomes, especially when the odds are stacked against you. Trophies are just an ego-inflating symbol of success.

---

*By SWOT analysis, I'm referring to the age-old business practice of exploring the strengths, weaknesses, opportunities, and threats facing your brand. It's important to understand these four operational areas because they will influence the creation of your overall brand narrative, as well as inform how, when, and where you tell your stories.

If I were a Russian despot hatching a cunning plan to weaken a generation of Americans, I'd encourage the culture, in the name of fairness, to give every child a participation trophy regardless of their ability to contribute to a common cause. It's brilliant. Because in man's quest to counter natural competitive forces with participation trophies, we temporarily short-circuit the pervasive evolutionary dynamic of survival of the fittest, which wins out in the end. The meek inherit a trophy, and they may even inherit the world, but they will be trounced by committed market competition.

When have you ever received anything of value for nothing? It is just these antagonist forces, the ones punching us in the nose on the playing field of life, that imbue our offering with value. The adage "No conflict, no story" rings true with your brand.

These headwinds provide the lift every fulfilling life requires, the unique problems every brand solves, and the tension every story needs to propel the journey forward. Think of an airplane — it can't take off unless it is accelerating into a headwind. It requires determined thrust from its engines while maintaining the proper attitude to use air pressure to overcome the relentless tug of gravity. Only when thrust and attitude are aligned does it achieve its precise altitude. The higher, faster, and farther it wants to go, the greater the natural forces the pilot must overcome.

Attitude and effort are the only two things you really control in life, no matter what it chooses to throw at you. So embrace the villains, fog, and crevasses that are trying to stop you and capitalize on their energy to transport you, your brand, and your people to another world.

As Nietzsche wrote, "What does not kill me makes me stronger."

HOW SOCIAL RESISTANCE PROVIDES BRAND LIFT

In September 2016, Luis Miguel contacted me about helping refine Avantpage's brand story. For the previous 22 years, Luis and his team had provided language translation services for government, elections officials, and healthcare and educational programs to help immigrants assimilate in this country. Avantpage is headquartered in Davis, California, and has offices in Mexico City and Warsaw, Poland.

In 1973, Luis Miguel traveled from his home in Mexico City to the Ozark Mountains in Missouri for summer camp. It was his first visit to the United States. He was 15 years old. He was excited to experience America, but his excitement quickly dimmed when a boy at camp referred to Luis using a term he had never heard before. Being bookish, Luis returned home and looked up the meaning of wetback.

Five years later, with imperfect language skills, Luis returned to America to study at the University of Colorado at Boulder, but the university seemed cold and intimidating. So he moved to the University of California at Davis, to study agriculture and worked with migrant families in appalling farm conditions. Luis graduated and earned his PhD in computer science at the University of California at Berkeley. But he never forgot those migrant families. A few years later, Luis and his wife began a family of their own.

"I realized that the difference for kids is where they are born. These experiences made me sensitive to the plight of immigrants in the US and especially those who need special language support to connect with the people and institutions of America."

In 1996, Luis started Avantpage, an international translation firm. He combined the need for linguistics with compassion and empathy for immigrants. Luis, following many rough experiences assimilating into America, wished to help others realize their American dream. He wanted to create a translation company like no other that connects people, cultures, and communities. And the nationalism and polarization he sees growing around the world gives him the will to make an even greater difference in immigrant lives.

But Luis realized that their specialized translation work wasn't being recognized. The Avantpage brand blended in with myriad other translation firms. He knew it was time to refresh the company's brand story to ensure its growth and sustainability. But many obstacles stood in his way, including the risk of being commoditized in a crowded translation market. This market pressure, like other incidents that have propelled Luis' story forward, are what prompted him to seek us out and write the next chapter of the Avantpage story. He refined his brand in 2017 using the Story Cycle System.

The return on his new brand story has already been impressive, including:

1. Thirty percent more new business prospects since launching Avantpage's refreshed brand story.

2. Avantpage's organic search rankings dramatically improved because its new brand narrative focused on the SEO terms most relevant to its offering.

3. The website conversion rate quadrupled because now Avantpage is speaking the language of its ideal customer.

4. Since rebranding, Avantpage has experienced a 200 percent increase in applicants who mention that they feel connected to the brand's new mission of helping immigrants.

5. Avantpage reports a "massive increase" in employee interaction and enthusiasm for its refreshed brand.

This all sounds great, but you're probably interested in what exactly Luis did to achieve these things. Let me detail how the Avantpage brand story came together. We'll go through the entire Avantpage story cycle, and you can then use this example as yet another guide to help you craft your own brand narrative.

STEP 1: BACKSTORY—WHERE IN THE WORLD HAVE YOU BEEN?
Claim your #1 position in the market to focus your story.

What do you do differently—and therefore better—than your competition? We arrived at Avantpage's brand position statement by having them define what industry, category, and specialty they operate in:

Industry: Communications

Category: Language service provider

Specialty: Translation services

But this isn't enough to separate them from their competition. Avantpage, like all brands, must lay claim to their #1 specialty in their market. Declare your #1 position and you can become the go-to resource for your specialty. Here's what they arrived at:

Brand Position Statement: Avantpage is the #1 resource for translation services to help governments, healthcare, and democratic elections connect with and empower immigrant populations.

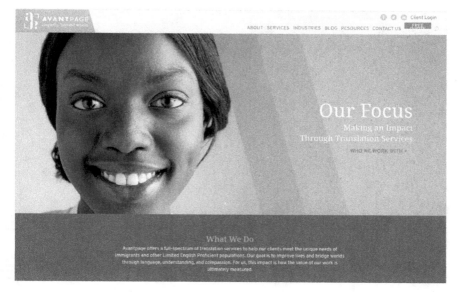

Figure 5.1 Avantpage website homepage

By declaring their #1 position in the crowded language translations market, Avantpage began to focus on what they do exceedingly well and, more important, why they do it: to empower immigrant populations. Can you see how their story is already starting to elevate the brand from just being another B2B translation company to one that stands for something greater?

STEP 2: HEROES: WHO'S YOUR AUDIENCE?
Identify your target audiences to make your message resonate.

Who cares the most about your product or service? Who are you for? These are the audiences you want to invite into and buy into your brand story. In Avantpage's brand story, they prioritized their audiences in this order:

Audience #1: Employees

Audience #2: Customers

Audience #3: Vendors/linguists

It often makes sense to identify your employees as your top audience when it comes to rebranding because you need to get them

Figure 5.2 An Avantpage employee shares her support
of the brand story.

to believe in and model your story before you share it with your customers. Sometimes brands place customers first before they get buy-in from their people, which can lead to an awkward and weak launch of your new or refreshed brand.

And don't forget your suppliers. They are an important part of your story because they operate as de facto extensions of your brand. You want them living into and prospering from your story, too.

STEP 3: STAKES: WHAT'S AT STAKE?
Clarify what your audiences seek so you can connect on a deeper level through understanding and empathy.

Once Avantpage identified their primary audiences, they clarified what was at stake for each: what they wish for and want relative to the Avantpage offering.

Audience #1: Employees

Employees wish to make a difference in immigrant lives and want to participate in a new brand story that they can live into and prosper from.

Audience #2: Customers

Avantpage customers wish to feel the satisfaction of helping their constituents by providing clear communication, and they want the most timely, accurate, and trustworthy translations possible from a caring provider.

Audience #3: Vendors/linguists

Vendors and linguists who serve Avantpage wish to be appreciated for the valuable service they provide and want to be treated with respect while applying their craft to a consistent volume of meaningful work.

As you may notice, what's at stake for each of these audiences is not so much about

Figure 5.3 Avantpage trade show panel

wanting/needing the physical translations that the brand provides (that's a given), but wanting the trust, integrity, and fulfillment that comes from engaging with an honorable brand like Avantpage.

By understanding these psychological needs, we elevate the Avantpage offering in the hearts and minds of its audiences. This leads to the next step of articulating what this all means through their unique value proposition.

STEP 4: DISRUPTION: THE CALL TO ADVENTURE
Declare your unique value proposition to create brand distinction.

To take your first big step out of the primordial muck of commoditization you must battle status quo by changing yourself. To do that, you either have to be the disruptive force in the market or position your brand as the answer to the disruption others are creating in the market. Either way, your goal is to become the most timely, relevant, and urgent offering in response to changing conditions.

But that takes guts.

Avantpage decided to separate itself from the pack by being the disruptive leader, having the courage to become an activist brand. This was an especially timely ethos in 2016, given the chaos in polarized leadership in DC, the proposed border wall between America and Mexico, and nationalism that was turning its back on immigration.

Avantpage isn't just about providing trusted translation services. They are the translation company to work with when you actually care about helping immigrants realize their American dream.

Once they got clear on this fact — that their brand story isn't about what they make (translations), but what they make happen (helping immigrants realize their American dream) — then everything else came into focus, including their unique value proposition.

Unique Value Proposition: Avantpage, with empathy beyond words, helps immigrants *overstand* their brave new world.

Yes, you read that right. Overstand!

Their UVP is based on the concept of "overstanding." Overstanding came from the global hip-hop culture. Artists coined the term to portray the distinction between the understanding that life is difficult and the overstanding that life is more difficult than it needs to be because it is in the interest of those in power to keep things as they are.

The Urban Dictionary defines *overstanding* as follows:

The distinction between overstanding and understanding is a matter of context and awareness. To overstand is to comprehend a thing itself AND to have knowledge of why it is the way it is and of its place or role in the grand scheme of things. If you can use something or do a job, you understand and memorize enough to act. One who understands may also be able to innovate or redesign but otherwise accepts the boundaries of a thing as given. Those who overstand appreciate the bigger picture and their rightful place in it.

The concept of overstanding became the linchpin of the Avantpage activist brand story. It led to its brand theme: *overstanding with empathy beyond words.*

STEP 5: ANTAGONISTS: VILLAINS, FOG, AND CREVASSES
Take advantage of opposing market forces to strengthen your brand performance.

As we've explored in this chapter, every story has its obstacles and antagonists that stand in the way of the hero's success. For Avantpage, these competitive forces included:

Villains = what they termed "big wig" vendors, "fly-by-night" operators, and DIY online platforms.

Fog = Many of Avantpage's customers didn't realize that these competitors provide impersonal, transactional, and often imprecise translations.

Crevasses = The competition not only vies for Avantpage's customers, but often soils the industry's reputation through unreliable service and shoddy translations.

These kinds of market dynamics are important to your brand story. This story tension is what you position your brand against to strengthen your UVP: what you stand for and how you deliver on your promises. Your effort and attitude.

You can stop here if you like and start doing the worksheet at the end of this chapter to determine your villains, fog, and crevasses. But a lot of clients ask for examples of how others have used the Story Cycle System, so here's the rest of the Avantpage story.

STEP 6: MENTOR
Humanize your brand with its promise, gift, and personality to build belief and trust.

At this halfway point of the Story Cycle System, we focus on the personality of your brand. I'm getting a little ahead of myself here, because we will detail the following five Story Cycle System steps in the following five chapters. But I'm including Avantpage's final brand story elements here as an easy reference for you to return to.

Your findings in this stage, which will be covered in Chapter 6, will shape the personality of your brand, including look, feel, tone, and content, etc.

Emotionally, what does your brand provide to every one of your audiences? What is the psychological thread that weaves them all together? For Avantpage, that emotion is trust. It's important to define your brand promise because it becomes the aspirational North Star that your employees will steer toward.

Again, the brand gift is a reflection of our brand mantra: "It's not what you make, but what you make happen." For Avantpage, what they make happen in the lives they touch is the phenomenon of overstanding. Understanding is knowledge, while overstanding is wisdom from experience: the intrinsic brand gift Avantpage provides. As an activist brand, Avantpage provides overstanding to everyone they encounter.

Now that you have determined physically and philosophically what you provide to your audience, it's time to determine the personality of your brand. In working with Avantpage, we used Swiss psychologist Carl Jung's 12 primary personality archetypes. We'll cover brand archetypes in the next chapter, too.

Avantpage selected the Caregiver as its primary archetype, which is a direct reflection of the earnestness of its founder, Luis. Then they selected Regular Guy/Gal and the Hero as supporting archetypes, which speaks to their easygoing but activist mentality. Kind of like President Teddy Roosevelt's famous line, "Speak softly and carry a big stick."

In the case of Avantpage, they operate with empathy beyond words through their Caretaker archetype with a hint of Regular Guy/Gal for depth. Then the Hero archetype colors its attitude toward helping immigrants overstand their situation to provide them agency to act. These personalities are combined to reflect the character of Avantpage, which encourages immigrants to find their personal agency in their quest for the American dream.

Brand Promise: Trust

Brand Gift: Overstanding

Brand Personality: Caregiver (secondary archetypes: Regular Guy/Gal and Hero)

STEP 7: JOURNEY

Increase customer engagement through the stories you tell.

Once you have arrived at your brand's promise, gift, and character archetype, find nine one-word descriptors that support your personality. These are important because you'll use them as story themes throughout your customer engagement to move your audience from brand awareness to adoption to appreciation and beyond. I'll take you through an exercise in Chapter 7 to help you find your nine one-word descriptors.

Think of three words that describe your company, three words that define your offering, and three words that detail your customer service. Here's what Avantpage arrived at:

Brand Descriptors:

Excellence

Rigorous

Trusted

Empathy

Camaraderie

Opportunity

Empower

Advocate/Activist

Knowledge

Avantpage used their descriptors as one-word themes to find and share their brand stories. The resulting true stories demonstrate the real-world impact Avantpage has on its customers and the communities they serve. By exploring the Avantpage website, you can see for yourself how Avantpage uses their descriptors to support their personality and guide the creation of their creative communications.

STEP 8: VICTORY

Celebrate wins on the Customer Journey Of Brand Awareness to Adoption Through Appreciation.

One of the big mistakes your brand can make is not planning for the small success milestones your audiences will experience as they engage with your company. Consider how you will celebrate each success point with your customers when they pass through the thresholds of brand awareness, adoption, and appreciation.

I won't divulge how Avantpage is building bonds with its audiences, but suffice it to say that having a plan in this area helps you move your customers from brand appreciation to evangelism. You'll learn how to do this in Chapter 8, "Victory."

It was at this point that we brought together everything from the first seven steps of the Story Cycle System and captured it in Avantpage's brand statement:

> **Brand Statement:** Avantpage — with empathy beyond words — empowers immigrants to achieve their American dream through trusted language translations. We help them grasp the nature and significance of an ideal or issue, strive for complete and intuitive comprehension so they can connect with and navigate through their brave new world, and truly *overstand* their journey.

STEP 9: THE MORAL

Articulate your purpose to elevate the meaning of your brand.

Through the first nine steps of the Story Cycle System we humanized the Avantpage brand narrative and we elevated the visceral meaning of Avantpage to a level that would make Maslow proud.

In Step 1 we identified Avantpage's features and functions, or their physiological needs, to determine their #1 position in the world: what Avantpage does differently and therefore better than their competition.

Then we stepped up to safety in Maslow's hierarchy by understanding their audiences and what's at stake for them in their journey. We leveled up to life/belonging, as captured in Avantpage's unique value proposition: Avantpage, with empathy beyond words, helps immigrants overstand their brave new world.

Russian
"Я достану тебе звезду с неба"
"I will get you a star from the sky."
-Daria Toropchyn

Figure 5.4 Russian promotional poster

And then we developed their personality in the Mentor phase to create esteem around the brand supported by its nine descriptors. Here Avantpage activates its personality by mapping customer engagement and celebrating the victories, large and small, along the way.

Now we're at the self-actualization step in the Story Cycle System, as we define Avantpage's brand purpose.

Brand Purpose: Avantpage exists to help all immigrants realize their American dream.

In Chapter 9, we will ask you to declare your brand purpose: why your brand exists to help people beyond making money.

It's worth repeating: It's not what you make, but what you make happen that is what your brand story is about. Avantpage exists to help all immigrants realize their American dream. They just happen to do it through precise translation services to help their customers overstand what's really going on in their world.

STEP 10: RITUAL

DESIGN YOUR BRAND RITUALS FOR REPEAT BUSINESS

Now your goal is to make your brand a significant part of your customers' lives. How do you build repeat business by becoming a ritual? The answer to that question is: through evangelism. Make your story their story, and they will share it with their world. Word-of-mouth marketing is your most powerful and least expensive form of advertising. It leads to referrals and a growing business. Once you have people evangelizing your brand, you will have elevated your customers from brand awareness through adoption to appreciation.

This is how you humanize your brand. Stand for something greater. Connect with audiences and customers on a deeper level by speaking their language. And exercise your own empathy beyond words.

NOW IT'S YOUR TURN

Here's how we at the Business of Story have outlined the villains, fog, and crevasses in our own journey. Our steps will provide a template for you to follow. First, you want to outline what your brand is up against, and then identify the obstacles and antagonists that your audiences are trying to overcome.

	Villains	Fog	Crevasses
Business of Story	Lots of emerging "gurus" and the need to differentiate the Business of Story brand	Clarifying our brand story online to feature our consulting, masterclasses, and speaking services	How to scale our enterprise with extremely efficient resources
Founder/CEO of an Emerging Enterprise	Emerging competition is eroding your market share and internally there is confusion about the direction of the brand	Your people aren't bought in to a consistent brand narrative which is adversely impacting performance	You are unable to clearly articulate your brand story to shareholders and stakeholders
Director of Marketing, Sales, or HR	Your external and internal competitive forces are keeping your teams from pulling together on a focused mission	People are unclear about the brand story and how to use storytelling to grow sales, marketing, and internal initiatives	People are telling lots of different stories because they lack the tools to create a unified storytelling culture
The Industrious Executive	You face much competition for mindshare and need personal brand differentiation	You haven't clearly identified and communicated the moments/ stories that define your character	You aren't using your storytelling skills to connect on a human level with the people you're trying to influence

Table 5.1 An example worksheet of the villains, fog, and crevasses that confront our brand and our audiences

Now identify the villains, fog and crevasses that confront your brand and audiences:

Fill out the worksheet identifying the villains, fog and crevasses your brand must overcome and those same obstacles and antagonists in your audience's life that you help them overcome.

	Villains	Fog	Crevasses
Your Brand			
Audience #1			
Audience #2			
Audience #3			

Worksheet 5.1 Villains, fog, and crevasses your brand must overcome

FINAL THOUGHTS

You're halfway home. Your brand story is evolving from one of logic, reason, features, and functions to fulfilling the emotional wishes of your customers. But, as you've experienced in this chapter, it's not always easy. We've raised the stakes by making you call out your villains, fog, and crevasses, and those your audiences encounter with your brand. The only way to overcome these obstacles and antagonists is to get real about them. Denial leads to a drubbing. Plus, when you call them out you co-opt their power and use their energy to make your offering all the more compelling. The tussle strengthens your character. No participation trophies here. And defining the character of your brand in determining your promise, gift, and personality is exactly what you're going to tackle next.

ADDITIONAL RESOURCES

If you would like to venture deeper into the dragon's cave to determine your villains, fog, and crevasses, then visit businessofstory.com/antagonists for these additional resources:

- Read Vol. V of the *Business of Story* online magazine: "Obstacles & Antagonists: How to Profit from Adversity."

- Listen to Jonathan David Lewis on "Embracing a Survival Mindset in Your Brand Storytelling."

- Watch my quick explanation video on how to create your UVP: bit.ly/StoryCycle-Antagonists.

STORY ON ACTIVITY

Create an Instagram story that features three of your obstacles and antagonists, including a villain, a fog blind spot, and a crevasse performance gap. Then share it with me: instagram.com/parkhowell.

6

Mentor

How to Humanize Your Brand with Its Promise, Gift, and Personality

"The intuitive mind is a sacred gift and the rational mind is a faithful servant. We have created a society that honors the servant and has forgotten the gift."

— Albert Einstein

YOUR CUSTOMERS BUY *YOU*

I'm a fool.

I took the Heroic Myth Index test in Carol S. Pearson's book *Awakening the Heroes Within: Twelve Archetypes to Help us Find Ourselves and Transform our World* to better understand my personality. According to Pearson, I could've been the Innocent, Orphan, Warrior, Caregiver, Seeker, Lover, Destroyer, Creator, Ruler, Magician, or Sage. But what is the archetype personality currently prevalent in my life? Yep, the Fool—also known as the Jester or Trickster or, with age, the Wise Fool.

But that's a good thing. Pearson describes the Fool archetype as essential for the balance of the kingdom. A king or queen wouldn't think of running their empire without the entertainment and counsel of the court jester, because these fools can speak truths, puncture sacred veils, and break rules of etiquette and decorum, "thereby allowing an outlet for forbidden insights, behaviors, and feelings."

To me, our world is oppressively serious. Perhaps that's why the Fool is prominent within me. You have the Fool in you, too—maybe just to a lesser degree. It is the archetype that expresses itself as a primitive, spontaneous, playful creative.

"The Fool is the archetype most helpful in dealing with the absurdity of the modern world and with faceless, amorphous modern bureaucracies — places where no one takes personal responsibility, rules are expected to be followed no matter how absurd they might be, and the tables are incredibly stacked against individual effectiveness."

—Carol S. Pearson

And it's true — I pretty much rail against all those things. Always have. But the Fool isn't the only archetype present in my life. I also score high on Seeker (curiosity), Creator (industriousness), and Magician (personal power).

BRAND ARCHETYPING

In this chapter, I want to help you define the character archetype that reflects the authentic personality of *your* brand. Remember in Chapter 2, "Heroes," when I may have shifted your paradigm by placing your customers at the center of your brand story rather than you? Well, now in this chapter, you will learn how to reveal your brand as your audience's mentor or guide. Think about it: Luke Skywalker would never have overthrown the evil empire without the wisdom, tools, and instruction of Obi-Wan Kenobi and Yoda. How about Dorothy? She would've been stuck in Oz without Glinda the Good Witch of the North. You play the same role in your customers' lives. You equip them with your offering and wisdom to help them on their journey to fulfilling their wish. And since stories are what make us human, we use compelling character-defining archetypes — such as those in Carol Pearson's list above — to articulate and humanize your brand.

Early in my career I was taught to ask my customers insipid questions like: If your brand was a dog, what kind of dog would it be? What kind of car reflects your personality? How about a drink? Are you a cocktail? A beer? Diet soda? Energy drink?

This accepted branding process never sat well with me. *From all our insightful exploration, we have determined that your brand is a five-year-old green goldendoodle named Hazel that drives an Audi Q3, enjoys Manhattans, reads Vogue and Outside magazines, and gives her Nordstrom personal shopper birthday presents.*

Seriously, man, that was nuts. This put me on a quest for a more authentic exploration, which led to my discovery of brand archetyping. Here at last I found a foolproof way of sculpting and authenticating a brand's distinctive, enticing personality.

It is important to understand your brand personality because it informs the creative expression of your communications. How do you currently look, sound, and feel to your customers? Are you a Ruler brand like American Express, a Creator personality like Lego or Ikea, a Regular Guy/Gal persona like Charles Schwab, a Caregiver identity like Oprah and her OWN Network, or do you represent the character of the Hero archetype like Patagonia?

This guidebook provides you with 12 archetypes to choose from to determine the personality of your brand. But you have some introspection to do first. I'll summarize the steps here, in order, and the rest of the chapter will provide the details:

1. Define nine one-word descriptors for your organization, offering, and outcomes.

2. Embrace the emotional promise people experience with your brand.

3. Determine the intrinsic gift you provide in people's lives.

4. Reveal the personality of your brand by selecting its personality archetype.

1. FIND YOUR BRAND DESCRIPTORS

Think of your nine one-word brand descriptors as your brand's character traits. Defining them is the first step in determining your brand's personality archetype. This is where you start to create real meaning for your brand through the themes and stories you tell. And you do it to make it easy for your customers to understand the character of your organization, and the offering and outcomes you deliver.

You may be wondering why I'm insisting these descriptors be just one word. Well, think how often you have asked someone about something they experienced and they described its impact on them in one word.

"How'd you like the movie?" "It was *touching*."

"What'd you think of her personality?" "She's a *beautiful* person."

Or that time when I asked a friend about a show he saw and he replied, "*Brilliant!*"

I've had people describe my Business of Story workshops as *enchanting, intriguing,* and *mind-blowing.*

Remember the Seven Dwarfs? Each of them has his own one-word descriptor that defines his primary archetype: Happy, Sleepy, Doc, Bashful, Sneezy, Grumpy, and Dopey.

The point is, your mind automatically sifts out unimportant details to categorize information for easy assimilation and recall. We want to compartmentalize our knowledge about something, so we boil it down to one or two words that capture the essence of the entity or the experience. What words do people use to describe you, your brand, and your offering? What words would you like them to use?

DO THE "OOOH" EXERCISE

The OOOh exercise—"OOO" stands for Organization, Offering, and Outcomes—helps you determine the nine one-word descriptors that express your brand's character traits. The "h" underscores the exclamation point each of these words makes on your brand personality.

We ultimately want to get to the *one* word that expresses the emotional promise of your brand, but we start by figuring out the nine. Why? Because your company, product, or service and the customer engagement methods are multifaceted. These initial nine words are important storytelling themes that will help support your overall brand narrative. They become the essential building blocks of the true stories you will tell about the impact you make in the world.

Your anecdotes will not only demonstrate your brand ethos in action but will become the foundation for your content marketing. As you and your colleagues spot these stories in the wild, you will also begin building a storytelling culture. (Remember the ROI of story from Chapter 3 and what it can mean to your organization?)

For example, by performing the Oooh exercise, we derived the following nine one-word descriptors for the Business of Story:

Organization	Offering	Outcomes
Mage	Primal	Clarity
Industrious	Dynamic	Connection
Optimistic	Truth	Trust

Mage: At the Business of Story, we teach the applied science and bewitchery of storytelling. I also believe that if content is king, as so many content marketers profess, then storytelling is the kingdom's sorcerer — because telling stories is where the magic happens. That's why I believe our people are mages of sorts, magicians or learned people who are steeped in activating the mechanics and charisma of storytelling.

Industrious: Our expertise comes from being industrious. Synonyms include diligent, hard-working, and studious, which further underscores our approach to helping people reignite their inner storyteller. But I particularly like its root meaning: skillful, clever, and ingenious. We've experienced that the use of storytelling in branding is an ingenious skill to make your brand marketing points in a brilliant way that enchants the human mind.

Optimistic: As an organization, we are optimistic. While the world seems to be overwhelmed with information and interpersonally disconnected by technology — and has become polarized, nationalized, and ideologicalized — we've seen how an anecdote is the antidote that brings people back together, finding common ground through a shared story. So we encourage you to tell stories *on purpose.*

Primal: The three words that describe our offering naturally begin with "primal." *Homo sapiens* are the only creatures we know of that think in story. We use narrative as our central organizing force, creating imagined realities that we collectively live into. That's why storytelling is not a gimmick but has been a proven evolutionary tool since the beginning of recorded time. We are storytelling apes — therefore it makes sense to evolve as storytelling leaders.

Dynamic: Like thermal dynamics, storytelling has an energy and force all its own. Inspired by the definition of physics, story dynamics is the narrative science that studies imagination and its motion and behavior through the space and time of a story and its related entities of energy and force. Story dynamics is one of the most fundamental communication disciplines. Its main goal is to help us understand how the universe behaves through the stories we tell and live. We help you use stories to nudge the world in any direction you choose.

Truth: The singular purpose of a story is to reveal a truth. From truth comes trust. Sure, you can use stories to tell untruths. Comedian Stephen Colbert even coined the term "truthiness," describing something that is masquerading as genuine. But the fact is, with story the truth eventually prevails.

Clarity: The sole purpose of the three proven narrative structures—the And, But & Therefore framework, the five primal elements of a story which we will cover in Chapter 7, and the Story Cycle System taught by the Business of Story—is to evolve from an intuitive to an intentional storyteller to clarify your message. Clarity amplifies your impact because you make it easy for your audience to understand you and be open to your "ask." Plus, a clear and concise story helps you simplify your journey by focusing your mission on what's truly important to your success.

Connection: Storytelling is the Velcro of collaboration. As the storyteller, you start by understanding your audience's journey and empathizing with what they wish for and want. Then you share a story that they can appreciate to hook your two worlds together, creating a stronger whole. There is no more powerful uniting force between human beings than experiencing a shared story.

Trust: The truth about storytelling is that you use it to become confident in the authenticity of your personal narrative and the direction of your journey while gaining the trust of your audiences. Stories reveal truths that create trust.

You have just reviewed the nine one-word descriptors that are the narrative pillars for the Business of Story brand story strategy. In Chapter 7, you will see how these themes show up every day in our work. I'll share real-world anecdotes that reveal the truth about the impact we have on people through our storytelling offering and outcomes. But for now, let's get to work defining *your* brand's descriptors.

To find your descriptors, make three columns on a white board titled Organization, Offering, and Outcome. Give each of your team members nine Post-It® notes (three for each column) and ask them to individually write down three words for each of the categories. Wait until everyone is finished, and then place the Post-It notes under their respective categories on the white board. You will naturally group the same words together as you guide a dialogue about what nine words you will ultimately use to describe the character traits of your brand. This discussion is invaluable to building consensus in your organization about what your brand stands for. It reveals agreements and divisions within your ranks, and the resulting exploration helps you bridge those gaps and create unity around your brand narrative.

2. EMBRACE YOUR EMOTIONAL PROMISE

Inspired by your nine brand descriptors, we move on to the second step, inching closer to revealing your brand's personality and archetype.

Please find a single word that reflects the emotional promise people experience with you and your brand. This is important because while your nine words describe the breadth of your offering, your one-word promise takes us to the depth of your brand's soul.

For the Business of Story, our one-word emotional promise is *enchantment*. Nothing in the Business of Story makes sense except in the light of enchantment. Our goal is to enchant you with the wizardry of storytelling so that you can use its primal power to delight your customers, who in turn will experience a more captivating narrative. When we are all engrossed in these stories together, our individual and collective human potential grows.

By the way, the antonyms for enchantment are repulsion, misery, and boredom. Yikes! But these negatives strengthen our promise because they represent the antagonists we are pushing against. I mean, when was the last time you were bored into buying anything? Now we have a common foe: boredom.

So when you and your team select your one-word promise, review its antonyms and see those as the human emotions you are helping your customers overcome. By having your team work with you on this exercise, it will further ensure their buy-in to your entire brand narrative. They need to believe in it as strongly as you do.

3. PRESENT YOUR GIFT

OK, so you've now arrived at your one-word brand promise through your nine one-word descriptors. Your descriptors capture the character traits of your organization, its offering, and its outcomes, all of which are built upon your unique value proposition (see Chapter

4) that artfully articulates your position statement (see Chapter 1). Let's now define what you actually make happen in the world.

Your emotional brand promise is about how people *feel* when interacting with your brand. Your gift is what it delivers beyond your product or service. Remember earlier, when I said your brand story is not about what you make, but *what you make happen* for your customers? This is the intrinsic gift we seek.

For instance, in 1982, in Austria, Dietrich Mateschitz developed the first energy drink. His brand manifesto was and remains today: "We give wings to people and ideas." Red Bull isn't just an energy drink that commands nearly 50 percent of the global market, it's an organization and a product that Gives You Wings. The drink is just the vehicle to transport you to someplace bigger.

Another example I love is Booking.com. In 2013, this Amsterdam-based company connected travelers to 425,000 hotel rooms, did $8 billion in mobile transactions, and hailed itself as "Planet Earth's #1 Accommodation Site." Today, Booking.com has more than 950,000 participating properties, including hotels, luxury resorts, bed & breakfasts, and even tree houses and igloos. They make booking your stay easy through their website. But what they make *happen* is captured in the campaign theme that replaces their name Booking.com with "Booking.*Yeah!*" They captivate their audience by easily connecting them with the exhilaration of an epic adventure.

Yes, Apple produces computers and other digital devices. But what they really make happen is to help you express your creativity and individuality by demonstrating how you *Think different*. Grammatically, it should really be Think Differently. But that wouldn't be expressing the brand gift of thinking different, now would it?

At the Business of Story, we make brand and business storytelling more accessible through our proven storytelling framework. By teaching you the applied science and bewitchery of storytelling we are conjuring your latent storytelling superpowers to strengthen your connection with people and move them to action. Ultimately, what we make happen is to enable you to *excel* through the stories you tell. We enchant you internally with our promise and help you excel externally by becoming a more confident and influential communicator.

So how do you unwrap your brand gift? Brainstorm with your team what your customers actually achieve when they use your product or service in their lives. Go all Maslov on this exercise and determine how your audiences find a part of their self-actualization through your offering. In gamer's terms, you declare how you "level them up." Walt Disney would call it "fulfilling wishes."

4. EXPRESS YOUR AUTHENTIC PERSONALITY

Figure 6.1 The 12 brand personality archetypes used in the Story Cycle System

Now let's dive into character development so we can create and express your brand's unique personality traits, including its attitude, appearance, tone, and feel. This is your brand archetype: the consumer-facing personality that needs to be bold and consistent from the initial contact of "Hello, there" to the wedded bliss of a fully immersive customer experience.

Archetypes are universally understood characters, personalities, symbols, or patterns of behavior. All of the strong characters in our myths and stories take on distinct archetypes that are recognized across cultures, religions, and races — and, more to the point, target markets.

Swiss psychologist Carl Jung characterized archetypes as "ancient or archaic images that derive from the collective unconscious." He believed that archetypes are mythic characters imprinted on our collective psyche to help humans make sense of the characters, patterns, and fundamental motifs of our experiences as we evolved. Archetypes therefore evoke tremendous emotion unique to the characters they represent.

From what I have found in my travels, there appear to be 12 fundamental archetypes that pervade our stories. Some researchers suggest that there are 12 families of archetypes, and five subarchetypes within each family that share similar qualities. But that gets way too far into the psychic weeds for what we're accomplishing here. As you will see, your brand has a dominant personality reflected in at least one of the 12 archetypes, and it probably has supporting character traits of one or two of the other archetypes.

As I mentioned, archetypes are important because they evoke emotion. Emotion creates meaning, even with inanimate objects and organizations. Creating brand meaning for your customers is your core mission. With greater meaning, you create a stronger connection. With a more resilient bond, you develop a purposeful mentorship between your brand and your customers as they venture through their journey with you.

I sometimes find it difficult to convince nuts-and-bolts, features-and-benefits-type people that the emotional side of archetypes is more important for their brand than the analytical side of product attributes. In fact, I usually have to prove it to them. So, I ask them to consider actors James Dean and Clint Eastwood, who most often played the characters of hero, rebel, or outlaw. Aren't these the same archetypes reflected by Harley-Davidson, Greenpeace, and Apple? Dorothy in *The Wizard of Oz* portrayed the Innocent archetype, which you might ascribe to brands like Hallmark, Charmin, and Tom's of Maine toothpaste. Adventure pilot Amelia Earhart and entrepreneur Richard Branson share characteristics of the Daring Explorer archetype, much like Virgin Airlines, North Face, and Red Bull.

Archetypes are reflected in each of us, who in turn are reflected in the characters we are attracted to in the stories we create and consume. Therefore, when you arrive at the authentic personality archetype for your brand, your audiences sense it. Feel it. There is a truth in it that transcends your brand storytelling even while it animates your narrative. You become more attractive to the customers you actually want to attract. They care about what you have to offer because you are connecting with their basal, albeit subconscious, need to connect with people they feel are like them and with organizations they can trust. This is a completely different approach to traditional features-and-benefits marketing.

The single greatest asset of a brand is its meaning: how it resonates in the hearts and minds of its customers. Brands such as IBM, BMW, Coca-Cola, Ben & Jerry's, and Ralph Lauren nurture, manage, and defend their meaning, and they vastly outperform companies that operate with faceless bottom-line thinking. Carol Pearson and Margaret Mark reveal proven techniques for creating and managing brand meaning in their book *The Hero and the Outlaw: Building Extraordinary Brands Through the Power of Archetypes*. They write:

> **"Archetypal psychology helps us understand the intrinsic meaning of product categories and consequently helps marketers create enduring brand identities that establish market dominance, evoke and deliver meaning to customers, and inspire customer loyalty — all, potentially, in socially responsible ways."**

Pearson and Mark outline what they consider to be the 12 primary brand archetypes and their functions, shown in Table 6.1 on page 110. I've also attached a plausible brand to each archetype to demonstrate how they've matched the meaning to their offering. See if you can add another example to each archetype.

As you might imagine, many brilliant minds have written books on archetypes for branding, and my objective here is simply to introduce you to the concept and provide resources to help you define the right archetype(s) for your brand. There are many ways to approach an archetyping session. One of the most thorough I've found is through the workbook *Archetypes in Branding*, created by Margaret Pott Hartwell and Joshua C. Chen. They state:

> **"While archetypal stories have enormous impact in marketing and communications, there is also a commensurate value in observing how archetypes function within business and leadership style and, subsequently, how they affect the authenticity and trust of a brand and its outreach efforts."**

In both design and narrative, this is one of the most beautifully illustrative toolkits I have found that underscores the importance of, and provides the tools for, creating the proper archetype for your brand.

So far in this chapter you have found your one-word brand descriptors. Next, you landed on the one word that defines the emotional promise you make and keep with your customers. Then

Archetype	Meaning	Brand
Creator	Creators are individualists, crafting something new everyday.	Lowe's, Apple, Lego
Caregiver	Caregivers are the protective kind, soothing and taking care of others.	Johnson & Johnson, Volvo, Campbell's Soup
Ruler	Rulers exert total control and expertise in their largely luxurious fields.	Rolex, Mercedes, American Express
Jester/Fool	Jesters are always good for a laugh and just want to have a good time.	Ben & Jerry's, Taco Bell, Old Spice
Regular Guy / Gal	The Regular Guy is your everyday man who is comfortable in his own skin.	Ikea, Budweiser, Levis
Lover	Passionate, sensuous, and unafraid to indulge in excess, Lovers give and receive love.	Haagen-Dazs, Godiva, Victoria's Secret
Hero	Fearless, Heroes show power and strength through courageous acts.	Teach for America, Nike, Army
Outlaw	In true rebellious spirit, Outlaws aren't afraid to let loose and break the rules.	Harley Davidson, Urban Outfitters, MTV
Magician	Magicians are dreamers who face the impossible and bring about transformation.	Axe, Redbull, Disney
Innocent	The Innocent evoke nostalgia, retaining or renewing faith through their pure image.	Coca-Cola, Dove, Cheerios
Explorer	Explorers are adventurous, independent, and always up for a challenge.	Jeep, The North Face, Starbucks
Sage	Like a master sensei, Sages possess an all-knowing sense of wisdom and understanding.	Charles Schwab, PBS, Google

Table 6.1 Examples of the archetypes associated with popular brands

you unwrapped the intrinsic gift you provide: the important thing you make happen in their life. Now it's time to reveal your brand's archetype to inform how you express your promise, gift, and personality to the world.

To make this exercise easier for you, simply use the archetype chart I provided. Read through the character traits of each and determine which is the best fit for your brand. Just like the Oooh exercise, give everyone in the room three Post-it notes and ask them to write down what they believe is the dominant archetype for your brand, as well as up to two supporting archetypes. Only write one archetype per Post-it. On the wall, sort archetypes by dominant and supporting and let the conversation begin as your team shares how they arrived at their recommendations. Before you know it, you will have consensus on the most authentic personality for your brand.

Revealing your archetype(s) is important because their character traits will inform everything you do in how you consistently express your brand's personality to the world. This includes everything from color palettes and typefaces to logo design, imagery, and tone of content, to website design and user experience, to advertising creative, sales materials, and presentations, to inbound and outbound marketing strategy, to—well, you name it. Your archetype(s) become the face of your brand and guide how you interact with your audiences.

You have just taken the next step in humanizing your brand.

FINAL THOUGHTS

Whew! You have covered a lot of ground in brand character development. You have unearthed your nine brand descriptors and explored the emotional promise your brand makes and keeps with its customers. You have considered the intrinsic gift it provides to reinforce the promise. And you have excavated the brand archetype(s) that will be the most apt reflection of its personality and its authentic meaning. Your important relationship as mentor to your customer has arrived.

Can you see how your brand is being humanized? It has evolved from differentiating your features and functions in Chapter 1 to revealing its humanity here in Chapter 6. In Chapter 7, you will test the character of your brand's emerging personality by finding stories in the wild that support your one-word descriptors, promise, and gift, making your personality all the richer. And you'll explore ways to connect these stories with your customers at the right time and place on their journeys.

I may be a fool. But who better to create a foolproof system to humanize your brand?

ADDITIONAL RESOURCES

Explore ways to express your brand's unique personality by visiting businessofstory.com/mentor to review these additional resources:

- Read Vol. V of the *Business of Story* online magazine: "Connect with Your Brand's Promise, Gift, and Personality"

- Listen to Margaret Mark and Carol Pearson on: "How to Use Archetypes to Create Deeper Customer Connections"

- Watch my quick explanation video on how to create your UVP: bit.ly/StoryCycle-Mentor

STORY ON ACTIVITY

A great way to explore archetypes is to select one of your favorite actors and define what their personality is from the 12 archetypes. Then think about yourself: Which one best defines you? And what are your supporting archetypes? For further exploration, read Carol Pearson's book *Awakening the Heroes Within: Twelve Archetypes to Help Us Find Ourselves and Transform our World.*

7

Journey

How to Increase Customer Engagement Through the Stories You Tell

"Stories have a way of summoning forces . . ."

—Christopher Vogler, The Writer's Journey

HOW TO MAKE YOUR STORY THEIR STORY

In October 2015, I was riding in a cab from SeaTac Airport to my folks' home in Woodinville, Washington. We drove through hallways of glistening cedar and Douglas fir trees dripping in a cool autumn drizzle. The taxi driver spoke in a thick Greek accent with bulbous syllables folding into English like a baker kneading a baklava—messy but sweet. He asked what I did.

"I'm in the storytelling business," I said.

"Ooooh, you tell stories for leeeving?" he asked.

"Not quite. I teach business leaders how to become more effective communicators by using storytelling."

"Ahhhhh, very good." He cocked his head toward the rear-view mirror, his dark eyes fixing on me in the backseat as if the cab would drive itself.

"Do you know what all stories begin with?" he queried, bushy eyebrows rising.

"No, what?"

"Eeem-pa-thy," he emphasized, squinting a knowing smile. He looked back to the road. Finally.

"Why empathy?"

"Because how two people share same world in story if not connected through eeempathy? It's same everywhere." He shrugged with a nonchalant wisdom.

This is a moment that I will not forget: seemingly inconsequential but profound. I've found, as Christopher Vogler wrote in *The*

Writer's Journey, that the act of telling a story summons forces. I've also learned that when you study storytelling, the universe delivers these little wisdom bombs in the most peculiar circumstances through unsuspecting messengers. Vogler, true to Campbell's Hero's Journey, calls these characters Threshold Guardians, because they are the gatekeepers to new worlds of knowledge and experience where wisdom resides. Some threshold guardians try to block your progress, such as the threshold guardians of doubt we introduced in Chapter 3, while others act as wise sentries to prepare you for the journey ahead.

What if you and your people can be persuasive threshold guardians for your customers by sharing intentional stories about your brand that reveal the wisdom of your offering? That's what this chapter is all about: building understanding, empathy, and connection with your audiences through your true stories, well told, that will usher them into a new world.

First, we will explore how you find the stories that support the nine one-word descriptors you identified in Chapter 6. These anecdotes will become powerful brand content. By having your people find their own versions of these stories, you will build an immense library for content marketing. And with your stories in hand, you will plan when to share them during the three phases of your customer journey: Brand Awareness, Brand Adoption, and Brand Appreciation.

When you and your team start finding the stories that support your brand story strategy, you will:

> Witness how your brand story is alive and well within your organization, proving that you're headed in the right direction with your narrative strategy.

> Build a storytelling culture as your team sees these true stories materialize all around them.

> Co-create your branding campaign as you use these stories to get your people to buy in and align with your focused mission, while you build real-world content for inbound and outbound marketing and sales.

Connect your stories with your customers and where they are on their brand journey from brand awareness, to adoption, to appreciation.

Encourage all your people to find their own personal nine stories that they've experienced with your brand, and before you know it you will have hundreds of tales to choose from in a story library that is uniquely your own.

Now, in just a moment, I'm going to share with you the nine one-word descriptors we developed for the Business of Story. And I'll give you an example of each in play (I have dozens of these stories). But before we get started, this is a great spot to expand on something I briefly mentioned in the previous chapter—namely, the elements of a small story, which can create a *big* impact. I learned this structure from my friends Shawn Callahan and Mark Schenk, who are from the international business storytelling consultancy Anecdote in Melbourne, Australia. I am a certified coach with Anecdote's Storytelling for Leaders training program. They helped me understand how to break down the structure of a brand-supporting anecdote by using these five primal story elements.

When: Provide a specific time stamp for when the story you are about to tell occurs. A precise time alerts your audience's subconscious limbic system that it's about to be presented with an experience that it should pay attention to so it will know what to do in case it ever happens to them. Think of your brain as your system's hard dive and your stories as its software. A time stamp provides the "Go" command to start sifting meaning out of the coming tale.

Where: What is the exact location where this moment happened? Callahan coaches that you can use either a time stamp or a location stamp to capture the attention of your audience. But I like to double down and use both whenever possible to prime my audience for the story.

Character: Who is the central character in your story? Is it you? A colleague? A customer? Or someone else? The most important thing about the singular character in your story is that your audience must be able to empathize with him/her so they will live vicariously through the tale and embrace the learning moment the tale conjures.

Action/surprise: Something has to happen in your story to make it a story. Think of the first three primal elements as the setup for your story, the "And" in the ABT, as discussed in Chapter 4, to set the context. But then describe in quick detail the surprising outcome that reveals a truth.

Aha!: The universal truth of the story supports the business point you are making with this short story. Audiences can and will argue against data, stats, charts, and graphs. But they find it difficult to refute a true story, well told. In fact, anecdotes invite your audiences into your view of the world through the moments you experience. These are the scenes that support your larger brand narrative.

See if you can find these five primal elements in the stories I share about Business of Story's nine one-word brand descriptors. As demonstrated in the previous chapter, I've grouped these nine anecdotes into the three categories of Organization, Offering, and Outcomes from the OOOh story exercise.

Organization	Offering	Outcomes
Mage	Primal	Clarity
Industrious	Dynamic	Connection
Optimistic	Truth	Trust

ORGANIZATION:
THE BUSINESS OF STORY IS A *MAGE*

I've learned that to benefit from the full force of storytelling you have to understand the applied science and bewitchery of the craft.

Russell Goldstein, CFP, CAP, is an institutional client advisor at U.S. Trust, Bank of America, and a graduate of my storytelling course in the Executive Master of Sustainability Leadership program at Arizona State University. In 2017, he started my 12-month program, thinking storytelling in business was a joke. A gimmick. But once he got educated on how to be an intentional storyteller using proven narrative frameworks, his whole world changed. He sent me this note following the course.

> Park,
> A couple of weeks ago I presented to about 80 people at the monthly meeting for the Planned Giving Roundtable. They sent me the audience reviews from Survey Monkey. Look at what they said:
> "Engaging, motivating, and energetic."
> "Russ is a great storyteller."

"Enjoyed the fact that there were personal stories interspersed with the relevant topic."

"Russell is a wonderful presenter and a true professional."

Park, I never realized the power of story in business until I took your class. Now I'm trying to teach my colleagues how to use stories, too. Thank you. Storytelling is like having a big 'ol bonus check sitting in my top drawer.

Thank you, Russell

You can see how Russell applied the science of storytelling to bewitch his audiences.

THE BUSINESS OF STORY IS ABOUT BEING *INDUSTRIOUS*

The Business of Story approach is both the product of an industrious assemblage of proven narrative frameworks and the platform by which humans can become more effective communicators in our overcommunicated, tech-driven world.

Let's use an example that I presented in the preface (just in case you skipped that part in your eagerness to get your story straight). In his 2012 predictions for the tech industry, pundit Mark Anderson, CEO of Strategic News Service, said, "Steve Jobs didn't really invent anything at all. But he was great at integrating things into a product." He argued that most of the technology that created the Mac, iPod, Next cube, etc. was already available. Jobs was simply able to see things others couldn't in combining disparate technology advancements to create new products. Apple's innovation was not so much a product of invention, but observation and integration.

I've found the same concept of invention via integration to work in business communications, too. Specifically with brand storytelling.

In 2006, after running my ad agency for over a decade, I realized that the advertising paradigm as I knew it no longer worked. While brands used to own the influence of mass media (broadcast, print, outdoor), technology turned their world upside down. The Internet handed control of communication to the consumer. The masses became the media. And by the way, they now own your brand story, too.

Desperate to find an answer for how to get our clients' messages to cut through the noise, I first turned to Hollywood. There I learned about Joseph Campbell and the universal framework of story he called The Hero's Journey. Then I saw how screenwriters like Christopher Vogler, Blake Snyder, and Randy Olson used various forms of the Hero's Journey and other narrative structures to capture their audiences.

These same narrative forms began to materialize around me in marketing and sales, especially in the work of Dr. Robert Cialdini, author of *Influence: The Psychology of Persuasion*. I noticed that all the most powerful campaigns—from the likes of Apple, Nike, Virgin, Airbnb, and others—were all story-based and used these same templates, whether they intended to or not.

Finally, I dove into the neurophysiology work and studies of folks like Dr. Daniel Kahneman, Dr. Paul Zak, and American moral psychologist Jonathan Haidt to understand the intersection of brain structure and story structure.

When people ask me how the proven Story Cycle System™ came about, I say:

> "The Story Cycle System is distilled from the timeless narrative structure of the ancients, inspired by the story artists of Hollywood, influenced by masters of persuasion, guided by trend spotters, and informed by how the human mind grapples for meaning."

This is the foundation for the industriousness of the Business of Story platform.

THE BUSINESS OF STORY IS ABOUT CREATING *OPTIMISM*

You know storytelling is powerful when you see how people get inspired when they learn to craft, tell, and appreciate a good story. They naturally become more optimistic about having an impact in the world they seek.

On Sunday, July 29, 2018, I was working with 110 Air Force generals and their staff at Lackland Air Force Base in San Antonio, Texas, during a half-day Business of Story workshop. When I asked some of the attendees to share the stories they were working on, Brigadier General Christopher "Mookie" Walker raised his hand. He said that he would be speaking to the West Virginia State football team on the following Sunday. He told me he typically just gets up and wings it because he is good on his feet and a confident speaker.

But now that he had been introduced to the And/But/Therefore foundation to storytelling and to the Story Cycle System, he completely changed the approach to his presentation right there in the workshop. He realized he needed a more focused narrative to connect with the football players. His message was that he himself had been a reluctant hero, ignoring the universe's call to him until he spent several years in the Air Force. He learned that we all have the capability to be effective leaders.

His point to the players was that when they stepped onto the football field they became leaders in the eyes of the West Virginia State football fans, especially the kids. And that it is their duty to act like leaders, especially during those times when they didn't feel like it. General Walker stressed that their leadership was important because West Virginia has the highest rate of opioid addiction in the country, and that these players could play a major role in turning that around by taking a stand against drugs and working with youth to encourage them to make the right choices.

General Walker got a huge ovation from his fellow generals when he had finished describing the theme and approach to his upcoming presentation. He said it was inspired by the work we were doing in this Business of Story communications workshop.

Become an intentional storyteller, and your leadership will inspire optimism in your audiences.

For more ways to create your own inspiring stories, download our fun and FREE eBook with five storytelling exercises: "The 5 Stages of Grief in Telling Your Business Story" at businessofstory. com/storytelling-tools.

OFFERING:
THE BUSINESS OF STORY IS *PRIMAL*

The various narrative frameworks you can use to tell a story have a rich, proven history of effectively connecting with people and moving them to action. In fact, they are primal to us storytelling monkeys.

In the fall of 2018, I was working with 60 engineers and executives at the Palo Verde nuclear generating station in Phoenix. They were a smart and very logic-driven crowd, so I shared with them how our minds are hardwired for story by telling them the tale of Thog the Caveman:

One evening, Thog returned to his cave looking a little worse for wear. His plump cavern roommate, Larry, grunted, "Thog, you no look so good. What happen?"

He explained, "Thog go to stream to catch saber-toothed salmon for dinner."

"Uh-huh," grunted Larry.

"But saber-toothed tiger show up!"

"Uh-oh!" belched his roommate.

"Thog give tiger salmon. Tiger like salmon better than Thog, so here I am, safe in cave with you."

"Aha!" said Larry, nodding at the insight.

And there you have it: a perfect three-act story structure delineated by Larry's "Uh-huh" (setup), "Uh-oh!" (conflict), and "Aha!" (resolution).

Thog's story is a fun way to illustrate the three-act structure of every compelling story. Plus, it underscores that storytelling is more important for our survival than our opposable thumbs. After all, stories are what helped us navigate and survive the savannah 90,000 years ago and what helped us evolve from cavemen to consumers.

Remember, this is essentially the same story structure you used in Chapter 4 to suss out your unique value proposition in the form of the And, But & Therefore foundational narrative framework. You can learn more about the And, But & Therefore framework by listening to my podcast with Dr. Randy Olson: "The Science of Storytelling."

THE BUSINESS OF STORY IS *DYNAMIC*

The dynamism of storytelling through the use of metaphor is precisely how you become a more persuasive communicator, because stories can link two disparate worlds into a third, more powerful collective point of view.

For instance, in late March 2018, I was greeted by 100+ skeptical software developers at the MuraCon conference in Sacramento, California. I kicked off my Business of Story keynote by asking the audience this question: "Who thinks storytelling is bullshit?" I was not surprised when half the programmers in the room raised their hands.

But instead of ducking their skepticism, I acknowledged it. I said that I didn't understand their life of coding but I felt like our two worlds were not so dissimilar. We agreed that great developers seek to design and write the cleanest, purest code in order to create the best user experience. I mentioned that storytellers do the same thing. We want to craft and tell clear and compelling stories to create optimal user experiences between the teller and their audience.

"In fact," I said, "stories are simply the software that drives the hardware of our minds, which are constantly whirring as they make meaning out of the madness of being human."

They laughed, nodded in agreement, and gave me permission to teach them how to write better code for storytelling over the next 90 minutes.

Storytelling is one of the most powerful tools for overcoming entrenched, anti-story viewpoints. And the only way you are going to overcome these polarized views is with the dynamism of a better story and the positive energy and force it creates.

You can read more about this by pulling up the resources on our website at the end of this chapter. Read "How Storytelling 'Soft Skills' Can Create Better User Experiences in Technical Careers."

THE BUSINESS OF STORY IS ABOUT *TRUTH*

A true story, well told, reveals a truth about ourselves and the world around us.

Per Olef Bengtzen was bobbing in his boat at the mouth of a precarious channel in the Galápagos Islands. He was only 22 years old, standing by himself in the stern of his 24-foot sailboat on his solo journey from Stockholm, Sweden, to Melbourne, Australia. It was getting dark and in 1982 he didn't have a GPS. So he decided to anchor in a small bay and wait for the safety of morning light to navigate the passage.

"Have you ever heard that weird screech dolphins make in the wild?" he asked me with the accent of a salty seagoing Swede.

"I can't say that I have," I answered.

"I woke up about five in the morning and a dozen dolphins were scurrying around my boat, screeching that eerie sound at me. I climbed up on deck to see about the commotion and realized that the tide had gone out. I had just minutes before we'd be crushed upon the volcanic rock."

"We?" I asked.

"Me and my boat," Per replied. "I had to pull anchor and get out of there immediately."

"Whoa. Do you think the dolphins were warning you?"

"Yes, I think they knew I was in trouble and they wanted to wake me."

Just then, a subtle smile of recognition washed across his face.

"What?" I asked.

"I've spent my career as a car wash salesman and I just realized that every big sale I've ever made in my life came after telling a sailing story."

"Why do you think that is?" I prodded.

He shrugged. "I don't know."

"Because," I suggested, "stories like the one you just told reveal a truth about you, your character, and the universe around us. Truth and trust are at the core of every relationship. Your story tells of your courage and persistence. Isn't that exactly what I want in my car wash salesman? Because I know, like those dolphins, you'll be there for me when I need you."

At the core of every story is a truth.

OUTCOMES:
THE BUSINESS OF STORY IS ABOUT REVEALING *CLARITY*

When you clarify your story using the Business of Story tools and techniques, you will reveal insights that are invaluable to furthering your personal and professional ambitions.

On Thursday, February 24, 2018, I was presenting a 90-minute Business of Story workshop to 400 professionals during Social Media Marketing World at the San Diego Convention Center. Entrepreneur Saul Nir stepped to the microphone to share his And, But, & Therefore statement with the audience, which would be the foundation for his personal brand story.

He stood tall. But as he read, his posture changed. His head dropped. He became confused. His ABT statement about becoming a coach for entrepreneurs wasn't clear or convincing. So I pressed him to see if he could clarify, but he couldn't. I asked him if coaching entrepreneurs was truly where his heart was right now. He shrugged and said, "I don't know . . . Thank you." And then he sat down.

The next day, I received this pivotal tweet . . .

wikijoy @thewikijoy · Mar 8

@ParkHowell Hi, I was at your session at #SMMW18 I got a lot out of it, I asked a question & you guided me to clarify my purpose, next day I realized my heart isn't coaching entrepreneurs right now. Instead I'm going to do a goofy You Tube channel and just have fun, Thank You!

Figure 7.1 Wikijoy's tweet following my storytelling session at Social Marketing World 2017

I believe Saul is now following a more powerful story for himself through the insight he gained in this simple story exercise. Ah, the power of clarifying your story.

THE BUSINESS OF STORY IS ABOUT *CONNECTION*

Intentional storytelling connects you with yourself and your audiences on a deep, primal level.

In early June 2018, Jennifer Russo called me to discuss some job opportunities. She had spent 15 years as an international marketing communications executive for Rio Tinto mining. But now she was leaving her position to spend more time with her two young boys.

As a single mom, she still needed a full-time job, but one involving less travel. When I asked her what kind of position she was looking for, she mentioned a high-level job where she could work with a multinational company and use her communications skills right there in Phoenix. "And maybe something in diversity and inclusion," she said.

"You have an amazing background," I said, "but I think your job search criteria are too vague." I could tell a bit of coaching was in order, so I encouraged her to clarify her personal brand story to amplify her impact and simplify her life. "Because you don't want to spend the next 15 years, the prime of your business life, in another job that doesn't play to your curiosity and passion."

As her brand marketing agency-of-record for five years, I experienced the energy and positive attitude Jennifer brought to all of her work relationships. She was too close to her own attributes to appreciate them. So I suggested that she excavate her personal brand story by filling out the DIY Brand Story Strategy workbook.

Once she was finished, Jennifer sent it to me so I could help her refine her story. Clarifying her story was important to define the position she was looking for, which would attract the right opportunities and save her time from chasing the wrong gigs.

I suggested that her unique personal brand position in the market of corporate communications professionals is as the "Kinetic Communicator," with an energy that attracts professionals of diverse thinking and backgrounds to help people and organizations outperform in the market. Jennifer mines the untapped capital in a company's collective diversity.

Her personal brand story now connects her to her authentic offering as the Kinetic Communicator, and it has helped connect her with the right kinds of job opportunities to help companies connect with their people through diversity and inclusion initiatives. As of this writing, Jennifer is Director of Corporate Communications for Banner Health, and she loves her position and is making a difference.

You can experience Jennifer's story at JenniferRusso.me

THE BUSINESS OF STORY IS ABOUT *TRUST*

The only way to truly live into your most powerful stories is to have the courage to share the truth that creates the trust, especially if that truth makes you feel vulnerable.

In March 2018, I met Anjella Crowe, a soft-spoken thirtysomething Ukrainian immigrant. She works for Silverline, a fast-growing high-tech customer relationship management firm in New York. I was doing a Business of Story workshop with 50 of their top sales and marketing people when Anjella volunteered to tell her story. She said that her sole purpose at the company was to build important alliances and partnerships within the organization and its customers.

That was all fine and dandy, but I pressed her to recall the specific moment when she knew this was her superpower. But she pushed back, perhaps because we were working her story in front of her colleagues. Or maybe it was too painful a moment to share in public.

After the session, she came up to me and said, "I didn't tell you everything."

"I know. How come?" I asked.

"I've been told that businesspeople wouldn't think it is appropriate to talk about my hard times in the orphanage."

"Orphanage? Wait a sec. You grew up in a Ukrainian orphanage!?" I asked.

"Yes, since birth until I was 18. It was hard. People picked on me and abused me, so I don't talk about it. I'm told no one wants to hear it."

"How'd you cope?"

She recalled the moment when she realized she had to surround herself with kids she could trust and with adults who didn't just care for her, but *about* her. Anjella built groups of these people to help her rise above the harsh conditions of her environment.

"Oh, my God, no wonder you excel at building alliances and partnerships," I said. "You grew up doing it to survive." I encouraged Anjella to talk about her life in the orphanage without going into all the difficult details. I mean, come on. "Ukrainian orphanage." *That* story tells itself. She nodded in agreement.

I learned that Anjella moved to the States when she was 18, earned two degrees from the University of Georgia, and then a master's in International Business from Georgia State, and has had a successful career in technology. I told her, "Have the courage to tell your story, because you *are* the epitome of the American dream. Never let anyone quiet that. And here's how you use it . . .

"Just imagine looking into the eyes of your next prospective client and asking them, 'When was the last time your vendor orphaned you? Didn't do what they said they'd do? Left you feeling abandoned? I promise you, that will never happen with me.'"

She smiled and seemed relieved. When I asked her if I could retell her story during my TEDxGilbert talk, she said, "Absolutely!"

Anjella's story is an excerpt from my TEDx talk: "Start Looking for Your Scenes and Your Story Will Find You."

YOUR BRAND ENGAGEMENT STORIES

Now it's time for you and your team to find nine stories, one tale for each of the brand descriptors you identified in the previous chapter. Use one of your words, as I have above, as the singular theme and start capturing those stories in the wild using the five primal elements of story.

Once you have begun capturing your anecdotes, categorize them in three groups (some of the stories may be used in more than one category): brand awareness, brand adoption, and brand appreciation.

When and where do your audiences become aware of your brand? What is their first contact and which stories do you have in the queue to pique their interest? Think back to what your customers wish and want for themselves, and then determine the stories that will help them find the *will* to go for it with your product or service.

I heard a definition recently that I liked about the difference between sympathy and empathy. Sympathy is liking someone and being concerned for their plight in life. Empathy is that feeling you get when someone is like you. You can empathize with them because you've experienced something similar to what they have experienced. You want to demonstrate empathy for your audiences so that they'll feel, Hey, she's just like me.

That's why you tell your stories from your audience's perspective. Give them a character they can live vicariously through. Help them realize that you understand what they wish for and want because you are sharing stories about individuals that they can root for. This is how you connect their world with your world.

As you unearth your stories based on each of your nine brand descriptors, you and your team will be amazed at how your overall brand story comes to life, how you are already walking the talk. And in the process you'll notice that you're building your innate storytelling muscles to grow your organization and your people.

You will feel yourself becoming more of a messaging mage as you deploy the primal frameworks of story to clarify your collective journey. When you become industrious about viewing the entirety of your business strategy, team alignment, and customer acquisition through a narrative lens, you will see how dynamic your interpersonal connections become through storytelling. Optimism increases when you help your audiences envision a shared reality that they can buy into and prosper from. And this only happens by sharing true stories—good news or bad—that build the ultimate test of a brand: trust.

Now here's a quick test for you: Can you find the nine one-word descriptors of the Business of Story in the paragraph above? I use them to not only help me find my stories that began this chapter, but as narrative buoys to navigate my story in a sea of noise. How am I different? How do I impact the lives of others? How do I transport leaders of purpose-driven brands, their people, and the communities they serve to new worlds? Did I capture that overarching narrative in one paragraph using my descriptors? You be the judge.

NOW IT'S YOUR TURN

I have two exercises for you. First, pull together your nine one-word descriptors and ask each of your team members to select three of the words and find three true stories (one story per descriptor) to share with everyone. You are now proofing your brand story strategy by seeing it in action through the stories they select. Plus, you are starting to build your story library for use in all your internal and external communications.

Next, map the customer journeys for each of the three primary audiences you identified in Chapter 2. Their journey includes brand awareness, brand adoption, and brand appreciation. Once you determine when and where they come in contact with your brand, decide to purchase your product or service, and then return for more, you'll have a new supply of anecdotes to add to your growing story library. The more stories, the merrier.

	Awareness	Adoption	Appreciation
Audience #1			
Audience #2			
Audience #3			

Worksheet 7.1 Write in what your audiences experience in each stage of brand awareness, adoption and appreciation.

FINAL THOUGHTS

You are now squarely in the action portion of Act II of the Story Cycle System, as your brand narrative has taken flight through the stories you are capturing in the wild. Campbell calls this the test and trials of the Hero's Journey. While you've set the context for your brand story and humanized the personality of your offering, you've now truly brought it to life through the true stories you make happen in peoples' lives. Next up is to map the victory milestones along your customer journey of brand awareness, adoption, and appreciation to demonstrate to your audiences that they are on the right path with you.

ADDITIONAL RESOURCES

Visit businessofstory.com/journey to explore more ways to express your brand's unique personality, as you:

- Read Vol. VII of the *Business of Story* online magazine: "The Road of Trials: Mapping Your Customer's Journey."

- Listen to Greg Chapman on: "How to Combine the Science of Data With the Art of Storytelling to Create Meaningful Customer Experiences."

- Watch my quick explanation video on how to map your customer journey: bit.ly/StoryCycle-Journey.

STORY ON ACTIVITY

Pick a favorite story that supports one of your descriptors and outline it using the five primal elements of story. Then tell it three times to three different people: a close family member or friend, a colleague, and a stranger. See how it evolves with each telling. As Christopher Vogler wrote in *The Writer's Journey*, "Stories have a way of summoning forces." See how your stories conjure the energy of your brand offering to help all who come in contact with it to grow.

8

Victory

How to Celebrate Wins on the Customer Journey from Brand Awareness to Appreciation

"You can have everything in life you want if you just help enough people get what they want."

—Zig Ziglar

YOU'RE BUILDING TO SOMETHING BIG

When you craft your brand narrative, two important forces are summoned. First, you create meaning for your offering, which is critical to customer engagement. Otherwise, you remain mired as a meaningless commodity in our world of abundant choices. You can't afford to be just another NUMBer.

But something else magical happens when you create meaning for your fellow *Homo sapiens*. They begin to care. And when you unwaveringly deliver on the promises you make in your brand storytelling, they turn caring into love.

You began to rise above commoditization in Step 1 of the Story Cycle System™ when you declared your #1 position in the marketplace: what you do differently, and therefore better, than your competition. This is a crucial first step in brand awareness.

In Step 2, you prioritized your top three audiences, placing them at the center of your brand story. Isn't that where everyone wants to be, the focus of the story?

Then you explored what's at stake for your audiences in Step 3: what they *wish* for in their lives and what they *want* to buy to fulfill their needs.

You began to humanize your brand position by articulating your unique value proposition in Step 4. This is important because you want to clarify why your offering is the most timely, urgent, and relevant option for your audiences, especially in their time of need. Your UVP is what triggers their *will* to act.

In Step 5, you embraced the obstacles in your respective journeys. The goal, as you now know, is the jujitsu move of turning those antagonistic forces into narrative energy to propel your customer engagement forward.

You continued to humanize your brand as your customer's mentor in Step 6. You determined the foundations of its character through your nine descriptors. Then you arrived at your emotional promise, intrinsic gift, and archetypal personality. We meaning-making machines love to see how your brand persona meshes with ours.

In the previous chapter, Step 7 of the journey, you began finding true stories based off your nine descriptors to demonstrate your brand in action—how it walks the talk, so to speak. These stories become powerful anecdotes that connect your world with your customer's world to build brand adoption.

Here, in Step 8, you will learn the three pivotal customer engagement scenes—brand awareness, adoption, and appreciation—and which stories to tell to whom, when, and where in their journey with you. This is important because you want to anticipate the little victories your customers will experience along the way so you can celebrate with them. In the Hero's Journey, this is where Campbell describes the road heroes take back home to their ordinary world as they return with the boon. They've grown through experience and have acquired new wisdom about themselves and the world around them. Think about Maslow's hierarchy of needs. This is when you are moving your audience up from esteem into self-actualization. I know that may sound grandiose, but consider the little successes in your life that have given you a bigger appreciation for who you are and what you stand for.

For instance, how have the small successes on your journey through the previous seven steps of the Story Cycle System created clarity and excitement in you about the prospects of your brand? You're no longer just a provider of a product or service. It has become self-evident that you make powerful things happen in the lives of your employees, customers, and the communities you serve. Your brand is becoming self-actualized.

HOW TO CREATE SMALL SUCCESS SCENES FOR BIG IMPACT

Little wins along your road of trials are critical because they demonstrate to your customers that their relationship with you is progressing. But we're often so focused on the big triumphs that we overlook the small successes that bind people to our brand. In this chapter, we help you map your success moments that advance your story and lead to customer engagement and loyalty with your audiences.

Think of these moments as success scenes. For instance, when I drove up to the pickup window at D'Lite Healthy on the Go in Phoenix, a healthy fast-food restaurant—which is not an oxymoron—the dude in the window surprised me. He asked if I wanted a dog treat for my passenger, Hazel, our goldendoodle. That represented a simple success scene for me. I now go to D'Lite often for my Man Salad. That's right, "Man Salad." And I'm sharing their story, which, you'll notice, has become my story. Brand awareness, adoption, and appreciation served up in a drive-thru.

Another example is when I arrived in Chicago the night before a daylong Business of Story master class for DiMeo Schneider and Associates, a large financial firm. I had packed my power blue suit but forgot my shoes in Phoenix. It was 7 p.m. when I realized my gaffe, so I hustled down to Michigan Avenue to find a shoe store before closing. Brand awareness came as I happened upon the Johnston & Murphy in Water Tower Place, the first time I've set foot in one of their stores. The dapper salesman actually came across the room and greeted me with a smile and a handshake. His was a rare welcoming gesture in our hurried world that made for a nice moment. I shared my predicament. He sized me up and suggested a conservative pair of wing tips.

"But what about those?" I pointed to a dashing pair of Stacy Adams Dickinson navy suede cap toe Oxfords.

"Really? Those are sweet," he said, trying to hide his surprise at my choice. (They are sweet. Look 'em up.)

I bought the shoes (brand adoption). The next day, I was happy to get a couple of compliments on my new blue suede shoes, which helped soothe the blister brewing on my right heel. Six months later, remembering my great experience with Johnston & Murphy, I bought another pair of black dress shoes at their store in Scottsdale Fashion Square. In the window were the Oxfords I had purchased in Chicago marked down 40 percent. I casually mentioned my story to the saleslady in the busy store. Then she voluntarily took 40 percent off of my new shoes. Obviously, Johnston & Murphy empowers their people to make such a decision on the spot. I was impressed. So I shared my experience on my podcast. Their exceptional customer service led me to brand appreciation for Johnston & Murphy. I made their story my story. Who do you think I'm going to buy my next pair of snazzy shoes from?

Do you see how these success scenes weave together for a sharable brand narrative? From the welcoming gent in Chicago (brand awareness) to purchasing the stylish navy Oxfords (brand adoption) to the empowered saleswoman in Scottsdale who provided me the discount based solely on my word, my different interactions with Johnston & Murphy have taken me on a journey that has culminated with me sharing my story with the people in my world (brand appreciation) — a victory for both me and them.

Think like a screenwriter. Script your small success scenes and connect them together to create the narrative arc of your customer engagement story. These success scenes anchor the three acts of the customer journey in the Story Cycle System:

ACT I: Brand Awareness

ACT II: Brand Adoption

ACT III: Brand Appreciation

André Martin-Hobbs uses success scenes for exceptional customer engagement in his Quebec-based used-car company, Prêt, Auto, Partez. By first clarifying their brand story using the Story Cycle System and then mapping their success scenes, they doubled their staff and tripled their size in two years, with significant month-over-month sales growth from the previous year. Let's examine how they did it.

SCENES SELL

André's brand story journey began when he introduced himself to me in the crowded corridor of the San Diego Convention Center. I had just finished my first appearance at Social Media Marketing World, producing a 90-minute Business of Story workshop that kicked off the 2016 conference. Essentially, my presentation was Act I of Brand Awareness for André and the Business of Story.

"Park, I am interested in working with you to help us devise our brand story," André said to me in his Québécois accent.

"Cool. Where are you from and what is your business?" I asked.

"I am from Quebec, and we sell used cars to financially challenged Canadians."

Great, I thought. *Clunkers sold to desperate people usually add up to someone getting run over – namely the buyer*. I handed André my card.

"Thanks, I'll follow up in a couple of weeks," he said. I was kind of hoping he wouldn't. Although André came off as a solid guy, I was skeptical about what I considered his potentially smarmy business model. Did I really want to get involved in an enterprise that didn't support my raison d'être of helping purpose-driven brands clarify their stories to amplify their impact and simplify their lives? But it turned out I was ignorant (which, by the way, is spelled the same way in French). I had no clue what he was up to. My ego nearly detoured an amazing brand story because I had made up a fictitious story in my head about André and his company by jumping to an erroneous conclusion. I hate it when that happens.

André called and I began to understand and appreciate the incredible impact he and his company were having on their customers. They were selling used cars in great condition to subprime car buyers for a bigger mission: to help their customers repair their credit.

He explained that his customers were good people who had experienced bad times. They had gotten T-boned by the global recession, or by a job loss or costly medical treatments, or maybe by a devastating divorce. Many of the buyers lacked the fiscal sophistication and wherewithal to weather their financial blows. Others simply collided with bad luck.

"We want to help them get back on their feet by finding a vehicle they can afford and use to restore their credit," André explained. That's a compelling purpose I hadn't anticipated coming from an unlikely source like a used-car dealership. At the heart of their brand story was an amazing market differentiator in the traffic-snarled car sales business. André walked me through the customer journey and the successes they experience along the way.

"People show up because they've been taking the bus for a few years. They've saved a little money and they want the freedom of having their own car again," he said. "They aren't even thinking about their long-term finances when they walk in. They just want the self-respect an auto represents now.

What's at stake for the car buyers is that they *wish* to feel the freedom of driving. They *want* a car to provide that freedom. And many are willing to risk default again for the luxury of owning their own car. Unbeknownst to André's car buyers, they come in for a ride but leave with a personal financial plan.

Unlike predatory used-car salesmen who burden credit-risk buyers with high-interest loans, Prêt, Auto, Partez (which translates to Loan, Car, Go, a play off "Ready, Set, Go") educates their customers in a three-hour financial planning session. They won't sell a car to a customer until that person has a clear understanding of their budget and determines which car they can actually afford. The goal is to make their monthly payments for two years, which is the benchmark to repair your credit in Canada. Their interest payments are still high—the unavoidable reality of being a subprime buyer—but the overall price is determined by what they can afford. No predatory BS.

Remember arriving at your unique value proposition in Chapter 4? When we crafted Prêt, Auto, Partez's UVP, it practically wrote itself:

Prêt, Auto, Partez is your vehicle to financial freedom.

The mark of an authentic value proposition is not just how it amplifies your differentiation in the market, but how it clarifies and simplifies your life with your operations. André doesn't hire car salesmen. Prêt, Auto, Partez attracts employees who are interested in helping people fix their credit. The cars they sell are simply the vehicle for their greater purpose. In the next chapter we'll cover your purpose statement, which cements the self-actualization of your brand.

Remember, your brand story is not about what you make or offer (in André's case, the purchase of a used car), but what you make happen in the lives of the people you serve (for André's customers, that's financial freedom). Prêt, Auto, Partez operates at the intersection of freedom and peace of mind: the freedom created by the convenience of owning your own car and the peace of mind that comes from knowing that you can not only afford it, but that it will help you repair your credit. This is how we landed on the brand gift covered in Chapter 6: *transporting* customers to a better place, both physically and philosophically.

CELEBRATING SUCCESS MILESTONES

Now that the brand story elements became clear, we explored how Prêt, Auto, Partez celebrates the victories, large and small, in their customers' journeys.

In the brand awareness stage (or Act I of our "movie"), customers arrive at Prêt, Auto, Partez to buy a car. But what they get first is a financial plan. Some customers are startled by this approach and quickly depart. This is actually good for André and his team because they are only interested in helping people who want to help themselves out of their financial challenges. These are also the same car buyers who will pay their monthly lease, which is good for everyone. See how clarifying their brand story to help those buying a car who want the help simplifies Prêt, Auto, Partez's operations? It's a deadbeat filter.

The first big win for customers is that they get the peace of mind of understanding their financial position and how to budget for their car accordingly. They've replaced the worry of the unknown with the courage that comes with taking ownership of their finances. Even if they don't buy a car from Prêt, Auto, Partez, at least they are educated about how to get out of their financial predicament.

What can you offer your audiences when they first become aware of your brand that will represent a win for them? Is it a free tool, knowledge, insight, or a giveaway that they'll find immediate value in?

The next act, Act II, brand adoption, happens at Prêt, Auto, Partez when both the buyer and the company representative agree that a car and its monthly payments make sense, given the customer's finances. The customer doesn't always get to buy the car they wanted due to cost, but they do get a car they can afford. As I mentioned earlier, Prêt, Auto, Partez doesn't hire car salesmen who will sell any sucker anything. They employ people motivated to help people improve their finances. Customers win with that rush of freedom they feel when they pull off the lot in their car. Plus, they enjoy the confidence of having an advocate on their side who will help them stay on their road to financial freedom.

And finally we come to Act III, brand appreciation. This happens when customers share their Prêt, Auto, Partez story with others. You know this phenomenon as word-of-mouth marketing (WOM). I call WOM a phenomenon because it is the most valuable, least expensive influential marketing you can do. That's why it's so important to help your customers make your brand story *their* story through the wins they talk about with their family and friends. It's easy to visualize a happy Prêt, Auto, Partez customer driving off the lot in their new car, eager to show off their purchase to the important people in their life—people who themselves may be ideal customers for André and his team.

André has extended what he learned by clarifying the Prêt, Auto, Partez brand story with the Story Cycle System to each of his representatives. He is helping them build their influence by sharing their own unique personal brand stories on LinkedIn and Facebook to make them even more confident advisors to their customers and effective extensions of his brand.

That's the beautiful thing about stories: they scale.

The success scenes André and his team have scripted into their customer journey at Prêt, Auto, Partez incorporate little victories all along the way, including:

ACT I: BRAND AWARENESS

Setting the stage with a welcoming salesperson more interested in helping than selling (a surprisingly refreshing initial customer engagement in the cutthroat used-car business).

Acknowledging the customer's excitement about the freedom that comes with car ownership. (This is usually a step forward in the buyer's personal journey of finally having the ability to buy a car again and their growing self-respect it represents.)

Taking an important detour from buying any automobile to pinpointing a car they can actually afford. (Although they may not have expected it, buyers are appreciative of the financial advice they receive.)

ACT II: BRAND ADOPTION

Growing the customer's understanding of their personal financial situation through their three-hour free planning session, with the aim of repairing their credit in two years so they can purchase the car they want.

Working together to find the right car that the customer will be proud to drive.

Following up after the purchase to see how the financial plan is working for them.

ACT III: BRAND APPRECIATION

Brand appreciation begins by taking great care of the potential buyers their now-proud customers happily refer to Prêt, Auto, Partez. (Everyone loves to be the person who refers a friend or family member to a great experience.)

Being there for the customer in two years when they are ready to upgrade their vehicle.

These are Prêt, Auto, Partez's high-level customer engagement victories. Each of these small interactions supports their brand story elements. They instill the brand's promise of "peace of mind" while demonstrating its gift of "transporting" the customer to another world of financial understanding and physical freedom. Themed success scenes are experienced through the brand personality archetype of the "Caregiver." And of course these moments support their UVP and brand purpose of providing their customers with a vehicle to financial freedom.

André has many more smaller success scenes he and his team celebrate with their buyers along the way to building customer engagement. The point is, never discount the power of the moment and the momentum it can create for your brand.

In the first three years living into its new brand story, Prêt, Auto, Partez has grown by 100 percent and is building its fourth dealership. Customers travel as far as eight hours to buy one of their cars with the promise of repairing their credit.

"We don't even have to sell them," André told me. "Our customers arrive convinced we have a car and a plan for them; and we do."

You can review Prêt, Auto, Partez's brand story elements at the end of this chapter. Use their brand narrative as yet another example to help you craft your own purpose-driven story.

HOW VICTORY IS AT HAND WITH THE BUSINESS OF STORY

As illustrated above with Prêt, Auto, Partez, it's important to map the ways you plan to activate and celebrate your small customer engagement victories. For instance, here are the three gifts we at the Business of Story provide along the journey of brand awareness, adoption, and appreciation:

1. Act I: Brand awareness = Invaluable *free* advice

2. Act II: Brand adoption = Story eurekas

3. Act III: Brand appreciation = Story scaling

Brand awareness for the Business of Story primarily happens in three ways: online with our podcast, blog, and website; in person during speaking engagements; and through referrals. Now that this book is published, I can add to the list a fourth experience where brand awareness can happen.

In each interaction, we offer as much invaluable *free* advice as possible. You can download free eBooks and storytelling tools. You can listen to and learn from the more than 200 story artists we've featured on our weekly *Business of Story* podcast, which is among the top 10 percent of downloaded podcasts in the world. You can reference the extensive library of books, audios, and videos I have collected, all of which profoundly influenced my growth as a story-teller.

At the Business of Story, our goal is to reignite within you the one true superpower we all possess — storytelling — to nudge the world in any direction you choose. So we give away our knowledge and tools to help you develop your storytelling muscles from the very moment you begin interacting with us.

The responses we receive from people letting us know how our frameworks have helped them excel through the stories they tell is rewarding to us. They tell their stories through email or social media, sharing their small victories, and telling us how they are crafting their brand stories using our resources. That's a win.

Figure 8.1 on the next page shows an example of a small victory as captured in our private Facebook group. Eric Relyea was trying to use the And, But & Therefore narrative framework to clarify his brand story. He was wrestling with it, so he shared his ABT with me. I could see where he was headed with his story, but he was having a hard time clarifying his message. So I helped him with this ABT, and we both won in the transaction.

I have never met Eric, nor is he a client, so I would place this conversation in the brand awareness act of the customer journey. By joining our private Facebook group, Eric is bordering on brand adoption. He may never buy anything from us, but that's OK. By helping him get what he wants and needs, we grow our influence as we demonstrate how our proven narrative frameworks work in real time. We help a fellow professional in the process. His success moment is another convincing scene in our story. Plus, his brief story unfolded before all the members of our Facebook group so they could learn, too. It's a perfect example of the scalability of story. That's a win/win in our book.

Figure 8.1 Thread from the Business of Story: Storytelling for Leaders of Purpose Driven Brands private Facebook Group

In my speaking engagements, the room is typically filled with people who are just becoming aware of me and the Business of Story. I provide my keynote participants with as much value as possible by teaching them the applied science and helping them experience the bewitchery of storytelling. Each attendee works on their story using an And, But & Therefore worksheet. They learn and apply the five primal elements of story. Plus, they walk through the Story Cycle System in the *What's Your Story?* field notebook we provide for free. By the end, they will understand why storytelling is more important now than ever if you want your brand to rise above the noise of the attention economy. They will appreciate how stories work in their lives to connect with people and move them to action. And they will have at least outlined their own story and have three proven narrative frameworks they can use to build their storytelling muscles: a win/win/win.

BRAND ADOPTION

Giving away our invaluable *free* advice leads to what we call "story eurekas" These are those energizing aha! moments that lead to brand adoption, where you experience even more energizing story eurekas! I love the term *eureka*. It comes from the Greek word εὑρηκα (heúreka), meaning "I found it." It is an interjection used to celebrate a discovery or invention, an exclamation attributed to ancient Greek mathematician and inventor Archimedes. *Eureka* is closely related to *heuristic*, which refers to experience-based techniques for problem solving, learning, and discovery.

For me, this definition of eureka concisely describes the power of story. Storytelling is an experienced-based technique that shares anecdotes about real-world events to advance problem solving, learning and discovery. When our audiences experience these story eurekas through their exposure to the Business of Story narrative frameworks, they become eager to learn how to create these same reactions in their own audiences—so they adopt our storytelling practices.

Brand adoption happens when a customer purchases a Business of Story product or service. This includes investing in the DIY Brand Story Strategy workbook, hiring us to help craft their brand story, or immersing their marketing, sales, and leadership teams in a Business of Story master class or eight-week story mastery program. In each case, we design in success scenes that progress the customer through the brand story creation process, creating more and more story eurekas. These include the inspiring story appetizers we send before every session to familiarize them with the content and spark their imagination. Each engagement is tailored to their needs, and we share specific added-value resources to help them grow as brand and business storytellers.

Customers experience success in each step of the Story Cycle System as their brand story becomes increasingly clear. With clarity comes simplicity and excitement about where the brand is headed. This clarity and focus are also experienced by participants in the master class and story mastery programs. We celebrate our customers' successes as they share their stories with their cohorts and colleagues, learning from one another and growing as storytellers.

To mark their achievements, brands *define* their story elements, as demonstrated by the Prêt, Auto, Partez brand story elements presented at the end of this chapter. Course participants leave with newfound communication skills to help them connect with audiences on a primal level and move them to action.

BRAND APPRECIATION

How do you make your story their story? You do so by helping them get what they want out of life, which inspires them to eagerly share their experience with others. For the Business of Story, this means helping people become crystal-clear about who they are, what their brand stands for, and where they are headed. We help them amplify their impact in the market by differentiating their offering from their competitors' and making it immediately relevant to their customers. And we help them simplify their lives. When you dial in your story, you know what to say yes to and, more important, how and when to say no. If the request does not honor your vision and service your mission, it's not meant to be in your journey. Then we ask our customers to share their new narrative wisdom with the world through their stories. Each tale is a moment of success that both models the storytelling techniques they've learned and demonstrates the power of the process.

In fact, this book is a story of stories about those who have learned the applied science and bewitchery of storytelling through the Business of Story. Each anecdote is about a moment when everything changed for them. As I mentioned up top, stories are about the scenes that transform us. So look for those moments of success your customers experience. Capture them. Celebrate them. Then string those scenes together and watch your brand story come to life.

In April 2018, I performed my first TEDx talk in Gilbert, Arizona. My talk was for the young students and professionals in the audience, the twentysomethings, to help them align with their calling. So I asked them to stop looking for their story and start finding their scenes. These are the moments we all experience that have shaped who we are today.

"Find your scenes and your story will find you," I encouraged. Or another way to think about it is that stories are made of scenes, but it is the scenes that make the story.

The script for my talk itself follows the Story Cycle System. To see how you can use the Story Cycle System to guide your long-form communications and presentations, I've included my TEDx script in Appendix One of this book. I'm confident you'll find more story eurekas in the presentation to help you scale your storytelling.

NOW IT'S YOUR TURN

Map the success moments on your customer journey for each of your audiences. Where do you celebrate little victories with them during the three phases of brand awareness to adoption through appreciation? Think of these moments as scenes in your customer journey. How do you show up in these scenes to help them celebrate their success?

Success Matrix	Awareness How will you welcome them into your story?	Adoption How will you make them a part of your story?	Appreciation How will you help them share your story?
Audience #1			
Audience #2			
Audience #3			

Worksheet 8.1 Map the success milestones for your audience from brand awareness to adoption to appreciation.

FINAL THOUGHTS

If we break the Story Cycle System down into the three-act structure of story, then you have just come through Act II and are entering the final act. You began Act I by setting the stage for your brand story when you defined your #1 position in the market. You introduced your three audiences as the main characters at the heart of your story. You determined what's at stake for them—their wishes and wants—so that you can make your story compelling.

Then you broke into Act II in Chapter 4 by describing the disruption in the market your brand is responding to: the problem you solve in your customers' lives. You boldly crafted your unique value proposition to declare how you are the most timely and relevant offering to help your audiences get what they wish for and want. But then the antagonistic forces showed up. Instead of letting these obstacles thwart your progress, you strategized on how you will co-opt their energy to propel your brand and its story forward in the hearts and minds of your customers.

Then you put a face on your offering when, in Chapter 6, you revealed your brand's emotional promise, intrinsic gift, and unique personality. You mapped how you and your brand, as your audience's mentor, will guide them on the journey of customer engagement, experiencing its highs and its lows. Act II wraps up with acknowledging the victories your customers achieve, and how you celebrate with them along the way.

Now it's time for Act III of the Story Cycle System. As with every story, this is when you clearly reveal the moral of your story. Hollywood calls this the "promise of the premise." What is the universal truth underscored in your story? In branding, this is when you define your brand's ultimate purpose: why you exist beyond the basal need of making money. Your brand purpose is the ultimate expression of the self-actualization of your offering and how it lifts the people you serve.

ADDITIONAL RESOURCES

Explore ways to express your brand's unique personality with the additional resources at businessofstory.com/victory:

- Read Vol. VIII of the *Business of Story* online magazine: "Victory Is at Hand: Celebrate Success with Your Customers"

- Listen to Barry Kirk on: "How to Build Customer Loyalty Through a Shared Brand Narrative"

- Watch my quick explanation video on how to map your customer journey: bit.ly/StoryCycle-Victory

STORY ON ACTIVITY

Create success moments at home. Design three things you can do in the next two days for the one you love. Activate those scenes and write down their outcomes. Then watch a personal story about an important relationship grow.

PRÊT, AUTO, PARTEZ

Brand Position

Prêt, Auto, Partez is the #1 resource for subprime car buyers to purchase a vehicle and begin repairing their credit.

Unique Value Proposition

Prêt, Auto, Partez is your vehicle to financial freedom.

Brand Promise

Peace of mind

Brand Gift

Transportation

Brand Personality

The Caregiver (secondary archetype: The Hero)

Brand Descriptors

- Trustworthy

- Insightful

- Integrity

- Respect

- Educational

- Honesty

- Authentic

- Friendliness

- Humor

Brand Purpose

Prêt, Auto, Partez exists to get people back on the road to financial freedom.

Brand Statement

For subprime car buyers who want the independence and pride of owning a like-new car, Prêt, Auto, Partez provides the vehicle to repair their credit through honest rates and a fiscal education program that increases the health of their purchase, transporting the buyer to greater peace of mind and self-esteem on their road to financial freedom.

Theme

Your vehicle to financial freedom

9

The Moral

How to Declare Your Brand's Purpose to Amplify Your Impact

"I believed that if people got out and ran a few miles every day, the world would be a better place, and I believed these shoes were better to run in. People, sensing my belief, wanted some of that belief for themselves. Belief, I decided. Belief is irresistible."

— Phil Knight

TELLING YOUR STORY ON PURPOSE

When I think of consumer commodities, I think of bottled water, aspirin, and vodka (not necessarily in that order). But how do you create meaning for an inherently meaningless product to create a premium offering? You craft a compelling brand story based on the purpose that is expressed through your product.

That's what this chapter is all about: finding the purpose that propels your brand. Because as you'll soon see, your customers buy your story before they buy your offering.

This brand story concept has never been more underscored to me than by listening to celebrity Dan Aykroyd pitch his Crystal Head Vodka on the Joe Rogan show. You can learn a ton from this gifted brand storyteller about how to spin meaning into your merchandise.

The entertaining two-hour episode rollicks through his beliefs and experiences. Aykroyd spoke at length about his religion of following spiritualists and mediums. He wrote *Ghostbusters* because he was raised in Ottawa, Canada, in a family that routinely performed séances and hung out with mediums. He believes in

Sasquatch and has had three of his own close encounters with unidentified flying objects.

But Aykroyd started the show shilling his premium vodka called Crystal Head. This award-winning vodka is an expression of his purpose, which as I understand it is *to tap into unseen forces to elevate your understanding and therefore your life.*

When it comes to selling an expensive commodity, I can't think of a bigger task than hocking a $55 bottle of vodka. According to the Planet Money Show on National Public Radio (NPR), a federal law requires all vodka to be pretty much the same. "Vodka must be distilled or treated until it is, quote, 'without distinctive character, aroma, taste, or color.'" Some distillers will add flavor packs, which is a separate category outside of "pure vodka."

The Planet Money team wanted to test this. So they bought some vodka concentrate and added water to create their homemade booze. Then they sent it to White Labs in San Diego for a comprehensive spirits test. Along with their bathtub batch, they sent a sample of the cheapest vodka they could find and a sample of the ultra-luxury brand Grey Goose.

Guess which of the three vodkas came in third for taste?

Yep, Grey Goose.

INTOXICATING BRAND STORYTELLING

Given this insight, I was intrigued by how Aykroyd told the story of his ultra-premium Crystal Head Vodka. His vodka has been on the market for 11 years and is in 70 countries with over 50 million bottles sold. It won the Gold Medal for Excellent Taste at the 2013 PRODEXPO exhibition in Moscow, out of 400 vodkas.

But what is even more impressive than the success of his tasteless spirit is his brand storytelling. Aykroyd extolled the virtues of their process.

"What we do is we take peaches and cream corn from Chatham, Ontario, and we put them in the truck in the mash. We ship it 90 percent alcohol volume at that point and we take it over and put it in the ferry boat and bring it over to the distillery in Newfoundland, Canada, one of the last state-owned stills in the world. And why are we there? Because the water from the original Wisconsin glacier is under Newfoundland. Vodka is an old Russian word for water. And great vodkas have sweet water."

Aykroyd went on to describe how his vodka has a "sweet, vanilla, dry crisp with a kick of heat off the finish. Our [flavor] notes are from Anthony Dias Blue."

But wait. The brand story only gets better. Aykroyd says that after distilling, they filter their vodka by pouring it over Herkimer diamonds. Not surprisingly, Rogan jumps on the thought. "You pour it over diamonds?"

I'll let the former Bass-O-Matic salesman take it from here:

CRAFTING BRAND MEANING THROUGH DIAMONDS AND UFOS

AYKROYD: "We do. We pour it over the Herkimer semiprecious stone. And the Herkimer semiprecious stone is one of our last purification processes. Now, if you asked a high school professor what does pouring alcohol over diamonds do to the alcohol, they'd probably say, 'Well, nothing.' But, our stones, after a certain number of pours, they turn yellow and we have to bleach them clean or replace them.

The Herkimer diamond is found in an anomalous area of upstate New York, also in Afghanistan and Oaxaca, Mexico. They're little semiprecious double-ended crystals and people love the taste of the vodka poured over the stones."

ROGAN: "Is there a chemical reaction with the stones that causes the crystals to turn yellow?"

AYKROYD: "You'd have to sit with a chemistry professor and say why does the alcohol turn the crystals yellow — is it doing anything, is it purifying it? We've done flavor profiles and people like it better poured over the stones.

Now, why I like the Herkimer diamond is of course because it's near Griffiss Air Force Base in Rome, New York."

ROGAN: (Under his breath) "Dun, dun, dun . . ."

AYKROYD: "That is where a lot of scrambles went up in the 70s and 80s against whatever was coming and going in the mountains there in Pine Bush, New York."

ROGAN: "UFOs?"

AYKROYD: "So I thought, this is great. Herkimer diamonds from that area associated with ETs, the Navajo, the Aztec, the Anasazi. They said that these skulls came down to them from the star children. They were given to them as scrying devices to help the tribe move forward, to give positive energy to the tribe. And so I thought, perfect tie-in. We pour our vodka over Herkimer diamonds; we're tied in a little to the extraterrestrial legend there with the skull. It's the neat kind of bow to our product.

But the most important thing is that the fluid in the bottle matches the beauty of the bottle, and the bottle is the idea of selling purity and enlightenment thinking. Enlightened drinking is what these skulls were made for."

THE THINKING BEHIND THE SKULL

Crystal Head Vodka is brilliantly packaged in an artisan skull bottle designed by notable Texas artist John Alexander, inspired by the crystal skull legend.

The crystal skulls are human skull hardstone carvings made of clear or milky-white quartz (also called "rock crystal"). According to National Geographic, many believe these skulls were carved thousands of years ago by an ancient Mesoamerican civilization. Others think they may be relics from the legendary island of Atlantis or proof that extraterrestrials visited the Aztecs sometime before the Spanish conquest.

However, these claims have been refuted for all the specimens made available for scientific studies. But what a story! And the folks at Crystal Head Vodka are undeterred. They have grown a community of bartenders they call "startenders," who share their unique experiences with this otherworldly brand.

"We are the vodka for the creative spirit," Aykroyd declares. He said the spirit comes from two artists: a writer and a graphic artist who is also a designer, painter, and sculptor. And then he defined the purpose behind the Crystal Head brand:

Enlightened drinking for the creative spirit

Rogan deadpans, "Dan Aykroyd, you may be the best salesman who has ever lived."

This is the power of a brand story told on purpose. Crystal Head Vodka is a clear example of how brand storytelling can levitate your brand's position in the marketplace for incredible success.

Because, as Aykroyd has proved, people will buy your story before they buy your product.

And while you might call B.S. on his story, Aykroyd is sharing his true beliefs in mystical forces to sell his spirits. It's authentic to him, whether you believe it or not—and there's nothing wrong with that. And if you do believe, well . . . the sky's the limit.

The purpose of this chapter is for you to declare what your brand ultimately stands for beyond just making money. I call it the moral of your story. As you will see, it's critical to declare your brand purpose to connect with today's jaded consumer. They just don't believe in the myth of profit-grabbing brands anymore.

WHAT YOUR CUSTOMER WANTS

Several studies, including one by Accenture that interviewed 30,000 consumers around the world, found that 63 percent are buying goods and services from brands that reflect their personal values and beliefs. In America, nearly seven out of 10 consumers say they are more loyal to purpose-driven brands, according to the 2018 Cone/Porter Novelli Purpose Study. But most brands have a hard time articulating what they stand for beyond just making money. They're not connecting with this ardent and growing customer mind-set.

Internally, employees are rising up to support the purpose of their organizations, and sometimes pushing back. I was recently driving home from a workout and heard on NPR that 1,000 Google employees have petitioned their company to not compete for a lucrative contract with the federal government to use its data science on the US/Mexico border. They feel basic human rights and privacy are at stake, a divisive social issue as of this writing. Providing their big data services for this endeavor would fly in the face of Google's original purpose, "Don't be evil."

When you have a clearly focused purpose for your organization, these kinds of issues are easier to navigate because you can vet them through a simple question: Does this initiative work or not work to support our purpose in the world?

Your brand purpose is the ultimate expression of the sentiment you've been building on throughout the Story Cycle System: It's not what you make, but what you make happen that your audiences will buy into and align with.

THE SKY'S THE LIMIT

The four-star Air Force general raised his hand. He was sitting in the top row of a packed 180-person theater at Joint Base Andrews outside of Washington, DC. "Yes, sir," I acknowledged from the stage. I had just completed a half-day Business of Story workshop to help generals with their storytelling skills. We were in the final Q&A.

He cleared his throat and said, "I have a correction to the first story you told this morning."

Oh, boy, I thought. *I must've messed up a call sign or squadron number or mispronounced a jet fighter reference.* I've found generals are particular about such details, especially when uttered by civilians. I was jumpy because I have never served in the armed forces. I admit this at the beginning of my workshop. That's why I open each Air Force storytelling workshop with a connection story. I explain that although I've never served, I did marry into an Air Force family that has had a tremendous impact on me.

The story is about my wife, Michele's, astonishing experience following the terrorist attacks of 9/11. She prayed to her long-deceased father, Major James Reynolds, asking him for solace after the falling of the Twin Towers in Manhattan.

Figure 9.1 Major Jim Reynolds

Figure 9.2 Model replica of Maj. Jim Reynold's F-86 Skyblazer

A week later, Michele was shopping for Legos for our boys in a Tuesday Morning store, the Tuesday morning following the previous Tuesday morning attack. But what she found stopped her in her tracks. It was an exact model replica of the F-86 fighter — right down to his name printed under the cockpit — her dad flew as the squadron commander of the Skyblazers demonstration team, the predecessor to today's Air Force Thunderbirds. To me, this was a sign that he was still looking after his little girl, even as he is flying through the heavens.

When I finish this story, I ask the generals for permission to be their storytelling wingman. They give it.

Now, fast-forward three hours to the general at the back of the auditorium. In his commanding voice, he said, "You stated that you have never served our country."

"That's right, sir."

"Well, from what I can tell you have served this Air Force honorably today. And for that, I commend you."

I stood there as the theater erupted in applause. For a moment, I was shell-shocked. A chill ran down the back of my neck. I looked at my toes. A smile peeled across my face.

No finer compliment about our work have I ever received. His reaction is the result of our brand purpose at the Business of Story: the reason we do what we do that is bigger than coaching and teaching storytelling.

We are brand story strategists who deploy our proprietary Story Cycle System to help leaders of purpose-driven brands clarify their stories to amplify their impact and simplify their lives. In addition to the Story Cycle System, we teach the And, But & Therefore narrative framework and the five primal elements of powerful anecdotes that grow individuals as storytellers and help them build storytelling cultures within their organizations.

We share our applied science and bewitchery of storytelling through speaking engagements, master classes, and an eight-week deliberate practice program. Plus, we consult one-on-one to help selected clients craft their brand story strategy. This book was written to show you how to develop your brand story on your own. We even prove our impact by helping you understand, plan, and measure the ROI of your brand and business storytelling endeavors.

Everything I've just mentioned about the Business of Story is what we make. What we coach. Teach. But what we make *happen* is vastly more rewarding. Our singular purpose is to help people live into their most powerful stories. With the Air Force, it's to help their leaders excel through the stories they tell. This is what we believe. What we do. How we do it simply supports what we believe.

I learned this from leadership guru Simon Sinek and his now legendary 2002 TEDxTacoma talk (nearing 45 million views on YouTube), "How Leaders Inspire Action." He said, "People don't buy what you do, they buy why you do it. What you do simply proves what you believe." Sinek said that most brands communicate from the outside in. They talk about what they make and how they make it. Rarely do they get to the Why, which is their purpose.

Take life insurance, for instance. Most life insurance ads say something to the effect of "We're one of America's largest/oldest insurers and we have a variety of life insurance plans for any need. Want to buy one?" Now ask yourself what differentiates Liberty Mutual, MetLife, and Northwestern Mutual from the rest of the market.

Nothing? Exactly!

Don't let this happen to you.

BUILDING BELIEF

We recently helped Phoenix-based commercial contractor Willmeng define its brand story to reveal its purpose. They operate in the commoditized commercial construction industry. All of their competitors look and sound the same. So we started asking questions:

What is Willmeng? A commercial contractor.

How do they operate? They specialize in tenant improvement, ground-up construction, and renovation in commercial buildings.

Why do they do it? Willmeng believes that people thrive when they find their genuine place of purpose, especially in how and where they contribute to their careers, families, and communities. Therefore, *Willmeng exists for people to build their genuine place of purpose.*

This idea of brand purpose was something that was lying latent within me early in my career. I sensed it, but I couldn't quite articulate it. Sinek's talk immediately released the idea of brand purpose, which fit perfectly in the Story Cycle System as the moral of your story.

Here's how Willmeng is guided by the beliefs and values of its brand story to help people build their place of purpose:

1. Show up every day as your genuine self

2. Attract talent with the right aptitude and attitude

3. Onboard new employees to set them up for success

4. Willmeng University provides robust, continuous training to grow talent, character, and culture

5. Serve like-minded clients

6. Preconstruction efforts to ensure the integrity of every project

7. Altruistic approach to customer service; care more than seems reasonable

8. Generous leader in thought and action for the industry

9. Invest in the community through philanthropy

10. Always do your genuine best

Willmeng's powerful purpose was arrived at by identifying the organization's why, which is captured in their UVP: *We build on character to create genuine success.* Their purpose-driven story even redefined what they do. Instead of being a commercial general contractor, which is a statement of commodity in and of itself, they are positioning themselves as *the* commercial *genuine* contractor. How they do this is captured in their position statement: Willmeng is the commercial general contractor when building with character is what you value most for the integrity of your project and the genuine success of your people.

These brand story elements come together to craft their ultimate goal of helping people build their place of purpose. Let's reexamine the brand purposes of the companies that you have been introduced to through this guidebook:

Airloom is an all-natural allergy supplement, but its greater purpose is to help people inhale a healthy dose of life. Let's take it a step further. The purpose of Oasis LLC, the makers of Airloom, is to ameliorate human suffering.

Ecodriving Solutions provides fleet driver training programs to fulfill its purpose of helping people arrive healthy, happy, and safe.

While most people think of Goodwill Industries as running thrift stores that fund their workforce development programs, they truly exist to help people realize the treasure of a good job.

Adelante Healthcare is a community health center fulfilling its purpose of providing sustainable healthcare for all.

Global Water is a water utility, but it exists to help people access the renewable resource of water so they can flourish.

Red Bull exists to give wings to people and ideas.

Airbnb exists to help people feel like they belong anywhere.

Prêt, Auto, Partez sells used cars to at-risk buyers. But this is just the brand's vehicle to serve its purpose of helping people get back on the road to financial freedom.

Crystal Head Vodka exists to help people enlighten their creative spirit.

From the list above, which is more intoxicating to you: the product or the purpose?

PURPOSE-FULL

In 2011, an important book was published which further inspired the idea of a brand purpose. In *Grow: How Ideals Power Growth and Profit at the World's Greatest Companies*, Jim Stengel used the term "brand ideals" to describe what I call the moral of your story in marketing. His book asks the following questions:

- What do you exist to do that is greater than your product or service?

- How are you bettering mankind through your offering?

- What compelling, fundamental need in the lives of your heroes do you service?

After years of research, Stengel uncovered 50 companies that, by passionately following their brand ideals, outperformed the S&P 500 by over 400 percent in the 2000s. What's even more amazing is that this was during the most significant worldwide recession in modern history.

Stengel's list of 50 top-performing companies includes organizations like Accenture, which exists to help people accelerate ideas to achieve their dreams. Apple exists to empower creative exploration and self-expression. Heineken exists to help men be worldly — resourceful, confident, open-minded, and cosmopolitan. Dove exists to help women celebrate their inner beauty. Pampers exists to help mothers care for their babies and toddlers and foster their children's healthy, happy development.

With each of the 50 companies, you can look at how they approach business and quickly fill in the blank to this statement: "Company X exists to_____." Their purpose reveals their higher ideal and why they're in business in the first place.

We all know Nike's fundamental Call to Adventure: "Just do it!" Nike exists to awaken the champion within us all. This brand ideal is at the heart of everything Nike stands for. It was particularly well revealed in a remarkable TV commercial they ran during the 2012 Summer Olympics called "Find Your Greatness." This story relies on minimalism. It has no edits, but one sixty-second shot that seems like several minutes of a heavy young man jogging on a country road. The narration intones as follows:

> "Greatness. It's just something we made up. Somehow we've come to believe that greatness is a gift reserved for a chosen few. For prodigies. For superstars. And the rest of us can only stand by watching. You can forget that. Greatness is not some rare DNA strand. It's not some precious thing. Greatness is no more unique to us than breathing. We're all capable of it. All of us."

The spot ends with a graphic that reads "Find your greatness." The moral of the story is to believe in yourself: Just Do It!

But just as Nike encourages the average athlete and weekend warrior to seek to be their best, you don't have to be a superstar brand to build a powerful purpose that helps you beat your competition. Just look inside yourself. Why do you do what you do? What was the inspiration behind creating your brand in the first place? Look to your origin story. Unearth the moments that have shaped who you are today. How did your curiosity, beliefs, and values materialize from those moments?

FOR WANT OF A STORY

In August 1485, King Richard III died during the Battle of Bosworth. William Shakespeare told the story in a history play around 1591. This is when King Richard III's horse was struck down on the battlefield and he reportedly said, "A horse! A horse! My kingdom for a horse."

This world-altering incident also spawned a proverb titled "For Want of a Nail," which teaches the importance of sweating the small stuff, like a horseshoe nail if you want to maintain your kingdom.

> For want of a nail the shoe was lost.
> For want of a shoe the horse was lost.
> For want of a horse the rider was lost.
> For want of a rider the message was lost.
> For want of a message the battle was lost.
> For want of a battle the kingdom was lost.
> And all for the want of a horseshoe nail.

I love this proverb for its poetic truth, which is as powerful today as it was in the 15th century. Many brands want to take short-cuts with the development of their story. Congratulations to you because you have gotten through nine of the 10 steps of the Story Cycle System. Your purpose-driven brand story will make all the difference between ruling your kingdom or succumbing to your competition. So I pose to you my version, which I call "For Want of a Story":

> For want of a story the purpose was lost.
> For want of a purpose the vision was lost.
> For want of a vision the passion was lost.
> For want of passion caring was lost.
> For want of caring the mission was lost.
> For want of a mission the business was lost.
> All for the want of a simple story.

NOW IT'S YOUR TURN

What's your purpose-driven brand story? Do this exercise to arrive at your purpose. Here's how it shakes out for the Business of Story.

Why: We believe people are more inspired, innovative, and industrious when they connect through their most powerful stories.

How: We use proven narrative frameworks to awaken within you the primal power of story to enrich your life and those you serve as you become an intentional and influential storyteller.

What: We are communication experts at the Business of Story.

The Business of Story exists to help people live into their most powerful stories.

Why: _____

How: _____

What: _____

Our brand exists to help people _____

FINAL THOUGHTS

You've been through nine steps of the Story Cycle System expressly designed to help you define your brand purpose. It's like archeology. You might even call it "brandthropology." You have been digging and sifting through all your operational and aspirational elements to reveal why you do what you do. On Maslow's hierarchy of needs, your purpose is at the top of the pyramid representing enlightenment. Everyone you sell to pretty much has their basal physiological and safety needs met. As social beings, they crave belonging and esteem, which you have built for your brand through the eight previous steps of the Story Cycle System. Those critical story exercises have been the building blocks for where you find yourself now, in that rarified air of enlightenment.

"What does it all mean and why are you here?" your audiences, at least subconsciously, ask themselves. Your brand purpose is the answer to that question: the moral of your story. Your brand purpose is the North Star that will guide everything you do from here on, navigating you into a more powerful story.

Welcome to humanity.

ADDITIONAL RESOURCES

Explore ways to express your brand's purpose at businessofstory.com/purpose:

- Listen to Avein Saaty-Tafoya on: "How a Purpose-Driven Brand Story Will Increase the Health of Your Organization"

- Watch my quick explanation video on how to identify your brand's promise, gift, and personality: bit.ly/StoryCycle-Mentor

STORY ON ACTIVITY

Think of three of your favorite brands and ask yourself what their purpose is. They exist to help people do what?

10

Ritual

How to Build Repeat Business to Simplify Your Life

"Do what you do so well that they will want to see it again and bring their friends."

—Walt Disney

SHOUT YOUR STORY FROM THE MOUNTAINTOPS

Imagine the exhilaration New Zealander Edmund Hillary felt when he planted his frozen toes atop Mount Everest. Picture the crystal-clear panorama he took in through his foggy goggles as the first human on the summit. I bet that's what you're feeling about now. Breathless jubilation, having made it this far with your brand story. Or am I just telling myself a story?

Regardless of your excitement level, you are in that lofty place of a brand storyteller who has mustered the resources, overcome competing forces, and is about to summit with the Story Cycle System. Suddenly your mission has become much more focused because your story is crystal clear.

The way most branders get through this guidebook is with a sturdy habit of huddling over the pages and doing the work. It's how you conquer any mountain. One repetitious step at a time. And you're near the top, but you have one more challenge ahead of you.

There was an infamous 39-foot cliff just before the summit of Everest called the Hillary Step, the mountain's last "Oh yeah, let's see what you're made of" obstacle. This treacherous frozen rock face, which was destroyed in a 2015 earthquake, stood between the climbers and their ultimate alpine conquest. But isn't that just the thing with the universe? Right when you think you're at the top, it punches you in the nose just to see how badly you really want it.

Well, I'm not going to sock you in the snout. But I am going to give you one more Hillary Step challenge. And I'll throw you a rope to pull you through it. It's called building brand rituals. Brand rituals are the ways you can seamlessly weave your offering into the lives of your customers, essentially making your story *their* story. It's like roping your mountaineers together as a team. You as the brand mentor look more like a Sherpa at this point, supplying the repeat behavior to help your customers achieve what they want through the routine use of your product or service and your guidance.

You start by enrolling your people, prospects, customers, shareholders, stakeholders, vendors, and community into your purpose-driven story. They need to buy in and align with your brand story if you hope to achieve your goals. This chapter will show you how to design and activate your brand rituals to increase customer engagement, build repeat business, and develop brand evangelists who will shout your story from the mountaintops.

BUILDING INTERNAL STORYTELLING RITUALS

You love it when you earn a loyal customer and they happily share your story with their world. But that typically begins by building a ritualized storytelling culture within your organization to amplify the impact of your brand story. You want to teach your front-line workers, staff, sales team, human resources personnel, and C-suite executives how to tell your brand story. They all need to embrace the brand purpose to get them pulling passionately in the same direction. If every member of your organization has not bought into your brand narrative — if they don't *own* it — don't expect your customers to buy into it either.

You've probably heard this old tale: When asked what his job was at NASA, the janitor replied, "I'm helping put a man on the moon, man." That's an employee who is enrolled in the organizational mission and story.

One of the first obstacles you'll face is what I call the "hot, thin air" syndrome. Your employees and even some of your executives may be skeptical about your new brand story. They will question how you arrived at your lofty brand position as articulated through your brand promise, gift, personality, and purpose. They may say things like:

"Where'd you pull that out of?"

"If it were only true."

Or the gut punch of all characterizations: "It's kind of *woo-woo*, isn't it?"

Hence, to them, your new brand story sounds like hot air that you pulled out of thin air.

But here's how you clear that up. You will immediately overcome their anti-stories by inviting them to cocreate true stories that support your new brand narrative. These are stories about employee engagement, customer service, product quality, community relations, etc., that you have already captured in Chapter 6 with your nine brand descriptors. Share these stories with your team to demonstrate how your brand is already fulfilling the promises it makes. And take note of how these stories also demonstrate areas where you can become stronger and more differentiated in the market.

Remember how Sean Schroeder did this with his blueriver team? They had no idea what the new brand narrative around "flow" was going to be, but they described it perfectly when Sean asked how they experienced flow in their jobs. Sean was simply testing the authenticity of blueriver's purpose-driven brand story.

Then you invite your employees to go out and spot, capture, and share their own stories in the wild that reflect each of your nine brand descriptors. In their story safaris they will experience these real-world anecdotes in action. They'll see how your brand is already walking the talk through exceptional moments of employee and customer engagement. And as I said earlier, stories scale. So not only will some of these stories grow in magnitude and importance for the sales, marketing, and legacy of your organization, they will also trigger stories in other people. Just think how a story you've heard always sparks a similar story of your own.

By doing this simple exercise with your team—asking them to spot, capture and share stories in the wild—you will prove your new brand narrative to your most important, and sometimes most skeptical, allies. Plus, you will begin building a storytelling culture through the ritual of finding and sharing stories that invites everyone to excavate the true stories you'll use in your inbound and outbound content marketing.

Here's what you'll do: Ask your employees to select one of your brand descriptors as a theme for a story. Then have them tell a true story that supports that descriptor. Coach them to tell their story using the five primal elements of storytelling in this order:

1. **When:** Stories are always about moments. Define when this story occurred — the more specific, the better. A time stamp tells our monkey brain that it's about to hear a true story that it should probably pay attention to because it might learn something.

2. **Where:** What was the specific location where this moment occurred? The location stamp works hand-in-hand with the time stamp to alert your audience that you're telling them a story.

3. **Character:** Introduce who is at the heart of the story that the audience can relate to. The story can be about you, a colleague, a customer, a vendor, etc.

4. **Action/surprise:** Describe what specifically happens in this tale that leads to a surprising outcome.

5. **Aha! moment:** Conclude with the business point about how this anecdote supports your brand descriptor.

MOM TO THE RESCUE

For instance, one of the brand descriptors for the Business of Story is *connection*. Stories, when they begin with empathy for your audience, are a proven way to find common ground to connect your world with theirs.

During the summer of 2019, I was presenting a 90-minute Business of Story master class to 60 of Banner Health's top human resources professionals at their headquarters in Phoenix. I wanted a connection story to link my world with theirs. But what tale would I tell them? Then it hit me with the force of a palm-to-the-forehead "Duh"! I would tell the story about my mom, the same one that I used to open my TEDx talk a year earlier. I rehearsed the anecdote in my mind just before my session.

A couple of years ago, I asked my 91-year-old mother, Pat, what was the moment when she knew she wanted to dedicate her life to nursing. She told me about when she was four years old sitting in a Wenatchee, Washington, hospital waiting room, eager for her new sister Diane to arrive.

"I was fidgeting in my seat," she recalled, "when all of a sudden this nice lady dressed in her nurse whites sat down next to me. She smiled, asked my name, and we started chatting. Then she reached into her pocket and pulled out an orange for me. Right then, because of that friendly gesture from a complete stranger, I thought I'd like to become a nurse."

Pat went to the University of Michigan and earned her degree as a nurse anesthetist. Following a decade of nursing, she got married to Keith and reared us seven kids. Pat had little time for nursing outside of mending our skinned knees, broken noses (in my case), and bruised egos. When most of us had moved away from home to follow our own careers, she volunteered for 30 years as a nurse at Overlake Hospital in Bellevue, Washington. Then she cared for our dad, who succumbed to Alzheimer's in 2018 after a courageous five-year donnybrook with dementia.

Yes, I thought, this would be my connection story to these Banner Health professionals. I walked to the side of the stage to hook up my computer and pull up my presentation. I glanced down to the side of the production table, and on the floor was a bag that rocked my world. It was a bag of oranges. I reached down, grabbed one, and put it in my suit pocket to reveal this serendipitous prop at the ripe time in my connection story.

In more than a decade of speaking on storytelling, I have never been greeted by a single citrus next to the stage, let alone a whole bag of oranges. Do you recall me mentioning how stories summon surprising forces and fortunes? Isn't it providential that it was the fruit at the crux of my connection story? The audience ate it up.

By the way, can you find the five primal elements of story in the anecdote above: when, where, who (character), what (action/ surprise), why (the aha! moment that makes your business point)? This is what you are looking for from your people. And here's the great part. As you are teaching them how to spot and capture these stories in the wild, and then retell them using the five primal elements of story, you are accomplishing more than just proofing your brand descriptors. You are starting to build a persistent story-telling culture in your organization to ritualize the collection of real-word stories that support your overall brand narrative.

As described in Chapter 7, I learned the five primal storytelling elements technique from Shawn Callahan and Mark Schenk of Melbourne-based leadership and sales storytelling consulting firm Anecdote. Shawn wrote a tremendous book titled *Putting Stories to Work: Mastering Business Storytelling* that shows you how to use simple anecdotes to make a big impact in business. I am also a certified coach for Anecdote's Storytelling for Leaders deliberate practice program. In it we teach four kinds of stories and how and when to use them: a Connection story to win over your audience; a Clarity story to communicate change; an Influence story to overcome an anti-story; and a Success story, which is a more human approach to your typical case study.

We live in such an information-overloaded world that I believe Attention Deficit Disorder has become communicable and we're all the viruses. But I've learned that the primal power of a simple story wins the day in our techno-driven world: *An anecdote is the antidote.*

Once your people see how the important moments of brand engagement are already happening as captured through these real-world stories, they'll understand how your brand story has come together. But these anecdotes do something more. In their telling, they inspire greater performance by your team members in creating more exceptional stories in the future.

THE VALUE OF BUILDING BRAND RITUALS

Your customer's first purchase from you means you've done a good job of communicating your value. But what is their *lifetime* value to your business? How do you keep them coming back for more to increase that value? You design the ritualistic use of your brand into their lives. Now it's time to help your customer take ownership of your story to generate repeat business and word-of-mouth marketing.

Brand rituals are the repeatable customer engagement moments designed into their journey with your brand. As you recall, stories are always about moments. Your goal is to create such memorable moments that your customers keep coming back for more—and bring their friends along, too.

Brand lore has it that in 1958, Procter & Gamble was worried about shampoo sales flattening out with the rise in popularity of the crew cut. They assembled their best marketing minds to determine how to bring the shine back to their sales. At the end of the table was a meek man named Quimby who nobody much paid attention to. After 45 minutes of heated brainstorming, Quimby raised his hand and muttered, "Why don't we just put instructions on the bottle to lather, rinse, repeat? We'll sell twice as much shampoo that way."

Go look at your bottle of shampoo. What are its instructions? On my bottle they are "Wash, rinse, repeat." And there you have it: a brand ritual designed into the use of a product. Can you think of other seemingly benign brand stories that trigger the habitual use of a product or service?

"Beef. It's what's for dinner."

"Buy it. Sell it. Love it."

"Just do it."

In short, rituals are purposeful, repeatable behaviors rich with meaning and belonging that connect us to something we perceive as substantive in our lives. They provide an unconscious reinforcement of the product or service upon which the ritual is created, and they often lead to passionate worship.

As Zain Raj, author of the number one marketing bestseller *Brand Rituals: How Successful Brands Bond with Customers for Life*, states, "Consumers no longer wish to be sold anything. They are looking for products and services that offer a new definition of value, which doesn't necessarily include having the lowest price, and for companies that share their values. You must create a bond with customers that actually changes their behavior and moves them from using your product occasionally to making it an integral part of their lives."

When we choose a brand, we hope it will somehow make us better or improve our quality of life. We wish for it to make us feel a certain way. We want it because we believe it will fulfill that wish. And the brand ritual around it creates the will we need to purchase it time and again, as long as it delivers on its promises.

Heinz Ketchup incorporated the ritual of waiting into their product with their famous "Anticipation" campaign. The primary visual in all its stories was the glacial pouring of its lusciously red, thick ketchup, as if a tongue were coming out of the bottle to foreshadow the taste that was about to explode in your mouth. The value of quality was vividly expressed.

Oreo built their identity around the common ritual of playing with our food. Oreo watched how customers naturally interacted with their cookies, and then celebrated the ritual by encouraging us to twist apart the two thin, dark mini-manhole covers of its cookie to reveal the creamy center, before eating it in our own peculiar ways.

Cracker Jacks has always been about the ritual exploring inside its box of sugary, popcorny, nutty goodness to find the prize. Cracker Jacks has even evolved with technology, and now one gets a personal code to key in on its website to redeem a prize from your mobile device.

HABIT, ROUTINE, RITUAL

What is the difference between a habit, a routine, and a ritual? There is no thought to a habit. For our purposes, it's a simple behavior with no personal attachment associated with it, and therefore it can easily be replaced with other offerings that fulfill the same needs with little regard for a customer's loyalty to any given brand. A habit evolves into a routine when it becomes a fairly fixed and regular occurrence in a person's day. A routine becomes a ritual when a consumer affixes a specific brand to that behavior.

For instance, one summer on a construction job I was a carpenter's apprentice to a guy named Don. Don was in the habit of packing his lunch. His routine was making the same lunch. Every day. His ritual was eating a peanut butter and white onion sandwich with . . . wait for it . . . Miracle Whip. Gak! His ritual brands were Skippy Chunky Peanut Butter, Miracle Whip, and Wonder Bread, washed down with Sunny Delight orange drink. I know — ascribing "delight" to any of this seems a stretch. But Don had ritualized these precise brands into his lunch box.

He said if a guy deviated from these exact ingredients, the sandwich would not live up to its "reputation for spectacular deliciousness." Don was confusing deliciousness with repulsiveness, I thought. He followed this exotic diet with his habit/routine/ritual, which was smoking unfiltered Camel cigarettes for "dessert," typically peppered with a joke so rank it'd make a whore blush (that was Don's high-water mark for joke telling). He was a rude, crude dude who loved this raunchy lunch ritual. (Try to say that three times.)

The true power of creating brand rituals is when marketers understand and tap into this human progression from simple habit to comfortable routine to cherished ritual. Think again of the three steps of brand awareness, adoption, and appreciation we discussed in Chapter 7, "Journey." Let's consider how you can evolve your customer from habit to routine to ritual using that same progression.

STEP 1. AWARENESS

It requires an enticing call to adventure in the customer's journey to cause her to switch brands or simply try a new one. To trigger this inciting incident, your brand must have created an outstanding value proposition through its positioning from its backstory. You must know what your customer wants and deliver on the brand promise to incite the change.

STEP 2. ADOPTION

Once the customer has chosen your new product or service, the journey down the road of trials begins. This is when the brand magnifies interest in its offering by being there to mentor the customer through the trials, tribulations, revelations and initial peak experiences with the product or service that start heating up brand loyalty.

STEP 3. APPRECIATION

As your brand interacts with your customer through exceptional customer service, greater brand bonding develops. The consumer experiences firsthand the brand ideal/moral of the story and attaches the brand values to his own beliefs and value, providing they are in sync or shared.

Creating a new ritualized behavior with your brand, the highest level of cognitive commitment, is essential to making your story *their* story to build repeat business. This is where brand evangelists are energized to help spread the good word for your offering. There is no more powerful form of advertising than word-of-mouth marketing. With brand rituals, not only are you developing repeat customers that you can count on, you are spawning independent salespeople to share your story.

DESIGNING YOUR BRAND RITUALS

Here are three ways you can design the ritualistic use of your product or service with your customers. Pick one that you think will be particularly powerful for your situation and go for it.

BUILD ON REALITY

Humans naturally ritualize behaviors. So capitalize on this tendency by ritualizing existing product functionality in consumer behavior. For instance, when we teach Business of Story workshop attendees about how to craft an And, But & Therefore statement to focus the theme of their message, I ask them to begin every future email they write with an ABT. We all write dozens of emails a day, so this natural activity becomes a perfect proving ground for ritualizing the use of a storytelling framework in a ubiquitous activity. I call it "curling your storytelling dumbbell" because using the ABT strengthens your narrative intuition. Try it. You'll find the ABT reduces your email writing time by as much as two-thirds. Plus, your readers will love you for it because they'll easily understand your communication and it will save them time interpreting your message.

What routine behaviors that intersect with your offering can you build upon with your customers?

EMBED MEANING

Don't confuse a ritual with a habit. You must make it meaningful to create a belief from the action, otherwise it's just a behavior. Supporters of breast cancer awareness wear the now-omnipresent pink ribbon because of the meaning and empowerment it represents toward the eradication of this awful disease. Apple's logo with the bite out of it has become synonymous with individuality as you disrupt the rules and "Think different."

How can you embed meaning in your offering? At the Business of Story, we embed meaning in our mentoring on the applied science and bewitchery of storytelling by giving every keynote, workshop, and master class participants a *What's Your Story?* field notebook to keep by their side long after the session. It's where they capture their notes and it becomes a meaningful reminder of the power of story in their life.

DEFINE RULES

Rituals often have a prescribed way of doing them. "Wash, rinse, repeat" clearly states the rules of use that shampoo manufacturers would like you to follow every time you're in the shower. Creators of these kinds of brand rituals leave nothing to chance. Is there a rule you can dictate about the use of your offering? I, for example, love using proverbs as rule conveyors.

Benjamin Franklin was brilliant with the life rules he defined by using proverbs. "Early to bed, early to rise, helps make a man healthy, wealthy, and wise." Proverbs are like little powder kegs of storytelling that communicate and make memorable a universal rule. Think of or make up your own proverb to communicate a defined rule for your offering. A proverbial rule I like to use to encourage the continual study and use of our approach to business storytelling is this: "You have to understand the magic to cast the spell." If you want to learn more about proverbs, read my good friend Ron Ploof's book, *The Proverb Effect: Secrets to Creating Tiny Phrases That Change the World.*

MOMENTS OF TRUTH

Rituals are similar to stories because they are always about a moment connected to a specific place and time. For instance, to anchor the Goodwill brand in the context of the second-largest retail shopping season of the year, we created a campaign that promoted Goodwill as "The Official Sponsor of Halloween" to ritualize the costume hunt for shoppers. Being the official sponsor of Halloween doesn't require any sponsorship payment or sanctioning by a governing body like, say, the Olympic Committee. We just simply invented the story of Goodwill being the official sponsor of Halloween to prompt the ritual of assembling your one-of-a-kind costume from their resale racks. And when you head to Goodwill for your goblin getup, American Express reminds you of the ritual around its credit card: "Don't leave home without it."

Other considerations when building your brand rituals include being consistent. Rituals are a behavior learned through repetition and positive reinforcement. The really good ones have a natural rhythm to them as well. Pringles potato chips says, "Once you pop, the fun don't stop." Pop too many, and you reach for another ritual: "Plop, plop, fizz, fizz, oh what a relief it is." Alka Seltzer.

Give your consistent rituals a finite length that accentuates the power of the moment. Dos Equis beer captured this essence in its "Most Interesting Man in the World" campaign, when he says, "I don't always drink beer. But when I do, I prefer Dos Equis."

Simpler is better when creating brand rituals. When we asked people to save water with our "Water—Use It Wisely" conservation campaign, our call to adventure was: "There are a number of ways to save water, and they all start with you." All we wanted people to do was to think about the water they were using every time they turned on the tap. Then we made these rituals actionable by creating environmental prompts in the form of 100+ surprising but highly effective water saving tips that make you think. For instance, water-saving device #32 is a toothbrush. How can a toothbrush save you water? It's an environmental prompt that reminds you that you can save up to four gallons a minute if you turn the water off while you brush your teeth. This is the idea of "habit stacking." Attach your ritual to an existing habit like brushing your teeth to infuse the activity with the meaning you're looking for. It works. The campaign, hopefully unlike your tap, is still running after 20 years.

Find product and service rituals that are uniquely your own and have shared value with your customers. Harley-Davidson sells a legendary motorcycle and imbues its rebel character with meaning through the bike accessories and apparel it wraps around the product offering. They famously turn workweek accountants into weekend warriors through their brand rituals.

Strategize how to create, nurture, and activate evangelists around your product or service by helping them embrace a brand ritual. The story they—your heroes—spread about you is vastly more potent than any story you will ever tell about yourself.

NOW IT'S YOUR TURN

How will you help your heroes create rituals around the use of your product or service? With your internal team, create the ritual of spotting and capturing stories in the wild that support your brand narrative using the five primal elements of story. That's a story creation ritual. This is a fun and engaging pursuit that helps them cocreate your brand story while building a rewarding storytelling culture within your organization. Plus, you will develop a ton of great content for your inbound and outbound marketing.

Then design rituals in the use of your product or service with your customers. Take cues from successful rituals other brands have created. Starbucks makes your "third place" easily accessible, comfortable, and habit-forming (the caffeine doesn't hurt either). Apple infuses its brand for daily use in our professional and personal lives through such tools as PowerBook, iPad, iTunes, the Apple Store and Apple TV. Ben & Jerry's ice cream provides a deliciously indulgent ritual, but at least you can feel good about consuming a purpose-driven brand.

As customers evolve and grow through repeated interaction with your brand, they progress into the next level of engagement and beyond. Although your brand rituals will be introduced in the first revolution of the Story Cycle System, it will typically take two, three, or four revolutions before your customer bonds completely with your product or service. And that bond is reliant on how well your brand mentors your customer in his or her journey and the potency with which an emotional connection is created.

In the form below, capture a moment that you can ritualize for each of your audiences to build repeat business and activate their word-of-mouth marketing on your behalf.

How You Ritualize the Use of Your Brand			
Audience #1			
Audience #2			
Audience #3			

Worksheet 10.1 Fill out this form describing how you can ritualize the use of your brand with your audiences.

FINAL THOUGHTS

Now what? You've navigated the 10 steps of the Story Cycle System. You've clarified your story, and it probably feels a bit like an epic at this point. I get it, because you've worked hard. So let's bring it all together in Chapter 11 with what most branding professionals would call a brand statement. But that's boring, so let's have some fun crafting your brand trailer instead to entice audiences into the bigger picture. I'll show you how.

ADDITIONAL RESOURCES

Visit businessofstory.com/rituals for these additional storytelling resources:

- Listen to Zain Raj on: "Creating Brand Rituals Through Story"
- Watch my quick explanation video on how to map your customer journey: bit.ly/StoryCycle-Ritual

STORY ON ACTIVITY

Think of your favorite brands and how they have ritualized the use of their product or service in your life. Consider how you can do the same with your brand in the lives of your customers.

11

How to Craft Your Brand Trailer to Hook Your Audiences

"Your brand is what people say about you when you're not in the room."

—Jeff Bezos, Amazon

IN A WORLD WHERE . . .

. . . you just settled into your faux-leather movie seat, a bucket of popcorn drooling with a butter-like substance warms your lap. You carefully place your flattish soda, the price of a flute of Dom Pérignon, in the cupholder to your right. Centering yourself, you drape napkins across your chest and thigh as if you were at an Amish picnic. To your left, you notice the lady in the next row feverishly texting on her iPhone. You hope she finishes soon. The theater dims in anticipation of the movie trailers. But this only makes the addicting self-indulgent glow of her digital demon even more annoying. (I digress with this public service announcement: Leave your damn phone in your car.)

"In a world where . . ." the ominous voiceover intones following the "This review is rated for all audiences" notice.

Hollywood knows they only have a moment to capture your attention and around two minutes to part you from $40 for your next movie ticket and requisite concessions. The trick is selling you on their coming $120 million blockbuster through an irresistible trailer, a mere 120-second tale. They intrigue you with the plot by teasing you with the movie's central mystery without spoiling the ending. The movie trailer must be compelling enough to overcome all the other distractions to win over the likes of that lady in front of you, who's finally put her phone away. Cuss all you want about her. We all have our moments in the shun due to the distraction of our digital devices.

And that's exactly the goal of this chapter: We're going to pull together all the story elements — the foundation for your epic brand narrative — that you've developed in the 10 steps of the Story Cycle System™ and use them to create your very own movie trailer to capture the attention of and set the stage for your audience.

GET YOUR BOON ON

You've been busy scripting and directing your brand story, and now you have returned to your ordinary world through this journey with what Joseph Campbell called "the boon." The boon you've earned — or you might think of it as a reward or treasure — is the clarifying of your brand story through the Story Cycle System. This hard-earned clarity will help you amplify your impact in the world and actually simplify your life. Plus, the boon represents the sum of knowledge you've gained in how to craft and tell compelling stories that sell.

You have learned the applied science of storytelling as you've conjured your important story elements. These foundational elements are what will create your epic brand narrative and guide your customer from engagement to evangelism. Your narrative ingredients include your position statement, unique value proposition, nine brand descriptors, and your promise, gift, personality, and purpose. The authenticity of your story elements is influenced by what you make happen in the lives of your target audiences (the heroes of your brand story). You've detailed what's at stake for them: what they *wish* and *want* and what triggers their *will* to act. You've also scripted how to make your story *their* story through the three acts of customer engagement, which consist of brand awareness, adoption, and appreciation. And to build repeat business, you're mapping how to ritualize the use of your offering through each of the three acts.

That's the applied science of storytelling. You've also seen its bewitchery in action through the anecdotes shared in this guidebook. Plus, you may have witnessed the magic of these story structures in your own life by wielding the And, But & Therefore narrative framework or the five primal elements of story when you relate anecdotes to your audiences and see their appreciative reactions.

Once you have completed this final story exercise, in the next chapter I will walk you through a communications plan that will help you determine how best to launch your epic brand story to the world. But first, let's hook them with your trailer to cast the storytelling spell. You will coalesce your story elements into a compelling brand trailer to capture the attention and interest of your audience. Plus your trailer works as a concise touchstone that all your content creators can refer to when crafting their brand stories.

CRAFTING YOUR BRAND TRAILER

Here's how the Business of Story trailer has come together. Use it as an example for the development of your own brand trailer.

BACKSTORY

Brand Position: The Business of Story® is the #1 resource for leaders of purpose-driven brands to clarify their stories, amplify their impact, and simplify their lives with the proven power of the Story Cycle System™.

HEROES

Target Audiences:

1. Founder/CEO of an emerging enterprise
2. Director of Branding, Marketing, Sales, or Human Resources
3. The industrious Executive

DISRUPTION

Unique Value Proposition: Excel through the stories you tell.

MENTOR

Brand Descriptors:

- Mage
- Industrious
- Optimistic
- Primal
- Dynamic
- Truth

- Clarity
- Connect
- Trust

Brand Promise: Enchantment

Brand Gift: Excel

Brand Personality: Magician

Secondary Archetypes: Jester and Sage

THE MORAL

Brand Purpose: The Business of Story exists to help people live into and prosper from their most powerful stories.

From all of the above, including exploration of the more operational chapters of stakes, antagonists, journey, victory, and ritual, I have crafted my final brand story trailer. Notice how I use the ABT to structure my problem statement for the solutions the Business of Story provides. This is a foolproof way (I should know) to formulate your brand trailer.

BUSINESS OF STORY TRAILER:

In a world where leaders of purpose-driven brands wish to make a significant social impact and seek a proven path to grow revenue, expand their reach, and inspire their people, but are frustratingly ineffectual because they don't operate through the lens of a focused brand narrative, the Business of Story communications training platform is their best hope. It's where industrious professionals learn the applied science and bewitchery of storytelling, summoning the optimistic forces of the Story Cycle System to clarify their stories by revealing a passion people can align with; amplify their impact by connecting communities with a common vision; and simplify their lives through a well-scripted mission—creating abundance for all through a powerful and prosperous story.

Theme: Excel through the stories you tell.

NOW IT'S YOUR TURN

From the previous 10 chapters, capture your brand story elements. Then write your brand trailer using the following template to get your audiences to turn their attention from their iPhones, popcorn, and soda pop to your story:

In a world where (your target audiences) wish to _____

_____

and want _____

_____/

But (the problem you solve for) _____

_____/

Therefore, (your brand name and solution) _____

_____

To help them achieve (live happily ever after) _____

_____.

HOW TO RELEASE YOUR BRAND TRAILER

You can have fun with this exercise. Be as theatrical as you like. Ways to use your new brand trailer with your people include:

Share the script with your people as you read it aloud in your best "In a world where" narrator voice.

Produce an audio recording complete with sound effects and music to send throughout your organization, demonstrating the passion for your new brand story.

Produce a short video or film just like a Hollywood trailer that expresses the personality of your new brand story in living color to all your audiences.

Regardless of the creative ways you will come up with to disseminate your trailer, leverage it to memorialize the exciting new vision and mission of your organization as told through your brand story. But now, how do you debut your epic brand story to the world? Turn the page and let's begin designing your comprehensive communications plan.

12

How to Debut
Your New Brand Story

The Seven Essential Phases
for Introducing Your Brand to the World

"Marketing is no longer about the stuff you make, but about the stories you tell."

—Seth Godin

HOW, WHEN, AND WHERE TO TELL YOUR BRAND STORY

Congratulations! You're now a brandthropologist, of sorts. You've used the primal power of the Story Cycle System™ to unearth your brand story. But how, when, and where do you share your new narrative with the world?

When my wife, Michele, and I were at "Engaged Encounter" 32 years ago in preparation for our marriage, one lady in the group asked the priest, "When is a good time to have your first child?" His response was classic. He said, "The first child can come along at any time. The second one usually takes around nine months."

The same is true with your brand story. As you've been birthing it, you may already be applying elements of it in your marketing. But if you have waited for it to come full-term, then this chapter outlines seven critical phases for launching your new brand story. But first, ask yourself these questions as you devise your communications launch strategy:

1. Do you need to name or rename your organization, offering, or initiative to reflect your new brand story?

2. Do you need to design or redesign your logo and business systems—including business cards, stationery, presentation templates, and brand style guide—to express your story?

3. Do you need to create or recreate your vision, mission, and values statements to frame your freshened brand ethos?

4. What are all the initial marketing, communications, sales, and human resources materials you will need to create/recreate to reflect the authentic look, tone, and feel of the character and personality of your brand through your internal and external storytelling?

5. Do you need to design or redesign your website to convey your brand story? (Probably.)

6. Do you need to create and install new business signage?

7. How will you get your internal audiences, including staff, employees, leadership, and stakeholders, to buy into and align with your bold new brand story so they own and willingly share it?

8. What communications channels, including paid and earned media, inbound and outbound marketing, direct mail, events, promotions, and public relations, will you use to share your story?

9. How will you deploy a concerted launch plan to announce your new brand story to the world?

I know, that's a ton to consider, so I've broken it into seven primary brand launch implementation phases to make the tasks easier to process. These phases include brand story strategy creation (which you've just completed), creative theme development, website creation, employee engagement, communications plan development, campaign elements creation, and external campaign launch. It's important to note that these phases can be executed simultaneously — as reflected in the timeline graphic below — all culminating in the external brand launch.

PHASE I: BRAND STORY STRATEGY CREATION
[FOUR TO EIGHT WEEKS]

If your brand story creation is a DIY project guided by this book, then it's probably taken you four to eight weeks to dial it in. That's typical. For reference, I find it often takes two months for the Business of Story to guide the brand story creation process with an organization and its leadership, depending on their availability and responsiveness. The fully guided brand story strategy creation process follows this pattern:

Figure 12. 1 Brand story strategy production and launch schedule

- The client captures their thoughts, as well as any relevant market and competitor research, in the DIY workbook and shares it with us.

- We review their input and then take them through a four-to-six-hour in-person discovery session, testing and sharing their assumptions with their team to begin building consensus.

- From what we learn, we take up to three weeks to explore their market research, consider their audiences, and formulate our initial brand story insights.

- We present our findings and what we believe to be their authentic brand story for their consideration.

- Within 48 hours of the presentation, the client provides us with their feedback on our brand story elements.

- We refine/revise the final elements and craft their brand story trailer.

Their brand story strategy is complete. Your own experience in Phase I will probably roughly correspond to this pattern.

PHASE II: CREATIVE CAMPAIGN THEME DEVELOPMENT [FOUR TO SIX WEEKS]

Now you must determine what your new brand story looks, sounds, and feels like as it is communicated through all of your internal, advertising, marketing and sales channels.

Once you have your brand story elements—including position statement, target audiences, unique value proposition, brand promise, gift, personality, and purpose—it's time to design the creative theme, which involves elements like color palettes, photographic or illustrative styles and other visual motifs, and the tone of the content for your storytelling. This is when your creative team explores numerous messaging themes to create the most compelling and consistent expression of your story. The final creative theme will inform the design and creation of your:

- Logo and business systems

- Signage

- Website

- Internal employee engagement campaign strategy and elements

- External advertising and promotional campaign strategy and elements

- Inbound and outbound marketing strategy and creative

- Sales and marketing materials and presentation strategy and templates

- Trade show displays and event graphics

- Public relations strategy and messages

This process of ideation results in the presentation of up to three different campaign theme directions, and then selecting and fine-tuning the winning theme. It takes four to six weeks. The goal is to arrive at a creative messaging theme that expresses your brand's character and personality and makes your audiences care about your celebrated purpose — what you make happen in their lives — through how you tell your story.

By the way, if you need to design or redesign your logo and business systems to reflect your new brand story, then plan on taking six to eight weeks for the logo design process. Some of this creative development and design time can be done during Phase II. But a word to the wise: Logos are so subjective that sometimes you find a winner quickly, and other times it can feel like a death march. But in the end, the right logo will bring your brand story to life.

PHASE III: WEBSITE CREATION
[THREE TO FOUR MONTHS]

Once your creative theme is selected, it's time to apply it to your most prominent storytelling medium: your website. The assessment, planning, strategy, and scoping of your new website can happen during the Creative Theme Development phase as well. That way you can design and build your site immediately upon the selection of your campaign theme. Depending on the size and scope of your website, you should plan three to four months for its creation and launch. Of course, this can be expedited, depending on the availability of content and resources and the responsiveness of your team to design and production deadlines.

PHASE IV: EMPLOYEE STORYTELLING ENGAGEMENT
INITIATIVE [10 TO 14 WEEKS]

Getting your internal audiences to buy into and align with your new brand story is critical. I hesitate to call this Phase IV, because hopefully you already started this process with the team you gathered to help you define your brand story strategy. But now it's time to enroll the rest of your people. The most successful employee engagement initiatives follow these three steps:

1. Build a guiding coalition of internal influencers

2. Celebrate early wins

3. Anchor behavior change

STEP 1: BUILDING A GUIDING COALITION OF INTERNAL INFLUENCERS

The goal of Step 1 is to identify and enroll the primary influencers in your organization who have the ear and respect of their colleagues. They will become ambassadors for the organization's mission as communicated through its refined brand story strategy. Selection of influencers will not be based on position or pay grade, but on how well they can unite their colleagues across all departments into the shared journey. This step has three objectives to be achieved in the first 10 weeks:

1. Inform influencers about the genesis of your new brand story to get them to buy in and own it. This is best done in small meetings where they can ask lots of questions. You will also get a good read from the exchange on how they are embracing your new brand story.

2. Teach them how to spot, capture, and share stories with your organization and the community that supports each of the nine brand descriptors you identified in Chapter 6, "Mentor," and how to activate those stories, as you learned in Chapter 7, "Journey." We provide an eight-week story mastery program to enroll your people into becoming brand story ambassadors. It starts with a half-day Business of Story master class that shows them why storytelling is now more important than ever to hack through the noise and hook the hearts of their audiences. I teach them the two proven narrative frameworks of the ABT and the five primal elements to story. And then I show them how to spot, capture, and share their powerful short stories based on the nine brand descriptors to support the overall narrative. As their stories come to life, they become cocreators of your brand story, causing them to buy into and align with your mission. This course also leads to objective 3.

3. Coach them how to train their colleagues to capture these same kinds of stories to prove the brand position, inspire the impact they're having on their colleagues, your customers, and the communities you all serve, and cocreate content for the overall campaign.

You can start building your guiding coalition of influencers any time. In fact, as you're crafting your brand story you may want to develop a list of the people you plan to recruit as your story ambassadors. Enrolling them into the brand story and subsequent training starts with a half-day session that kicks off the eight-week story mastery course I mentioned above. It's critical to inform them about the story, teach them storytelling techniques, and train them how to train their colleagues as you build a storytelling culture within your organization.

STEP 2: Celebrate Early Wins

You will start celebrating early wins as your influencers begin seeing your brand ethos and purpose in action through the stories they collect and share. Build on these wins through the training of your influencers to exponentially grow the belief in your brand story. They will in turn teach *their* colleagues how to do the same with the stories they experience and share. You are now scaling your stories and seeing the fruits of robust internal word-of-mouth marketing.

This is important because there is no stronger bond than when two people connect their worlds through a shared story, which helps them picture a more rewarding future together. Plus, these stories provide invaluable raw content to power both your internal and external campaigns. Your people will experience even more ownership—and you will be enjoying their buy-in—when they see how the top stories from their efforts are woven into your overall campaign. This further motivates your team of brand story cocreators.

STEP 3: Anchor Behavior Change

The first goal of these initial storytelling efforts is to get your people to buy into and align with your story. The second objective is to inspire them to grow their positive attitudes and behaviors in concert with your brand's core purpose. These stories are not just demonstrable, but aspirational. They act as examples of the kinds of healthy and productive interpersonal, customer, and community relationships you aspire to make happen in the hearts and minds of everyone your brand touches.

As your external brand campaign rolls out, you can launch a fun and empowering internal story quest competition among departments and colleagues. The idea is to have each group develop their own stories every week and then share them with your communications team. Then, on the following Monday, you can share the top stories with your organization to:

- Celebrate these moments that illustrate your brand purpose and the impact you're having in the world

- Demonstrate the new brand story in action (remember the "Hot, thin air" syndrome?)

- Encourage all team members to emulate these attitudes and behaviors

- Trigger other stories in colleagues that build on the brand ethos

- Inspire pride in their work and the adoption of the brand purpose

- Illustrate the uplift that is happening to colleagues, customers, and the community

- Build camaraderie to get everyone living into and prospering from your focused journey

- Help them excel through the stories they tell

OUTLINE: MASTER CLASS AND STORY MASTERY COURSE

As you know, storytelling is powerful in business. And more purpose-driven brands are using it to grow their organizations and their people. But story is difficult to master unless you intentionally use it every single day. Therefore, you can take advantage of Business of Story's proven story mastery course to help you and your influencers learn narrative skills, apply them daily in your work, and become an accomplished brand storyteller.

We kick off week 1 of the program with a half-day master class for your influencers, and then follow up with six weekly story quests that build their storytelling skills through real-world application. We culminate with a 60-to-90-minute live online workshop to coach your cohort. Through these activities, your influencers will:

- Understand how you arrived at your brand position, promise, gift, personality, and purpose

- Learn how to use the And, But & Therefore narrative framework to create a focused theme for every communications piece

- Make their communications more compelling by applying the five primal elements of storytelling to stories that are themed on your nine brand descriptors
- Create engaging presentations, proposals, white papers, and other longer-form communications using the Story Cycle System that follow a narrative arc your audiences can't resist
- Become adept at spotting stories in the wild for use in building internal trust and belief in the brand and serving as content for your inbound and outbound marketing
- Develop a story library for employee engagement, marketing and outreach

The interactive sessions are tailored, with your direction, to meet the exact needs of your influencers. Here is an overview:

Introduction & warm-up to activate the narrative mind of your attendees	:00
Why storytelling is more important now than ever to be heard and understood	:15
ACTIVITY: Experience how humans are hardwired for story	:20
Introduction to the *And, But & Therefore* (ABT) narrative framework to focus your story	:30
ACTIVITY: Create and share individual ABTs and workshop them with your gathering	:40
Introduction to the five primal elements of story to support your ABT	1:15
BREAK	2:00
ACTIVITY: Craft a short story to support your ABT	2:15
ACTIVITY: Workshop the short stories with your gathering	2:25
Introduction to the Story Cycle System	2:45
ACTIVITY: Outline a presentation using the Story Cycle System	3:00
ACTIVITY: Workshop a presentation with the gathering	3:20
Fin	4:00

Each attendee works from your brand story elements sheet and a *What's Your Story?* field notebook. Plus, they utilize links to additional resources to continue building their storytelling muscles.

Week 2: And, But & Therefore assignment and worksheet to encourage daily use

Week 3: Using the five primal story elements to create brand descriptor stories

Week 4: How to share your stories with others through watercooler moments, presentations, etc.

Week 5: Using brand descriptors to create story categories and organize your content

Week 6: How to teach colleagues to use the ABT and the five primal elements of story for their brand descriptor stories

Week 7: Building your story library for employee engagement, community outreach, and inbound and outbound marketing

Week 8: 60-minute live online coaching session with your team to bring it all together

Here's a nice bonus: Your team's work during the deliberate practice program will inevitably reveal powerful stories that you can use as content for your employee engagement initiatives, website, community outreach, advertising, sales, promotion, and inbound and outbound marketing. By following this employee engagement program, you are ensuring their buy-in and alignment with your brand story, teaching them how to spot and capture stories in the wild, coaching them how to enlist the support of their colleagues, and furnishing your marketing team with compelling content that will trigger additional stories—not to mention belief and pride—in your new brand narrative and purpose.

That's the beautiful thing about stories: They become self-fulfilling prophecies.

PHASE V: COMMUNICATIONS PLAN DEVELOPMENT [SIX TO EIGHT WEEKS]

You've determined how you will tell your brand story with the development of your creative theme. This creative exercise also inspires you with ideas about when and where you will share your story. But you must first determine your available financial and personnel resources to launch and maintain your brand story through your internal and external campaigns. I recommend creating an 18-month communications plan that includes:

- **Phase one:** Launch strategy and duration (brand awareness)

- **Phase two:** Customer acquisition and engagement (brand adoption)

- **Phase three:** Building repeat business and WOM through ritual and loyalty (brand appreciation)

Your communications plan will consider the use and timing of all traditional and digital channels, including:

- Internal communications including digital platforms, events, and training

- Brochures, sales materials, presentations, and other collateral

- Paid and earned digital media

- Social media

- Content marketing

- Email marketing

- Influencer marketing

- Broadcast: TV and radio

- Print: newspaper and magazine

- Direct mail

- Events and promotions

- Public relations

- Customer relations

- Vendor relations

- Shareholder relations

Ultimately, you will scope your 18-month plan, strategize your corporate communications as well as your inbound and outbound marketing efforts, create production and media schedules, and determine your overall budget. Your budget will also include the investment needed to create your campaign elements, including creative assets for advertising, marketing, sales, and social media.

PHASE VI: CAMPAIGN ELEMENTS CREATION
[EIGHT TO TWELVE WEEKS]

Guided by your media plan and the requirements of other planned outreach activities, you will need to create your campaign's creative assets. These assets will be built upon the consistent campaign theme developed in Phase II. The design, writing, and production of creative assets may include:

- Signage if you have a new or redesigned logo
- Internal posters, brochures, and training programs
- Sales brochures, materials, presentations, and other collateral
- Static ads, infographics, GIFs, and videos for digital advertising
- Blog writing, infographics creation, and video production for social media
- Content development for email marketing campaigns
- Materials for Influencer marketing
- TV and radio commercials
- Print ads for newspaper and magazines
- Direct mail production, lists, and postage
- Planning and materials for events and promotions
- Retainers or writing and placement costs for public relations
- Materials for customer, vendor, and shareholder relations

I know what you're thinking: *Wow, this brand storytelling thing is a costly, time-consuming endeavor.* But think of it this way: You will have plenty of time on your hands and less income if you do nothing. Because who knows what will happen to your brand if you remain in status quo or go about it half-heartedly? Besides, you want the true story about your real-world impact to be shared widely and wildly. Right?

PHASE VII: EXTERNAL CAMPAIGN LAUNCH

You've arrived and it's time to let the world know. You've crafted your brand story strategy and probably have a new or freshened logo and website. You have your team bought in, aligned, and excited about sharing your story because now it's *their* story. Your plan is in place, budgets finalized, creative work done and you're ready to hit the airwaves and Internet.

Make sure that your orchestrated external launch weaves seamlessly with your internal campaign. Celebrate how your team has come together to cocreate the campaign and find ways that they can share and scale your story on their terms in the communities you serve and where they live.

FINAL THOUGHTS

This chapter is a high-level overview of what to consider when rolling out your brand story. Please use this as a guide but don't be limited by it. I encourage you to be as creative as you like, tapping into the unique personality of your brand to inform other strategies and tactics that will help you stand out in our noisy world.

But most of all, remember this one thing as you grow as a confident and compelling storyteller:

The most potent story you will ever tell is the story you tell yourself.

So make it a great one.

Story on, my friend!

Appendix One

Using the Story Cycle System™
for Presentation Creation

"The art of storytelling can be used to drive change."
—Sir Richard Branson

WHAT I LEARNED ABOUT STORYTELLING WITH MY TEDX TALK

One thing I hope you experienced in the creation of your brand story is that you can use the And, But & Therefore foundational narrative framework, the five primal elements of story, and the Story Cycle System for all of your communications.

The following is an example—which happens to be my TEDxGilbert talk—of how you can use the Story Cycle System to guide the creation of a presentation or long-form communications piece. You'll spot ABTs and anecdotes throughout to make my points. But first, let me share a bit of background about the arduous process of getting my presentation in shape.

YOUR MOST COMPELLING PERSONAL BRAND STORY IS FOUND IN YOUR SIMPLE SCENES

Do you ever get cottonmouth when you speak? Nerves set in. Your armpits seem to suck all the moisture out of your kisser?

It happened to me.

I was the last of six TEDx presenters at TEDxGilbert on March 24, 2018. The theme we spoke to was Identity: Who We Are and Where We're Going. It was a standing-room-only crowd in the University Center Theater in Gilbert, Arizona. The place was a sauna when I stepped on the stage at 9 p.m.

About a minute into my presentation the plumbing department to my mouth experienced a shutdown. TED organizers don't like you packing around water on the stage, so I had to forge on as my tongue became carpet. But then I remembered a trick our master of ceremonies, Rachael Mann, had shared with us earlier in the day. When your mouth feels like it's wallpapered with Saltine crackers, imagine sucking on a lemon drop.

I carved out a section of my brain to picture that sour sucker without missing a beat in my presentation. My sprinkler system kicked on to rehydrate my gummy gums.

Try it. Picture yourself sucking on a lemon drop right now.

Wait for it . . .

What just happened in your mouth?

Such is the power of story. We're visual beings. Stories paint pictures that trigger our nervous system. Even making up a fictional narrative of a tart candy tricks your brain into thinking you're actually experiencing it, and your body responds appropriately.

HOW TO BE THE BEST AND BOLDEST NONFICTIONAL YOU

The lemon drop experiment is not only a lifesaver for cottonmouth, it's also a savory example of how stories transport us. From Saltines to lemon drops, your mind lives vicariously through the telling.

But the problem is that we often live into the wrong story due to the personal narratives we tell ourselves. We live into fiction. We are so busy living up to what we believe other people think about us that we don't remain true to our own authentic story. Social media fuels this fake world as we all try to keep up with the Joneses by posting perfectly coiffed images of our beach vacations, envious gatherings, and, for whatever reason, the coconut-crusted Mahi Mahi plate we had for lunch.

This was the TEDx topic I explored: In this fictional world, how can we be our best nonfiction selves, even when we think our audiences expect an epic adventure out of us?

So I asked the audience to stop looking for their heroic stories and instead start finding their scenes: those seemingly insignificant moments that have shaped who they are today. Find your scenes and your story will find you.

HOW TO FRAME YOUR AUTHENTIC STORY

I consult, teach, coach, and speak on the power of story for personal, professional, and organizational branding. But like Dr. Vo, my dentist who doesn't perform his own root canals, I needed help extracting my TEDx presentation from my cluttered mind. So I turned to Tamsen Webster, a brilliant presentation coach who has her own approach to storytelling she calls the Red Thread® Method. Tamsen was also the producer of TEDxCambridge, so she knows the TED stage well.

Her coaching was invaluable to help me frame my message. I've learned from my own story workshops that we get so close to our individual narrative that it is difficult to find our theme without the clear vision and input of others. (Plus, working with another story wizard helped reaffirm my appreciation that this story stuff is difficult without the proper guidance.)

When I thought I had finally arrived with my script, I sent it to Jen Dille, the producer of TEDxGilbert. But it didn't pass muster. Jen said that she liked my big idea, but that my message wasn't clearly communicated. Talk about taking a quill pen to the heart of a storyteller. Ugh! Mrs. Pintler, my fourth-grade English teacher, immediately popped to mind, giving me a fat red F on a paper I worked hard on. So, with just two weeks to go before TEDxGilbert, I tossed my first attempt and started over.

RELYING ON THE APPLIED SCIENCE AND BEWITCHERY OF STORY

I ruthlessly edited. But I was lucky. As I searched for the connective tissue in my narrative, the universe delivered a few choice insights and stories in my hour of need that are now reflected in my presentation.

For instance, Anjella Crowe's story (which you read in Chapter 7) presented itself during a Business of Story workshop I delivered to Silverline SalesForce Solutions just prior to TEDxGilbert. Her story was the ideal example to demonstrate the premise of my presentation.

I've learned that when you are following your true story, the universe will deliver in your time of need. The trick is to be paying attention and recognize the gifts when they arrive. While the Red Thread helped me frame my message, I returned to the Story Cycle

Figure A.1 The Story Cycle System script storyboard

System framework that I was so familiar with to put the final touches on my speech.

I even had artist Lisa Rothstein of drawingoutyourgenius.com illustrate my talk for three reasons:

1. Help me visually memorize my presentation

2. Illustrate the Story Cycle spiral in action

3. Demonstrate how to string together scenes through anecdotes that create your overall story

Here's how my TEDxGilbert script works within the 10-step Story Cycle System:

TEDXGILBERT TALK: HOW TO USE THE STORY CYCLE SYSTEM TO GUIDE YOUR LONG-FORM STORYTELLING

STEP 1: BACKSTORY

You set the stage for your premise to generate curiosity in your audience.

I know an amazing lady who will celebrate her 93rd birthday on April 5th. When she was just four years old, Pat was sitting in a strange and cold waiting room in a hospital in Wenatchee, Washington. She was eager for the arrival of her new baby sister, Diane, but the surroundings kind of creeped her out.

Then, out of nowhere, this nurse shows up, dressed in her nurse whites, like a guardian angel. She chatted with the little girl to set her at ease and then gave her an orange.

Pat never forgot the kindness of that complete stranger. In fact, because of it, she became a nurse after World War II. Got married at 29, had seven kids in nine years. And if you ever wondered if God has a sense of humor, he put HER in charge of starting the sex ed program at her children's school: St. Brendan's in Bothell, Washington.

After her brood had grown, she volunteered for nearly three decades at Overlake Hospital in Bellevue, until her mid-80s. Most recently, she has been caring for her husband, who is battling Alzheimer's.

Just imagine all the people she has helped over the past 70 years because of that seemingly insignificant moment in a waiting room: a thoughtful nurse and the warmth she bestowed through the symbolism of an orange.

STEP 2: HEROES

Connect your idea to your audience from their point of view as you make them the center of your story.

Do you know what your true calling is? As Pat showed, you don't need to craft some epic tale about love and loss to find it. Instead, look for the simple scenes that set everything in motion for you — those small moments that have shaped who you are today.

STEP 3: STAKES

Define what is at stake for your audience relative to your theme to increase its importance.

I started to realize just how important scenes are in our lives when, in 2006, I began studying the applied science and bewitchery of storytelling. I had been in branding and marketing for over 20 years and I watched as the advertising paradigm as we knew it was falling apart. Brands used to own the influence of mass media, but the masses had become the media, and it got difficult to rise above the noise, stand out, and be heard.

So I went looking for the answer. I discovered that an anecdote is the antidote.

"The human mind yields helplessly to the suction of story," says Jonathan Gottschall, author of *The Storytelling Animal: How Stories Make Us Human*. We've used storytelling as our most powerful survival tool to evolve from cavemen to consumers.

I believe it because I've experienced the magic of being a story-telling ape.

Science is revealing how stories shape us. Functional brain scans show that when we consume a story, the region of our brain called the left temporal cortex lights up, thinking we are actually playing a role in that story.

Blood tests show that good stories can trigger five neurotransmitters that make us experience what the protagonist is experiencing: serotonin, dopamine, oxytocin, cortisol, and endorphins.

For instance, when I was invited to speak at this TEDx event, I was pretty pumped. My mind was flooded with serotonin because I felt wanted and important. This made me happy.

Then I got excited about the task of finding my big idea and anticipating the rewards of sharing my experiences with you. This triggered dopamine, providing me with optimism and delight.

Recalling and writing the stories within this talk has released within me oxytocin, the drug that creates understanding, empathy, and connection.

When I experienced the crisis of being told that my final draft needed work—lots of work—my cortisol pump fired up, providing the focus I needed.

And when I had to burn the midnight oil because time was running out, endorphins kicked in for endurance, summoning my second wind and delivering the euphoria of overcoming this challenge.

Know these feelings?

Ira Glass, host of *This American Life*, who draws 1.7 million listeners every week to his stories, said, "The power of anecdote is so great that it has a momentum all its own." He contends, "No matter how boring the facts are, with a well-told story you feel like you're on a train that has a destination."

No wonder we call it the "theater of the mind."

Stories shape who we are individually and collectively. But be careful. Because when we hear them on the "Ira Glass scale," we're tempted to think that our stories don't measure up, even as our over-communicated world implores you to tell your story.

STEP 4: DISRUPTION

Restate your idea and illustrate why it is more urgent now than ever through a true story.

I say forget your story and locate *your* scenes first: those moments that have shaped who you are today, which created your superpower.

Your story will then find you.

Let me give you an example: Not long ago I met Anjella Crowe, a soft-spoken, thirtysomething Ukrainian immigrant. She works for a fast-growing, high-tech customer relationship management firm in New York. I was doing a Story Cycle workshop with 50 of their top sales and marketing people when Anjella volunteered to tell her story.

She said that her sole purpose at the company is to build important alliances and partnerships within the organization and with its customers.

That was all fine and dandy, but when I pressed her to recall the specific moment when she knew this was her superpower, she pushed back. Perhaps it was because we were working her story in front of her colleagues. Maybe it was too painful of a moment to share in public.

After the session, she came up to me and said, "I didn't tell you everything."

"I know. How come?" I asked.

"I've been told that businesspeople wouldn't think it is appropriate to talk about my hard times in the orphanage."

"Orphanage? Wait a sec . . . You grew up in a Ukrainian orphanage!?" I asked.

"Yes, since birth until I was 18. It was hard. People picked on me and abused me, so I don't talk about it. I'm told no one wants to hear it," she said.

"How'd you cope?"

She recalled the moment when she realized she had to surround herself with kids she could trust and with adults who didn't just care for her, but about her. Anjella built groups of these people to help her rise above the conditions.

"No wonder you excel at building alliances and partnerships, I said. You grew up doing it to survive."

I encouraged Anjella to absolutely talk about her life in the orphanage without having to go into all the difficult details.

I mean, come on, "Ukrainian orphanage" *That* scene tells a lot.

She nodded in agreement.

I learned that Anjella moved to the States when she was 18, earned two degrees from the University of Georgia, and then a master's in International Business from Georgia State and that she has had a successful career in technology.

I said, "Have the courage to tell your story. Because you *are* the epitome of the American dream. Never let anyone quiet that.

And here's how you use it . . .

"Just imagine looking into the eyes of your next prospective client and asking them, 'When was the last time your vendor orphaned you, didn't do what they said they'd do, left you feeling abandoned? I promise you, that will never happen with me.'"

She smiled and seemed relieved. When I asked her if I could retell her story tonight, she said, "ABSOLUTELY!"

As Anjella demonstrated, when you stop looking for your story and start finding and living into your scenes, your superpower will appear.

STEP 5: ANTAGONISTS

Raise the stakes by describing the universal conflicts that stand in the way of your audience members' success.

But as in every story, when you strive for something, the universe will push back. Punch you in the nose. Test you just to see how badly you really want it.

And the universe has become even better at it in the fictional world we live in today, especially with social media.

That "like" thumb is the opioid pusher of the Web, addicting us with serotonin, dopamine, and endorphins and causing us to wear our happy masks even when we're sad.

And of course there's FOMO: the Fear of Missing Out as we become fawning voyeurs to others' adventures.

Then we make the greatest personal narrative mistake: We compare what we think are our small stories to everyone else's fictional epics. But what this really leads to is epic alienation and loneliness.

Look, we're social human beings. Being connected to people is essential to our sanity and our survival. There's nothing more fulfilling than feeling understood, appreciated, and trusted by those who are close to us.

But what do we do to connect with others? We play roles in their lives, live into their stories to try to fit in, connect with them on their terms. But these roles are often inauthentic to who we really are.

The real problem when we're living someone else's story is that:

- We lose confidence in ourselves as we try to measure up to their expectations.
- We don't play to our strengths, weakening our impact.
- And we lose time toiling in fictional pursuits while our true journey waits for us in the wings.

We are so busy looking for the big stories to impress others that we don't appreciate the small scenes that have made an impression on us — our unique moments that have shaped who we are today.

STEP 6: MENTOR

Describe how you are uniquely equipped to help them get what they want by sharing a truth you've come to understand.

Believe me, I know the feeling. I woke up on Monday, September 14, 2015, with my stomach in knots. For the past 20 years, I had relentlessly worked to build my advertising agency. I'd started out in a little shack behind our first house, grew, purchased a building, added lots of employees, and created a business that I thought defined me.

I built a career I hoped my folks would be proud of, that my siblings would appreciate, that my peers would respect. But I wasn't happy. Because I realized I wasn't living into my story.

My answer was hiding in plain sight. In fact, I had been preaching and teaching it for five years.

As I mentioned, I was fascinated by storytelling, using it to craft brand story strategies to help our clients grow, and coaching leaders in how to use it for themselves and their teams.

In fact, Arizona State University even asked me to create and teach a curriculum around my Story Cycle System for its Executive

Masters of Sustainability Leadership program, which I did. What an honor.

The universe was now daring me to live into *my* most powerful story: to consult, teach, coach, and speak on how to use your unique, personal narrative to make your most profound impact in the world.

Which meant a career pivot. At 55. I thought, *Boy, this can either end in comedy or tragedy – though I was hoping for something greater.*

Because here's the truth I knew, but then had to learn for myself: Compelling storytelling is *always* about the moments. Those scenes are composed of the experiences that define your beliefs, which lead to your truth. When you unwrap your truth you find your superpower to nudge the world in any direction you choose.

STEP 7: JOURNEY

Here's the specific action you ask your audience to take despite all odds.

But here's the toughest part of this story/scene thing: Hollywood calls it "The Dark Night of the Soul." I prefer "The Belly of the Whale." I know someone who might call it "The Ukrainian Orphanage."

It is in these moments of struggle, when the universe is putting the screws to you and your character, that you'll find the pivotal scenes that propel your story forward.

But, like an archeologist, you have to dig 'em up. They're typically buried under the detritus of life, scrubbed from your immediate recall due to their unpleasantness, or hidden beneath the pile of scripts others think you should be playing to.

Picture one evening, a nine-year-old boy named James is in the kitchen with his aunt. While she's enjoying her tea, James stands at the stove by a boiling teapot.

He's fascinated by the steam coming out of the spout. So much so that he holds a silver spoon over the jet stream and watches as drops of water form on the spoon and run down the handle, marveling at this simple phenomenon.

His aunt is pissed — thinks he's lazy. She barks at him to go read a book or do something useful for a change.

"Aren't you embarrassed for yourself?" she scolds.

Imagine how James felt.

Fortunately for us, the boy was undaunted. Two decades later, in 1765, the then 29-year-old James Watt invented a new kind of steam engine that helped usher in the Industrial Revolution.

His teapot scene led to a marvelous journey that impacted all of humanity. And when you think of marvelous journeys, what TED talk would be complete without channeling Steve Jobs? His iconic odyssey started in seemingly insignificant moments, too—such as when his parents admonished him for wasting time studying calligraphy at Reed College in Oregon. Ah, but what did his fascination produce? The graphical interface that launched Apple and revolutionized our computing world.

STEP 8: VICTORY

Provide hope by describing what success looks like as you reiterate your theme.

You see, even revolutions begin in moments of discovery and inspiration. So stop looking for your stories and start finding your scenes.

STEP 9: THE MORAL

Reveal the truth you have found that is the pathway to their success.

When you own your unique moments, wonderful things happen. You will:

- Clarify your fundamental origin story that will help people understand who you are and where you are going.

- Amplify your impact with your personal narrative by enabling others to experience what you experienced, connecting your shared beliefs and values, which builds trust. And living into your authentic story simplifies your life by you just being you.

STEP 10: RITUAL

Connect your story to their story with a specific call-to-action.

So how *do* you find your scenes and live into your most powerful story? Before you go to bed tonight, jot down three moments that have shaped who you are today. Simply start by writing "That time when . . ."

- That time when something suddenly piqued your curiosity and you had to dive into it headlong.

- That time when a seemingly insignificant moment surprisingly became a major turning point for you.

- That time when you did something you thought you couldn't.

What was *your* enlightening "calligraphy moment"?

Your curious "teapot incident"?

Your episode of feeling lost and abandoned?

Or, as with my mom, Nurse Howell, what is that symbolic orange that inspired your purpose?

In the morning, start stringing those scenes together. You might even get a little pit in your stomach as *your* true calling awakens within you. I promise you'll learn, as I did, that . . .

The most potent story you will ever tell is the story you tell yourself. So make it a great one.

Story on, my friends.

THE 3-STEP TEDXGILBERT STORY EXERCISE FOR YOUR TEAM

Do you want to build more camaraderie within your team? Many of my clients are doing the following with my TEDx talk:

1. Gather your team and watch the video.

2. Have them spend that evening away from the office finding the scenes that have shaped who they are today and why they do what they do for you and your organization.

3. Gather again the next morning and have each team member share their story in under two minutes about a moment that shaped who they are today.

This simple story exercise creates understanding for what fellow team members are about. It helps people appreciate what others are going through. And it creates empathy that builds trust.

Clarifying your stories also helps you get focused on who you are and where you're going. And if for whatever reason you or some of your people sour on your current situation in life, it's simply because you are not yet living into your most potent story.

Think of this story exercise as your lemon drop to create a personal narrative you'll salivate over.

Appendix Two

My Origin Story

"Follow your bliss and the universe will open doors for you where there were only walls."

—Joseph Campbell

In the preface, I asked you if you found this guidebook or did it find you. The same question can be asked of me and my work with the Hero's Journey and my Story Cycle System. Here's how it found me, while I was looking for an answer to one big question: How do we connect in our over-communicated world? And I'll even retrace my odyssey using the 12 steps of the Hero's Journey.

WELCOME TO MY NOT-SO-ORDINARY WORLD

The haunting apparition appeared before me out of nowhere. I was careening down the searing farm road in my 1984 Honda Civic, its gold paint having long ago been burned off to a dull brown. The air conditioner suffered from chronic obstructive pulmonary disease, which wasn't cool, because it was 112 degrees that July afternoon in 1993.

Maybe I was hallucinating?

Heat waves radiated from the blacktop, creating an opaque landscape of gray gravel, green cotton fields, and the white hot sun. And then, like something conjured by Stephen King, the thing materialized in the oncoming lane. I leaned over my steering wheel, squinting as the distance between us closed. I muttered, "What the . . . ?"

I was returning from Buckeye, Arizona, a farming community about 30 miles southwest of Phoenix. I had spent the morning there with one of the largest advertising clients for the small ad agency where I worked. Schult Homes. They make manufactured houses. That's where my young, illustrious ad career had taken me — to a distant planet about as far from Madison Avenue as one could venture — selling mobile homes.

Following my meeting, I had grabbed lunch at a sad-looking Pizza Hut. I sat resigned over my single slice of pepperoni. It was all the $1.75 in my pocket could afford. My right elbow was on the table as I propped my forehead in my hand and looked past my smudged glass of water into the baking parking lot at my stupid little car.

My career can't get any worse than this, I thought. *Rock bottom in Buckeye.*

A quarter, dime, and two pennies sat next to my crumpled napkin. I got up, went out to the heat, and crawled back into my smoldering car, broke and broken. I tapped the pedal and squealed out of the parking lot, throwing a little defiant gravel in my wake.

Now I was racing down that road as if I were running away from my cruel predicament.

"What the hell IS that?"

Through the shimmering heat wave I saw a grotesque silhouette coming toward me. The phantom snapped into view. It was a fully dressed rainbow-wigged clown pumping his big ol' clown shoes on the pedals of a red Stingray bike, balloons trailing behind. As I raced by in disbelief, he just turned at me and smiled those yellow teeth old clowns flash behind their crusty white makeup. My eyes darted down to the side mirror. Then up to my review mirror. I wasn't seeing things. A clown was pedaling out of sight into nowhere.

I flumped back into my driver's seat. A smile surfaced at the realization. My mobile home meeting and measly lunch weren't rock bottom after all. This chance encounter with my freewheeling harlequin was the universe's way of having one more chuckle at my expense, as if to say, "Stop taking yourself so damn seriously, clown."

A CALL TO ADVENTURE

Two weeks later, a headhunter appeared out of nowhere. I had toiled in the advertising industry for eight years, working for small public-relations firms and ad agencies in Phoenix. My wife,

Michele, and I were raising two kids with a third on the way on a $26,000 salary—a pittance, even in the early 1990s. At one point earlier that year, I told a friend that I was going to venture out on my own and start my own ad agency. He looked at me over lunch and cautioned, "You're not ready yet."

Ugh, that hurt.

My career felt like it was in a death spiral. But even now I'm over-selling it. Because to be in a death spiral implies that it had actually taken off.

I was an impatient advertising wannabe fascinated by building brands. But my own brand wasn't defined well enough to land me a gig at the big, prestigious firms. At the five-person Petersen Communications agency where I worked, I did everything: concocted marketing strategies, wrote copy, managed clients, planned and bought media, produced radio commercials, organized special events, and pitched news stories.

I got to play attorney, too. When the savings and loan crisis of 1991 took down several of our real estate clients, sticking our little agency with their media bills, I was the guy the process servers served court papers to from angry media outlets that wanted to get paid. The first time I got served was 7:30 in the morning as we backed out of the driveway with our kids in the car going to Sunday mass. That was an awakening.

But I'm proud that we found fair settlements with all of the media outlets and retained our good name.

Perhaps my most profound lesson came one day in an innocuous car ride back to the office. Sandy Petersen, the agency owner, and I had just met with our client Warren Hess, founder of Robinett Roofing. (Yep, mobile homes and roofing contractors. A golden client list.) Sandy asked me what I learned from the meeting. I fumbled for an answer.

"That's your problem," he scolded. "You don't listen. You were so busy trying to be impressive that you didn't hear a thing Warren said."

Gah! I knew he was right. I stumbled into the rabbit trap that snares every young, ambitious, and insecure professional: trying to sound smart when you don't know shit.

But that was only one of my challenges. While I was learning tons about the various aspects of the business, I had no focused personal brand. Potential employers said, "I'm not sure where to put you."

Or, "You're not really a 'creative' because you've done all of this account service stuff."

One clearly myopic creative director dismissed my portfolio of work and told me I didn't have the creative chops to make it in advertising. I could always smell a fraud from 10 paces and didn't give his critique much purchase.

As I was turned down time and again for jobs that I thought I wanted, the biggest lesson I would learn about branding was staring me right in the face. But I couldn't see it. Only later did I realize that the best brands know who they are, what they do differently, and therefore better, than anyone else, and what they actually stand for.

I didn't know it at the time, but I had to clarify my story to amplify my impact and ultimately simplify my life. That's when my guardian angel headhunted me.

REFUSAL OF THE CALL

Michele and I had just returned from Rob and Carolyn Malinowski's wedding in Seattle. I had worked as an intern for Rob in the Fearey Group public relations firm in Seattle in 1983 while finishing my communications degree at Washington State University. Rob and I became fast friends. While standing at the altar as a groomsman, I remember being happy for them but remorseful about my job. I hear you – pretty self-centered, I know.

While Rob and Carolyn were saying their "I do's," I took advantage of the spiritual setting and put it out there to whomever might be listening above: "Is my career going to go anywhere, or is it time to find something else? Send me an answer, will ya?"

Returning to Phoenix, I walked into my office Monday morning and found a pink message note from the previous Thursday with a name and number on it: Bill Franquemont.

Bill Franquemont? Probably just another media rep, I thought.

I almost tossed the note because I wasn't up for another sales call or a trek into the unproductive unknown. But then something nudged me. It had been nearly five days since he called. Perhaps I was missing something? So I picked up the phone and dialed.

MEETING OF THE MENTOR

A proper-sounding receptionist answered, "DHR International, may I help you?"

Hmmm, potentially a new client call, I thought.

"Yes, Bill Franquemont, please."

"Who may I say is calling?"

"Park Howell . . . uh, returning his call."

"Of course. One moment, please."

That was weird. She sounded like she anticipated my call. Before I could give it much more thought, someone picked up the line.

"Hi, Park. This is Bill Franquemont." His friendly and determined demeanor struck me immediately.

"Good afternoon, Mr. Franquemont. I see you called."

"Yes, Park. I am an executive recruiter and I have a fast-growing client that is in need of an in-house Director of Creative Services to manage their new product branding and marketing campaigns."

Silence . . .

"Park? You still there?" Bill asked.

"Um, yes. And what does this have to do with me?" Being recruited was clearly out of my wheelhouse.

"Well, I've talked to a number of people and I think you might be a good fit for the job. I'd like to arrange an interview," he said.

"Really? When?"

"Tomorrow."

"Tomorrow?"

"They're moving fast," Bill continued, "and they will fill the position by next week."

"Next week?"

I wasn't exactly the picture of confidence on our first call.

"Perhaps you can come in at lunchtime, given your current employment situation," he suggested.

"Tomorrow?"

"Yes, Park. Tomorrow."

"Uh, ok."

Bill sprang from his desk with a big smile and a firm handshake as he welcomed me to his office. We had a quick and cordial interview. But I was still a bit dumbfounded by this turn of good luck. So I asked Bill how he had found me.

"I searched the *Phoenix Business Journal Book of Lists*," he said. "I found that Petersen Communications is ranked 25th among the top 25 ad agencies in Arizona. I noticed that you are listed as a principal with the firm."

I thought to myself, *Yep, and I learned that the glamour of being a corporate principal means you're also personally liable for all of those damn media bills, too.*

Bill continued, "I've had great success placing young executives from the *Book of Lists* because it tells me two things. First, that you come from a smaller firm, so you probably wear a lot of hats, which means you understand your business from many perspectives."

"That's for sure," I said.

"And second, the person in your position often finds themselves stymied and is looking to do bigger things."

Bad pizza and sinister clowns raced through my head.

"Is that you?" he asked as a man who knows his business and my expectant answer.

"Yep."

"Having met you, Park, I think you are the right person for this job. Can you meet their Senior V.P. of Marketing, Lynn Harper, this Thursday afternoon?"

"Thursday?"

"Yes, Park. Thursday."

"I suppose," I said, my head swirling in a heat wave of excitement, fear, and dread. Was I up to this opportunity?

"Are you ready for this to happen, Park?"

"Uh, yah . . ."

"Good, because I think this is going to happen for you."

As I was leaving for the interview with Ms. Harper, smartly dressed in my one suit—dark blue with a crisp white shirt, red paisley tie, and snappy red suspenders—I kissed Michele goodbye.

"I'll call you before I make any decision about the job, providing they even offer me one," I promised. She wished me luck.

Three hours later, Michele's phone rang.

"Hello."

"Hi, honey, it's me," I greeted.

"How'd it go?" she asked.

"Well, I'm calling you from my new office," I said.

"So much for talking it over," she mused.

"They wanted an immediate decision, and, well . . . a clown."

CROSSING THE THRESHOLD

I was the new Director of Creative Services for Quorum International, a marketer and direct seller of personal electronics and alarm systems. My salary was more than double what I made at Petersen. Plus, I received a monthly bonus on sales, which was nearly as much as my ad agency salary. And I was empowered to create a team of designers, writers, and producers to handle the myriad products Quorum would launch into the worldwide marketplace.

For the first time in my career my personal brand had been clarified to the singular moniker of "Creative Director." I was relieved to have a focused mission. But I underestimated the enormity of the position, which was revealed to me on my first day.

TESTS, ALLIES, AND ENEMIES

At 10 a.m., I met with the cabal of panicked product development managers. They were preparing for an international sales conference and the launch of five new products in just over six weeks. We had no package designs, no creative concepts or marketing materials, and no instructional manuals or launch videos. Bupkis! They looked to me with the optimism that befalls all newcomers: as if I was their savior. But I was the dumbest guy in the room. I knew little about the company or the people around the table. Nor did I have an inkling about the new products they were responsible for.

I suddenly channeled Sandy Petersen: "Shut up and *listen* to their needs." And for some reason, at that moment, a conversation I had had with Michele's dad popped into my head.

Major James Reynolds was a decorated fighter pilot in World War II, Korea, and Vietnam. He told me that when a pilot becomes lost in flight, they are instructed to follow the Five C's: Climb, Conserve, Communicate, Confess, and Comply. *Climb* to a safe altitude and throttle back to *Conserve* fuel. *Communicate* with local air traffic control. *Confess* that you're lost so they understand your situation, and *Comply* with their instructions.

So I relied on the Five C's to make me listen.

Instead of joining the conversation completely uninformed, I mentally *climbed* above the fray. I *conserved* my energy by simply listening to everyone's wants and needs. I must have sat there for 45 minutes scribbling notes without saying a word. My own assistant, whom I had known for all of two hours, kept shooting me nervous glances to see how I was handling the onslaught.

I was amazed at what I learned about the personalities in the room from this vantage point. I understood who had the power in the departments and deciphered their individual agendas. Who might be an ally and who might be a foe.

Then, I finally *communicated* my thoughts. To my surprise, they listened. My previous silence gave my words gravitas. But I *confessed* that I didn't begin to have all their answers. I was the new guy, somewhat lost at the moment. I told them that I was eager to *comply* with their wishes, but only after we crafted a creative production plan and a marketing and communications strategy.

They agreed. The tension in the room lifted. My heart sank.

What have I gotten myself into? I thought.

Six weeks later, we somehow launched all the new products to 15,000 boisterous sales professionals. They had gathered from around North America for a two-day sales and marketing conference, packing America West Arena in the heart of Phoenix. The direct sales convention was a spectacle of brand storytelling that I had never experienced before. There was a 16-piece orchestra. Quorum's V.P. of Distributor Relations was dressed in tails and crooned like a Vegas showman. The product launches were grandiose, the sales trainings inspirational. The sales folks were whipped into a fevered pitch. I sat amazed in the second row.

This marketing extravaganza turned my branding world upside down.

APPROACH

Quorum was founded by Raymond Hung, a Chinese national who amassed his fortune as the owner of an original equipment manufacturer (OEM) called Applied Electronics in Hong Kong. In addition to making Quorum's products, his OEM made parts for brands like Samsung, SONY, and Toshiba.

Following the sales conference, Raymond called me into his office to get acquainted. He was a formidable character who could be warm but intimidating, and not entirely genuine. Raymond was also a devout follower of fêng shui, the Chinese philosophical system of harmonizing everyone with their surrounding environment. He assessed his people to see if they might attract the good dragon or the bad one, which would affect business positively or negatively. Our offices were under constant renovation as his architect moved walls depending on sales forecasts to allow the good dragon to flow, bolstering the company's prosperity. If sales were down, another wall would be relocated or, like some of my fellow employees, disappear altogether.

Believe me, you didn't want to be that guy who attracted the bad dragon.

During our conversation, I asked Raymond why he established his global headquarters for Quorum in a remote building near the Deer Valley Airport in North Phoenix, when his family and OEM business were rooted in Hong Kong.

Raymond told me that although no one could "out-engineer" the Chinese, absolutely no one could "out-market" an American.

Raymond then leaned in and lowered his voice. In his broken English he confided in me, "You know, Paaak, Quorum is my *cup of baby*."

I grinned at his culturally challenged mixed metaphor. Was Quorum his baby or his cup of tea? It was charming. I realized Raymond was just like me. Despite our different stations in life, we want the same things: health and prosperity. I passed the fêng shui test, or so I thought.

CENTRAL ORDEAL

In early 1994, Quorum's sales experienced a natural slump. The architect and interior designer got back to work moving walls. Raymond sent his cousin Vincent, Chief Operating Officer, into my office with a directive. Vincent told me to get my diastema — the space between my two front teeth — fixed. He said I should close this "tooth space" because money will fly out of my mouth. "That is not good for someone in your position in Raymond's company," Vincent suggested.

He got up and left. I sat there and wondered what kind of sign the universe was sending me.

By the way, take a look at my current speaker headshot and you'll see how Vincent's directive went over with me. Oh, the stories we *Homo sapiens* tell ourselves.

Michele and I had our third child, a boy named Caedon, during this time. He joined our daughter Corbin, the eldest, and our son Parker. Our family was growing, as were my responsibilities at Quorum. But the problem with a high-flying money-making machine is that it can attract greed. There were a number of changes made in leadership over those first six months of 1994, and I became concerned for the direction of the organization and the credibility of the brand, which directly impacted my job. I voiced my concerns to some in the C-suite but was told to keep quiet.

One afternoon in October, just over a year into my career at Quorum, I looked up from my desk and my heart skipped a beat. One of the C-suite officers, I'll call him Jerry, stood looking down at me in my office. We had occasionally spoken in the past. Sometimes it was a light conversation about our families. But mostly it was about revising aspects of our marketing. These meetings were always on his turf, not mine. So having Jerry looming over me made me wonder if I was about to get fired for insubordination for not fixing that handsome hole in my mouth or for the overuse of said orifice.

With his right hand, he placed a small piece of paper on my desk.

"Park, if we were having this conversation, I'd tell you to call this person," he said, sliding the folded piece of paper toward me. "But since we're not, you can do anything you want."

He turned, and without another word slipped out of my office.

I looked down at the insignificant-looking note and unfolded it. On the inside was handwritten the name Navaz Ghaswala, and a local phone number. Given that the numbers weren't arranged in any mnemonic order, as most corporate phone numbers are to help you remember them, I assumed this was a direct line. But a direct line to whom and what?

The Arizona autumn sun streamed through the window of my second-floor office, warming it like a sauna. I got up and shut my door.

I read the name again: "Navaz Ghaswala." What a mysterious turn of events, I thought. So I dialed. After two rings, she picked up.

"Hello, this is Navaz," a deep Persian voice intoned.

"Good afternoon, Navaz. This is Park Howell."

"Yes, I've been expecting your call," she interrupted.

What the . . . ?

REWARD

Navaz Ghaswala is the right arm to Rex Maughan, the owner of Scottsdale-based Forever Living Products International (FLP), the world's largest grower, manufacturer, and distributor of aloe vera–based health and beauty products. In 1994, the company was nearing a billion dollars in annual sales. Despite their growth, they were looking for help with their branding and marketing.

Additionally, they recruited me to develop their satellite training network called ForeverVision.

Years before the Internet, corporations trained their people in classrooms and by mailing manuals and videos. At Quorum, we had created the first KU-band satellite network, broadcasting training videos weekly to the homes of our growing network of private direct-sales people. We branded it QSN for the Quorum Satellite Network. It was wildly successful for recruiting, motivation, and training. Given that QSN was under my direction, I was the natural go-to guy for FLP, who wanted their own satellite network.

But I didn't want another job. Thankfully, Navaz and her team weren't interested in hiring another employee. It was a marriage made in the geostationary satellite heavens. Because as I helped FLP launch ForeverVision, FLP helped me launch my ad agency, Park&Co.

Jerry from Quorum set in motion this whole chapter in my life. Only later did I realize he was looking out as much for my family as he was for my career when he slid that clandestine note under my nose in my stuffy office. And even later I learned from the mythology teachings of Joseph Campbell that when you follow your bliss, doors will open where there were only walls.

Pay attention to the threshold guardians that open doors for you, as Bill, Jerry, and Navaz did for me.

THE ROAD BACK

On March 1, 1995, I incorporated Park and Company Marketing Communications, Inc., and for the next 20 years operated as Park&Co. We grew from my solo act, working out of our 1930s carriage house in the backyard of our first home to 18 people working in a portion of the 10,600-square-foot building we purchased in 2003 in the heart of Phoenix's prestigious Arcadia district.

FLP was a client for 18 of those years, as we added local, regional, national, and international accounts, including Sky Harbor International Airport, Coca-Cola, Kiewit, and Chevron. And during that timespan I never once had a court-appointed process server show up in our driveway on a Sunday morning.

I was even named the Advertising Person of the Year by the Advertising Federation of Metro Phoenix in 2010. But I'm getting ahead of myself.

Business was good, until 2006.

Marketing and branding as I knew it wasn't working as it had. The paradigm was shifting. Our ad agency business was easy when brands owned the influence of mass media. All we had to worry about was creating effective advertising for TV, radio, print, outdoor, direct mail, events, promotions, and public relations. And there was no Yelp!

But the Internet democratized communications. The masses had become the media, and they took control of the bullhorn.

Clients started divvying up their accounts. Instead of one agency, they hired specialists to help them understand the new online world. We lost business. Plus, I had not effectively positioned Park&Co. Our agency was essentially a reflection of who I was back in the Petersen Communications days: a jack of all trades, a master of few. We did not have a differentiated offering that made our brand special. We looked like all of our competitors.

Our brand story was muddled. Our effectiveness diminished as we struggled to understand the Internet. And our journey to survive, let alone thrive, grew increasingly complex and cumbersome. We had become what we feared most: a commodity. A number.

NUMBer.

Then it got worse.

Do you recall where you were on September 15, 2008, the day Lehman Brothers collapsed, which triggered the global recession? I do. We were watching the calamity unfold online at the office. It was like reliving 9/11, only the tumbling World Trade Center buildings were metaphorically replaced with the devastating collapse of world trade organizations supposedly too big to fail. And this time the terrorists were us, the despicable men and women of Wall Street whose greed destroyed the only thing that will keep a society together: trust.

By November, our agency's income was slashed in half as our clients recoiled from the impact of the largest financial crisis since the Great Depression. I did what comes naturally in such a moment. I panicked.

It wasn't the full-blown flailing of arms and screaming like a lunatic before blindly running off a cliff into oblivion panic. No, mine was a slower churn of worry that led to the wrong decision of trying to land whatever business we could to keep us afloat. Instead of preserving our resources and directing our energies through a focused brand story to service a niche, we tried to be all things to all people, which of course meant we were nothing to everyone. I should've relied on the Five C's, Climb, Conserve, Communicate, Confess, and Comply. But now it felt like we were augering in.

RESURRECTION

Then I heard about a guy named Michael Gass. He is an ad agency business development guru. I reached out and expected a brash personality that typically befits a successful biz dev guy, especially in advertising. But what greeted me on our first call was the big Southern heart and pragmatic calm of a man from Birmingham, Alabama.

Michael had spent nearly 30 years developing new business for ad agencies the old fashioned way: cold calling and glad-handing. But he knew times had changed. He recognized the power of the Internet to attract new business long before most agency executives. His recipe was simple: Create a niche-driven blog that positions your agency as a leader in a specific market category, and then promote your wisdom through Twitter, Facebook, and LinkedIn. But to make the gymnastics of this communications floor exercise routine work, you had to first find the courage to have your brand stand for one — AND ONLY ONE — thing.

He didn't just profess a laser-focused brand position. He modeled it. Michael branded his new consultancy Fuel Lines, at fuelingnewbusiness.com, with a singular focus that quickly propelled him to the top of page one of Google for the term "Ad Agency New Business." Gass still dominates the market category of ad agency new business, helping hundreds of communications firms around the world grow because he clarified his brand story to amplify his impact and simplify his life.

He annoyingly stood for one friggin' thing: *Ad agency new business development online.* I say "annoyingly" because I felt like we were all over the place with our brand.

I was among Michael's first five clients in 2008. He flew out to Phoenix to spend the day with me to help refine the Park&Co brand story. Now, I know what you must be thinking. *You're a branding specialist. Couldn't you just do this for yourself?*

The short answer is no. Even Dr. Vo, my dentist, doesn't perform his own root canals.

What I've learned is that company leadership is too close to their own business, mired in their operational trenches, blinded by the competitive fog of war, to take a step back and accurately assess their brand position. They worry about becoming too specialized and losing out on ancillary business, when the opposite is actually true: The more you focus, the more you flourish.

Furthermore, they tend to talk about what they make, when their brand story is really about what they make *happen*. They're fixated on features and benefits. But what their audiences — customers, employees, and the communities they serve — really want are true stories about honest outcomes.

As I experienced with Gass, crafting your brand story requires an experienced, impartial outside observer with a proven program to help you see through the opaqueness of your imagined reality. Because, well, some have described their branding experience as something akin to a root canal. A necessary, painful evil. But it doesn't have to be. More about that in a minute.

I became embarrassingly aware of my own short-sightedness when Michael took me through his process in our conference room. He asked me to describe our greatest victories as an ad agency. Within these conquests he said we'd find our passions, our differentiated expertise.

I recounted our branding work that created the Water — Use It Wisely campaign in 1998. It grew to be the largest water conservation effort of its kind in North America, attracting more than 400 private and public entities to the program. After two decades, the award-winning campaign is still running today.

We reviewed our branding work for Goodwill of Central Arizona, which began in 2003 and grew the organization by more than 400 percent. We talked about how our success with environmental and social movements attracted advertising work for Resolution Copper, Maricopa County's Clean Air Campaign, and the Expect More Arizona education national NGO, among others.

Michael settled back in his chair and smiled at me.

"Well, it's obvious," he said.

"What is?" I asked.

"Your core focus at Park&Co."

"Huh?" I couldn't see what he was seeing.

"You are Arizona's 'green marketing' agency," he matter-of-factly said.

Michael pointed to the successes I was most proud of, which revolved around purpose-driven organizations. Each brand pursued environmental and social cause work. He said we weren't selling products and services, but promoting movements to activate behavior change for the good. And he suggested that our timing couldn't be better, because "Green" was becoming a thing.

But this was a market segment in its infancy. There were few agencies that owned this brand position. I knew his point was especially true in the conservative state of Arizona.

Michael's observation was so obvious that I felt like Bambi, with the branding truck barreling down on me. How could I have missed this core brand differentiator for Park&Co? I was simply too close to it, stunned by the high beams of a receding market, caught flat-footed before the accelerating online world, and nearly paralyzed in the intersection where these two market dynamics were colliding.

But I side-stepped calamity by clarifying our brand story. Only this was our first challenge. It didn't matter that we dialed in our focus if we couldn't get people to notice it and care. As I mentioned, two years earlier, in 2006, I realized the paradigm of advertising as I knew it had shifted. The masses had become the media. The competing cacophony of communication they created seemed impossible to rise above and be heard over.

RETURN WITH THE BOON

As luck would have it, this is when our son Parker became a freshman in the film program at Chapman University in Orange, California. He'd always loved making movies. In the third grade, he produced stop-action films with Lego men using our antiquated home video camera. He dived into the video program at Arcadia High School — the same school, incidentally, that Steven Spielberg attended. In his senior year, Parker made a film with his buddy Will Walsh that was featured in the annual Phoenix Film Festival.

Now at Chapman, I asked Parker to send me his books when he was done with them. (After all, we were paying for them.) I wanted to vet what Chapman taught these impressionable students to prepare them for the most competitive storytelling market in the world: Los Angeles. Plus, I wondered what Hollywood knew that I needed to know to become better at my craft of branding and communications.

Parker sent me textbooks, notes from important lectures, videos of compelling guest speakers, and a wealth of online resources to quench my curiosity. His study of the film world took me back to my own coursework at Wazzu. In addition to my communications degree, I also earned a Bachelor of Arts in music composition and theory. I found many similarities between the study of narrative structure and music composition. I was reminded that Mozart's sonata allegro form is based on three acts: exposition, development, and resolution.

This is when my storytelling mentor appeared, though he'd been dead for nearly 20 years.

Joseph Campbell was America's foremost mythologist. He defined a storytelling framework he called The Hero's Journey, or monomyth, as he described in his book *The Hero With a Thousand Faces*. I've seen The Hero's Journey detailed as everything from a 12-step story structure to a 19-step narrative form. At its core,

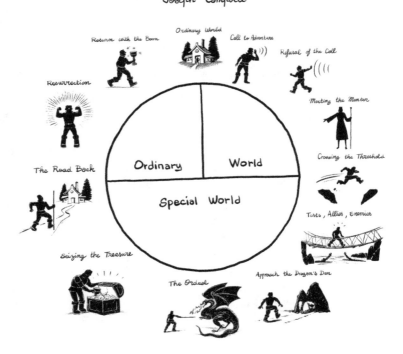

though, it is a story arc that covers the three acts of setup, problem, and resolution.

You will find similar constructs of this three-act structure in many forms. For instance, the humorist author Kurt Vonnegut, in his *The Shape of Stories* video on YouTube, describes what he considers the most popular story ever told: Man falls into a hole, man gets out of the hole. Setup: Before the hole. Problem: Falls into the hole. Resolution: He gets out of the hole.

Dr. Randy Olson, in his book *Houston, We Have a Narrative: Why Science Needs Story*, calls it the "And, But & Therefore" (ABT). The ABT comprises the same basal three-act story structure, based on agreement, contradiction, and consequence. More about the ABT and how you use it to develop your brand story in Chapter 4.

A story has a beginning, a middle, and an end, according to Aristotle.

It's important at this point in my story to establish in your mind this critical three-act structure. Because I've learned that story-telling is the most essential teaching device for our survival. We set the stage to create a context for the message we are trying to convey to our audience. Then we inflict conflict, contradiction, or complication to introduce the problem (man in a hole) that our hero (us, living vicariously through them) must overcome. Finally, we resolve the situation where we reveal the "Aha!" or teaching moment.

I love how Lisa Cron describes how our brains use story in her book *Wired for Story: The Writer's Guide to Using Brain Science to Hook Readers from the Very First Sentence*. She noticed that we live vicariously through the heroes in the stories we love so that we can try on their trouble just to see what we'd do in case it ever happens to us. And we get to experience their problems from the safety of our own easy chair.

The Hero's Journey is the larger story arc, based on the classic three-act structure, that is filled with plot points, narrative nuances, and assorted scenes that takes you on a journey of imagined reality to reveal a universal truth.

Blake Snyder, author of *Save the Cat: The Last Book on Screenwriting You'll Ever Need*, who sold more family-genre screenplays in Hollywood in the 1980s than any other writer, adapted The Hero's Journey to what he called the 15-beats of story. Snyder describes the kind of action that needs to take place at every juncture of a 110-page script, right down to the page number. By the way, Snyder was so fixated on story form that he claims a sellable screenplay has to be exactly 110 pages in length. You can remember that number because it's also the ideal weight of a jockey, 110 pounds. What a great metaphor he made to make his story point stick.

Perhaps the most obvious way for you to see The Hero's Journey in action is to watch the first *Star Wars* movie. As the story goes, director George Lucas was a disciple of Campbell's and wrote his senior thesis at USC's film school based on the monomyth template. It became the script to *Star Wars*. Use "The Hero's Journey" framework from page 228 as you watch the movie and see Luke Skywalker kick some Empire ass. Follow along with the infographic and you'll see the force of The Hero's Journey play out before you. Then watch movies like the *Indiana Jones* series, *The Matrix*, *O Brother, Where Art Thou?*, *Ready Player One*, *The Lego Movie*, or any Pixar flick. They all are based on this timeless narrative framework.

Blake Snyder's second book, *Save the Cat Goes to the Movies*, diagrams his 15 beats (his version of The Hero's Journey) in 40 movies. You can rent your favorites, follow along, and experience how the director is taking you by the hand through this epic narrative map.

If you're still an unbeliever, watch *The Wizard of Oz*. You will see Dorothy's trip down the yellow brick road back to Kansas as her Hero's Journey. But here's the magic: *The Wizard of Oz* was made in 1939, long before Campbell had identified and revealed the Hero's Journey structure. Yet it follows it exactly. In fact, this narrative form first appeared in 2100 BC in *The Epic of Gilgamesh*. Greek poet Homer followed the form in his epics *The Iliad* and *The Odyssey*. The Hero's Journey stands the test of time because it is *the* primal archetype or narrative framework that is embedded in our unconscious. We humans enjoy these stories because they are mirrors to how we experience life.

Do you get it now? You, me, and everyone are all on our own Hero's Journey. That's what I realized with my virtual Chapman film school classes.

In 1985, Hollywood story analyst Christopher Vogler wrote a memo to his bosses at Disney titled "A Practical Guide to Joseph Campbell's The Hero with a Thousand Faces." He realized that most of Hollywood's major hits resembled Campbell's monomyth, but in varying ways. Screenwriters innately knew the structure, but most weren't intentionally following it when writing their movies. Yet, the big movie hits proved that this story structure worked.

Vogler figured Disney could produce more hits than the other studios if they became intentional about following the Hero's Journey with their story development. The memo was leaked and soon it was the talk of Hollywood. It also prompted Vogler to write *The Writer's Journey: Mythic Structure for Writers*, which is now in its third edition. His seminal book details how writers can be guided by The Hero's Journey to craft compelling stories. But he takes it even deeper:

"I came looking for the design principle of storytelling, but on the road I found something more: a set of principles for living. I came to believe that the Hero's Journey is nothing less than a handbook of life, a complete instruction manual in the art of being human."

—Christopher Vogler, *The Writer's Journey.*

Here is a quick Hero's Journey primer using *The Wizard of Oz*, *Star Wars*, and my own story from the beginning of this book. Granted, my tale isn't as epic as Dorothy's or Luke's, but it absolutely follows the same primal pattern to narrative reflecting the fact that story mirrors life.

ACT I: SEPARATION

1. ORDINARY WORLD

You get introduced to the hero in their ordinary world to set the stage for the story and the contrasting world the hero must navigate ahead. Dorothy was a bored farm girl in a monochromatic Kansas before a tornado sweeps her into the colorful world of Oz. Luke

Skywalker was a bored farm boy on Tatooine before the murder of his aunt and uncle sweeps him into vanquishing the Empire.

I was a bored ad guy toiling in a fallow job in the farmlands of Buckeye, Arizona, before a headhunter sweeps me into the new international world of a Chinese-owned electronics direct seller.

2. CALL TO ADVENTURE

The hero is presented with a problem, a challenge, or an adventure. Dorothy runs away from her aunt and uncle's farmhouse to save her dog Toto from being put down by that nasty neighbor, Miss Almira Gulch, which leaves her vulnerable to a coming tornado. In *Star Wars*, Luke is asked by Obi-Wan Kenobi to join the quest following Princess Leia's holographic visit.

My Call to Adventure was a little pink note on my desk that said a stranger by the name of Bill Franquemont had called. OK, so it's not a tornado or holographic appearance by a princess, but it serves the same function in my journey: the mentor/herald has arrived.

3. REFUSAL OF THE CALL

As with all epic adventures that come our way, we're initially reluctant to take that first step because we face the fear of the unknown. A concussed Dorothy, upon awakening in Oz, is surrounded by Munchkins and pushes back on her calling to follow the yellow brick road. In *Star Wars*, Luke refuses Obi-Wan's call to adventure, and returns to his aunt and uncle's farmhouse (sound familiar?). But they've been toasted by the Emperor's stormtroopers.

My refusal of the call came when I nearly tossed Bill's message into the trash. And then I was dismissive of my abilities on our first phone call. A shrink might call this self-sabotage to deal with my fear of the unknown.

4. MEETING THE MENTOR

This is where the Merlin-like character who is the hero's mentor comes in. Dorothy's guide was Glinda, the fairy godmother–like good witch of the North who gifts her the ruby red slippers and their magical powers. Obi-Wan gives Luke his father's lightsaber and introduces him to The Force.

My headhunter mentor, Bill, coaches me on how to present myself for the Quorum job and imbues me with the magic of self-confidence when he says, "I think this is going to happen for you."

5. CROSSING THE THRESHOLD

You experience the hero fully entering the special world of the story for the first time. "We're not in Kansas anymore." Dorothy and Toto set out on the yellow brick road. Luke takes his Landspeeder with

Obi-Wan, R2D2, and C3PO to the spaceport town of Mos Eisley, the "Wretched hive of scum and villainy," according to Obi-Wan.

I set foot into the immaculate headquarters of Quorum International, interview with Lynn Harper, and accept the position on the spot. "I'm not in Buckeye anymore."

6. TESTS, ALLIES, ENEMIES

What journey is complete without the allies and enemies you encounter in your new special world? Plus, the hero must pass certain tests and challenges for his/her training. Dorothy locks arms with the Cowardly Lion, Tin Man, and Scarecrow, and off they go to be tested by the Wicked Witch of the West. "I'll get you, my pretty, and your little dog, too," she screeches. The Mos Eisley cantina is where Luke forges a crucial alliance with Han Solo and the start of an important enmity with Jabba the Hutt.

The Quorum boardroom on my first day was where I met my allies and the shadowy sycophants who would sabotage my progress. I was tested immediately with their branding and marketing demands.

7. APPROACH THE DRAGON'S DEN

The journey takes your hero to a dangerous place where the object of the quest is hidden. Dorothy has to confront the wicked witch in her own dark castle, replete with creepy flying monkeys. The Empire's tractor beam sucks Luke and his allies into the Death Star, where they must rescue Princess Leia.

For me it was the first meeting with Raymond Hung. Although he was a pleasant CEO, I didn't trust him. My Jabba the Hutt? Perhaps. In truth, my innermost cave was more cerebral—dealing with my own uncertainties about the efficacy of my employment and the company—than it was a physical place. That being said, I was painfully aware of the mythical good and bad dragons of fêng shui constantly circling about, looking to promote or devour me in the mystical world of Quorum.

ACT II A: DESCENT

8. THE ORDEAL

The hero endures the supreme ordeal. He/she reaches rock bottom, facing possible death. This is the black moment as you (as the audience) stand outside the cave, waiting for the victor to emerge. Dorothy must kill the wicked witch and bring her broom to Oz to prove it. In *Star Wars*, Luke's harrowing moment was in the bowels of the Death Star. He and his valiant crew are trapped in the trash compactor when a serpent drags Luke under the garbage gazpacho and you're waiting for the bubbles to stop.

My supreme ordeal was when Raymond's henchman, Vincent, visits me and strongly suggests that I get oral reconstruction for the good of the Empire, or else.

ACT II B: INITIATION

9. SEIZING THE TREASURE

Your hero survives death, bests the dragon, slays the Minotaur, and takes possession of the treasure he/she seeks. Dorothy dissolves the wicked witch and returns to the Emerald City with her broom. The broom represents a sword of sorts required for the wizard to return her home. Luke escapes the belly of the Death Star and becomes more worldly for the experience. He levels up to become a pilot for the rebel fleet — what he always wanted.

The absurdity of Vincent's request combined with the lunacy of a constantly changing leadership team of unqualified, greedy individuals, in my estimation, created a kind of courage in me that set my next chapter in motion. I realized that I had gained the experience, wisdom, and people skills required to venture out on my own. And as the Cowardly Lion roared: "The Courage" — or so I thought.

10. THE ROAD BACK

Right when you think your hero is out of the woods, the story turns for the worse. You know the feeling. The universe always punches you in the nose just to see how bad you really want your quest. Dorothy, after all of her travails, unmasks the wizard as a fraud and thinks she'll never make it home. The road back is also captured in chase scenes, as when Luke and friends are escaping from the Death Star with Princess Leia and the plans that will bring down Darth Vader.

Although I was emboldened to start my own agency, the reality of supporting Michele and our three kids tested my ambition. Before I could make a decision to leave, a plague of layoffs descended on Quorum. Sales were down and scores of employees

were let go. Each department took major hits, including mine. You could feel the despair of job losses slowly encroaching over the company like the shadow of a gleeful bad dragon gliding above. This leads to another dark night of the soul—the darkest before the dawn. In my case, the threshold guardian of Jerry arrived, much as Bill Franquemont did earlier in my journey, to offer a new call to adventure.

11. RESURRECTION

The hero emerges from the special world, transformed by his/her experience. Dorothy realizes that all she has to do to return home is to believe she can. She taps her magic slippers together and recites, "There's no place like home." Luke repels urges from the dark side and his own self-doubt to blow up the Death Star, Fris-beeing Darth Vader into the cold void of space.

My resurrection came when, following all my trials at both Petersen Communications and Quorum, I landed Forever Living Products as my first client. As I just wrote that sentence, something struck me: I realize what an apt name Forever Living Products is for the resurrection stage of my career's Hero's Journey. Oh, the universe!

ACT III: RETURN

12. RETURN WITH THE BOON

Your hero returns to their ordinary world, but not empty-handed. He or she brings back the elixir, treasure, or some lesson from their experience in the special world. Dorothy returned to Kansas with the appreciation that there is no place like home, and we all have it within us to center ourselves on what is truly important. Luke has vanquished the Empire, at least for now, and metaphorically we learn that a positive force will overcome a negative one.

I returned from nearly becoming a corporate drone in a high-flying international company to the independence of running my own ad agency. My elixir was the experience, knowledge, and courage I gained by working in a fast-paced global organization that created its own mythology. My ad agency, which I ran for 20 years, launched in 1995.

I'm a believer. The monomyth has become my storytelling religion. I'm Bilbo Baggins and The Hero's Journey is the irresistible mystical ring, but with a more positive motivation. I was drawn to the special world of Hollywood out of desperation because branding and advertising as I knew it stopped working in my ordinary world. I felt that this primal story structure was waiting for me. Once I found The Hero's Journey, I recognized it for what it is: a time-tested treasure map for communicators.

And here's the best part. While the mile markers for each step of The Hero's Journey remain relatively the same, the formula can be crafted in innumerable ways, limited only by the imagination of the storyteller.

Vogler underscores this in The Writer's Journey: "I'm retelling the hero myth in my own way, and you should feel free to do the same. Every storyteller bends the mythic pattern to his or her own purpose or the needs of a particular culture."

This is when I decided to map The Hero's Journey to branding and business. I used the core story elements but removed the more nuanced steps that work in movies. They are not needed in brand strategy. The following diagram shows you its evolution from Campbell to Vogler to The Story Cycle System.

The Hero's Journey	The Writer's Journey	Story Cycle System
Departure, Separation	**Act I**	**Setup**
World of Common Day	Ordinary World	Backstory
Call to Adventure	Call to Adventure	Heroes
Refusal of the Call	Refusal of the Call	Stakes
Supernatural Aid	Meeting with the Mentor	
Crossing the First Threshold	Crossing the First Threshold	Disruption
Belly of the Whale		
Descent, Initiation, Penetration	**Act II**	**Problem**
Road of Trials	Tests, Allies, Enemies	Antagonists
	Approach to the Innermost Cave	
Meeting with the Goddess		Ordeal
Woman as Temptress		
Atonement with the Father		
Apotheosis		Mentor
The Ultimate Boon	Reward	Journey
Return	**Act III**	**Resoltuion**
Refusal of the Return	The Road Back	Victory
The Magic Flight		
Rescue from Within		
Crossing the Threshold		
Return		
Master of the Two Worlds	Resurrection	
Freedom to Live	Return with the Elixir	Ritual

THE BOON OF THE STORY CYCLE SYSTEM

OK, if your head is spinning, no worries. Campbell's 19-step outline struck me that way, too. I feel like a greenhorn cop picking through Sherlock Holmes's cerebral forensic files to solve a case. That's why I prefer Vogler's simpler 12-step journey. It outlines the 12 story elements we all are used to seeing in the movies we love. Even though you may have not known of The Hero's Journey until now, your subconscious sure did. Does it somehow seem familiar to you?

THE STORY CYCLE SYSTEM™

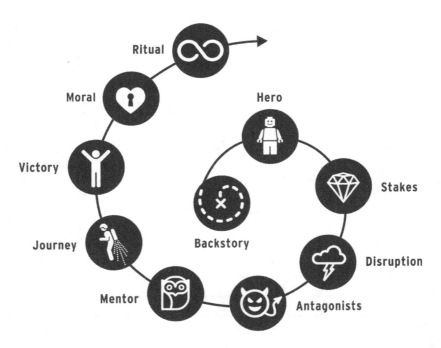

I've simplified the journey even more in the Story Cycle System. I mapped the 10 invaluable steps exactly to branding and business communications, while still holding true to the core anchors that make every story work. Let me do the myth for you:

ACT I: SETUP

BACKSTORY = POSITION STATEMENT: Set the stage for your brand story by first defining your #1 position in the market. What do you do differently, and therefore better, than anyone else? This helps you focus your brand offering for deliberate growth.

HEROES = TARGET AUDIENCES: Despite popular belief, you and your brand are *not* the hero of this journey. Your customers are. So as you're crafting your brand story strategy, prioritize your top three audiences and place them at the center of your brand story to understand your customers for faster growth.

By the way, this is a good time to tell you that I use the terms "customers" and "audiences" interchangeably because I feel that whenever you're telling a story you're trying to sell something to someone—a product, service, internal initiative, financing of your operation, or a promotion.

STAKES = CUSTOMER WISHES AND WANTS: Determine what your audiences want physically and philosophically so you connect with your audiences on their terms for greater growth. I think of their motivations captured in these three areas: What do they *wish* to feel emotionally; what do they *want* physically to have to make that happen; and what is their *will* to act to make that happen? Because—make no mistake—brands are in the wish-granting business.

ACT II: PROBLEM

DISRUPTION = UNIQUE VALUE PROPOSITION: Craft your Unique Value Proposition that articulates why you are the most timely, urgent, and relevant offering in your market. Get this right and your brand story will help you become the clear category leader to accelerate your growth.

ANTAGONISTS = MARKET DYNAMICS: Pinpoint the negative market dynamics that test the performance and delivery of your offering. By getting clear on how you help your customers overcome something to get what they want, you increase your importance in their hearts and minds to advance your growth.

MENTOR = BRAND PERSONALITY: Since stories make us human, doesn't it make sense to use storytelling to humanize your brand? Get out of your logical head and own your brand's emotional promise, spiritual gift, and unique personality to create deeper meaning with your customers. This is the first step to building a lasting brand bond with your audiences for accountable growth.

JOURNEY = CUSTOMER ENGAGEMENT: Map the journey your customers will undertake with you from brand awareness to adoption to appreciation. This will help you understand their journey, empathize with their wishes and wants, and captivate your audiences to amplify your growth.

ACT III: RESOLUTION

VICTORY = INITIAL BRAND BONDING: Plan your customers' success milestones and how you'll be there for them. Celebrate even their smallest victories to propel your brand story forward and sustain your growth.

THE MORAL = CONNECTING TO A HIGHER PURPOSE: Declare your brand promise: why you exist beyond making money. When you and your purpose-driven brand stand for something greater, you will amplify your impact through meaningful growth.

RITUAL = REPEAT BUSINESS AND WOM: Design ways for your audience to ritualize the use of your product or service to build repeat business. Plus, this is the point when you'll encourage your customers to share their experiences and your story with their communities. In doing so, you will simplify your sales through word-of-mouth marketing to compound your growth.

Now you have witnessed how the Story Cycle System came to life in my life. I hope you will use my journey in storytelling to help you on yours. Because what I've learned along the way is that my calling is to help you excel through the stories you tell.

Story on, my friend.

Glossary of Brand Storytelling Terms

Adoption Curve Scale: A sociological model marketers use to anticipate and describe the acceptance of a new product or innovation, according to the demographic and psychological characteristics of defined adopter groups we call customers or audiences. Use this guide to build greater understanding of your audience's predilection for buying.

Aha!: That eureka moment when you can say, "By George, I've got it!" These are the moments you want to strive for and share with your audiences in the stories you tell.

And, But & Therefore (ABT) narrative framework: A fundamental three-part story structure of Setup, Problem, and Resolution introduced to me by Dr. Randy Olson that I call the "DNA of Story": the narrative foundation for a crystal-clear message.

Ancients: The first Greek storytellers we know of, such as Homer, Sophocles, Plato, Aristotle, Euclid, Archimedes, and the rest of the sandaled and robed gang. They set the stage for all of humanity's storytelling structure.

Antagonists: Any obstacles or entities, animate or inanimate, that pose a real or imagined threat to the progress of your journey. Capitalize on these opposing forces to make your offering all the more attractive to those you help. *Nicorette: Make quitting suck less.*

Appreciating asset: Something of value—a person, property, money or a skill—that grows in value the more you nurture it. For instance, the ability to tell a story is the most valuable yet under-utilized business asset in your leadership communications arsenal.

Archetype: A defined personality expressing the unique character traits that humanize your brand. Select from the 12 universal archetypes as defined by Swiss psychologist Carl Jung to find your unique brand personality. *Virginia is for lovers.*

Audience: The person or group of people you are trying to connect with through the stories you tell. This book interchanges *audience* and *customers*, because when you think about it, every story attempts to *sell* a particular point of view.

Backstory: Creating the context for your story by introducing the theme, character(s), and setting. With your brand story strategy, sharing your origin story by describing where you have been, where you are now, and where you want to go is essential to launching your brand narrative.

Boredom: The ultimate villain we must all face as brand storytellers.

Brand: It's not your logo. It's not your tagline. It's not your website. Your brand is what you stand for philosophically in the hearts and minds of your customers—the stories they tell about you when you're not in the room.

Brandthropology: The unearthing of the true meaning and purpose for why your brand exists in the world. Your discoveries reveal the essential storytelling elements you use to become an instrumental contributor to the societies and cultures you serve.

Brand adoption: That critical moment when a new customer buys your product or service.

Brand appreciation: When your customers thank you by buying more and sending their friends.

Brand awareness: That moment when your prospect looks at your offering and thinks, *Hmmm, that's interesting.*

Brand essence: Amazon founder Jeff Bezos summed up brand essence when he said, "Your brand is what other people say about you when you're not in the room."

Brand descriptors: Vivid words that capture the essence of your brand. You use these nouns and adjectives in the "OOOh exercise" when you identify nine words that describe your Organization, Offering, and Outcomes. The descriptors begin to define your customer's core emotional experience with your brand. *GE: Imagination at work.*

Brand promise: What your customers experience emotionally when they interact with your brand. *Zappos: Delivering happiness. L'Oréal: Because You're Worth It. 3M: Innovation.*

Brand gift: The intrinsic gift your customers receive that elevates their experience with your brand. Remember, it's not what you make but what you make happen that is the gift delivered in your brand journey. *Booking.com: Booking.yeah. Apple: Think Different. De Beers: A diamond is forever. Disneyland: The Happiest Place on Earth.*

Brand personality: The culmination of the authentic character traits expressed through your brand storytelling based on one of the 12 universal personality archetypes. *Harley-Davidson: American by Birth. Rebel by Choice. GoPro: Be a Hero. Forbes Magazine: Capitalist Tool.*

Brand purpose: Why you exist, beyond just making money, to help people; it is your higher purpose that attracts and retains top talent and the best customers. *Love. It's what makes a Subaru a Subaru. The New York Times: All the news that's fit to print. SoulCycle: Find Your Soul. TOMS: One for One. Dove: Real Beauty.*

Brand story: The sequence of events you share, told through the voice of your authentic brand personality, that demonstrate how your product or service is the solution to the problem your customer wants to remedy so they can fulfill their wish for something more in their life. *Airbnb: Belong Anywhere. Nike: Just do it. What happens in Vegas stays in Vegas.*

Brand story strategy: The discovery, planning, development, and strategic telling of your overarching brand narrative to carve out your unique place in the world.

Category: The specific area in your market that you serve.

Crevasses: Those nasty gaps in performance that you close within your brand and the breaches you bridge for your customers to help them get what they want out of life.

Chassis: The narrative undercarriage your story is built upon.

Commodity: A ubiquitous product or service with such little emotional meaning that customers gravitate to the low-price leader and attach little to no brand loyalty. A commodity is brand boredom's sidekick.

Competition: Any market force, animate or inanimate, that competes for the attention of your customers.

Customer: The buyer or purchaser of or audience for your product, service, or brand story.

Disruption: The critical catalyzing market event that upends your customer's status quo and sets the stage for how your brand is here to help them on their journey.

Early adopter: An early customer who buys into your product or service and one you can rely on to provide credible feedback on the quality of your offering.

Early majority: The larger population of customers who follow the innovators and early adopters on the Adoption Curve Scale.

Eeem-pa-thy: Taxi cabbie Greek for "Empathy," the universal element for all storytelling.

Epic: A condition or achievement that is often sought after but seldom accomplished. Yet, your success comes in its quest.

Eureka: That sudden witnessing of a truth revealed by a small story or anecdote. Greek mathematician Archimedes coined the term *Eureka*, which means "I found it!"

Evangelizing: Customers whose wishes you have fulfilled so well that they make your story their story and share it with their world.

Five primal elements of story: The story elements — time, location, character, action/surprise, and Aha! moment — that make up a powerful anecdote told for big impact.

Flow: In positive psychology as defined by Mihaly Csikszentmihalyi, a flow state — or being "in the zone" — is the mental state of operation in which a person performing an activity is fully immersed in a feeling of energized focus, full involvement, and enjoyment in the process of the activity. A well-told story is one of the most effective triggers to transport your audience into the state of flow.

Fog: The blind spots — what you don't know you don't know — that your brand must clear up in how it sees the market, customers, and operations. You must also illuminate the blind spots your customers have about you and your offering. Fog is one of the three categories of obstacles and antagonists, also including villains and crevasses, confronted in Step 5 of the Story Cycle System™.

FOMO: The acronym meme for *Fear of Missing Out* popularized on social media.

FOME: My street-slang acronym meaning For Me!

Guide: Also known as the mentor, meaning your brand's role played in the Story Cycle System.

Guru: Someone an audience deems as all-knowing, regardless of their level of achievement in their subject matter.

Happy H: One of the most powerful examples of brand essence that I know.

Herald: An official messenger bringing news, or a person or thing viewed as a sign that something is about to happen.

Hero: Your customer or audience.

Hero's Journey: A popular storytelling template popularized by American mythologist Joseph Campbell, also called the Monomyth, that involves a hero who goes on an adventure, experiences a decisive crisis, wins a victory, and returns home changed or transformed.

***Homo sapiens*:** Latin for "wise man," *Homo sapiens* is the primate species to which we storytelling apes belong.

Laggard: Like flip phone users, laggards are the last audience in the Adoption Curve Scale who see any value in progressing with society regarding buying your stuff. Some frustrated CMOs like to invoke history by calling laggards *Luddites*.

Inciting incident: A Hollywood storytelling term for when a significant event happens that changes the fortunes of the central protagonist in a story. Step 4 of the Story Cycle System, "Disruption," is based on the concept of the inciting incident where something has changed in your customer's world to make your product or service their most timely and relevant option.

Industry: The most generalized term for the area of the market your brand services.

Innovator: The first customer segment on the Adoption Curve Scale and the quickest audience to buy into your brand story.

Journey: The mapped highs and lows of the customer experience, from brand awareness to brand adoption to brand appreciation, with the ultimate goal of brand evangelism leading to word-of-mouth (WOM) marketing and repeat business.

Late majority: Skeptical shoppers on the Adoption Curve Scale who wait for an innovation to be accepted by a majority of customers and the price to have dropped.

Mage: A magician or learned person.

Market: A specific customer base or audience segment that you seek to capture through your brand storytelling.

Maslow's hierarchy of needs: A motivational theory in psychology comprising a five-tier model of human needs — physiological, safety, belonging and love, esteem, and self-actualization — that marketers can be guided by when crafting their brand stories.

Moral: Step 9 of the Story Cycle System, where your shared beliefs and values coalesce to determine your brand purpose: why your brand exists beyond making money.

Mentor: You, as the brand, helping your customers get what they desire on their journey.

Metaphor: A powerful storytelling technique that connects two different concepts by revealing their hidden similarities to create a third, more compelling idea. For instance, storytelling is the Velcro® of collaboration that hooks two worlds together for a strong cooperative bond.

Meta: A creative work referring to itself or to the conventions of its genre; self-referential.

Mission: The decided quest of an organization and the determined steps required to accomplish its goals. Often confused with a brand's "vision" (see below) for lack of clarity in its storytelling.

Monomyth: Greek, referring to The Hero's Journey.

Narrative intuition: An innate understanding of the concept of contradiction and consequence in storytelling that the teller uses to ignite the curiosity of their audience.

Navel gazing: When brands think their story is about themselves and not their customers—i.e., selfies.

Negativity bias: The human predisposition to react to negative stimuli with more fervor than positive stimuli.

Nemesis: The Greek goddess who enacts retribution against those who succumb to hubris. In modern terms, nemesis is the inescapable agent of someone's or something's downfall. The lack of authenticity with Volkswagen's vehicle emissions reporting was its nemesis.

Obstacle: A barrier, real or imagined, that confronts you in your journey, but when hurdled contributes to the strength of your offering. *The United States Postal Service: Neither snow nor rain nor heat nor gloom of night stays these couriers from the swift completion of their appointed rounds.*

Obfuscation: Just say the word out loud. It's practically an onomatopoeia (the formation of a word from a sound associated with what is named). Obfuscation is the act of making something obscure, unclear, or unintelligible.

OOOh exercise: A process for helping you find your brand essence by defining nine words that describe your organization, offering, and outcomes.

Offering: The product or service you provide to the world.

Organization: The sum of your people, operations, and locations.

Outcomes: What you make happen in the lives of the people you serve.

Overstand: A term that emerged from the hip-hop culture that means to comprehend a thing itself *and* to have knowledge of why it is the way it is and of its place or role in the grand scheme of things.

Participation trophy: A totem that celebrates bad outcomes from good intentions.

Persona: The description of the core demographic and psychographic characteristics of a particular audience.

Position statement: Your declaration of what your brand does functionally different and therefore better than your competition. This statement is your first step out of the primordial muck of commoditization where so many organisms and organizations never evolve and then perish.

Primal: Relating to an early stage of evolutionary development; primeval. *"Storytelling is primal to what has made Homo sapiens the most aggressive invasive species known to man."*

Protagonist: The central character or hero in the story.

Relevance: The meaning you've manufactured through your storytelling that establishes your brand's connectedness to or appropriateness for your customer.

Ritual: Incorporating the ongoing use of your product or service into your customer's life.

ROI: The acronym for the financial term *Return on Investment.*

Semiotician: An expert in semiotics, a general philosophical theory of signs and symbols that deals with their function in both artificially constructed and natural languages and comprises syntactics, semantics, and pragmatics.

Scent-of-thrift: The odorous greeting of a second-hand store.

Shareholders: Investors typically driven by short-term financial gain rather than longer-term wealth, who therefore shortcut the power of brand narratives with marketing puffery.

Soft skills: Interpersonal skills of time management, networking, teamwork, creative thinking, and conflict resolution that flourish with business storytelling.

Specialty: The definition of what your brand is specifically good at providing in your market category.

Stakeholders: Anyone — including staff, employees, vendors, shareholders, customers, and community members — who has a financial or existential stake in your organization's success and with whom you need to gain buy-in and alignment with your brand story.

Status quo tipping: The inciting incident or disruption you cause that knocks people out of their comfort zone to propel your engagement with them forward.

Story artists: Guests on the Business of Story podcast who share their wit and wisdom on myriad approaches to brand and business storytelling to help listeners craft and tell compelling stories that sell.

Story Cycle System™: The proprietary 10-step brand story strategy creation process with the goal of clarifying your story to amplify your impact and simplify your life.

Story dynamics: The inimitable organizing force of story to advance society.

Story eureka: The excitement experienced when a universal truth is revealed through a well-told story.

Story scaling: The exponential impact a good story can make on humanity through the quality of its telling. *"I believe that this nation should commit itself to achieving the goal, before this decade is out, of landing a man on the moon and returning him safely to the Earth."* —JFK

#1 specialty: The one thing you do differently, and therefore better, than your competition as expressed in your brand position statement.

Stakes: What your customers wish to feel emotionally and want to purchase physically from your brand to achieve their goals.

Success scenes: Small victory milestones to be celebrated with your customers along their journey with your brand to scale your story through repeat business and word-of-mouth marketing.

Sustainability: That healthy place where efficiency creates prosperity for all players.

SWOT analysis: The study of organizational strengths, weaknesses, opportunities, and threats.

Threshold guardians: The forces that stand in the way at important turning points in a story, including jealous enemies, professional gatekeepers, or even your own fears and doubts.

Trend spotters: People who anticipate where social norms and sensibilities are emerging.

Trigger: The expression of a thought or action that ignites an idea to prompt a behavior.

Unique Value Proposition (UVP): A statement that describes why your brand is the most timely and relevant option for your customer.

Want: The seeking of a physical product or service to fulfill your customer's emotional wish. *"I want an Apple computer because it expresses my creative individuality."*

Will: The motivation to act often triggered by a compelling insight or need as communicated through your brand storytelling. *Dollar Shave Club: Shave time. Shave money. FedEx: When it absolutely, positively has to be there overnight. EF Hutton: When EF Hutton talks, people listen.*

Wish: How a customer hopes to feel after the purchase of a product or service to help them improve something in their life. *Coke: Open Happiness. Disneyland: The Happiest Place on Earth. Hallmark: When you care to send the very best.*

Vendors: Those important suppliers who support your organization and perform as an extension of your overall brand purpose.

Villains: The competitive forces, animate or inanimate, real or imagined, that stand to thwart your progress.

Vision: How an organization sees its purpose in the world; often confused with "mission" unless you've got your brand story straight.

Acknowledgments

Once upon a time, in 1987, Michele married me. I'm the luckiest.

Ten years ago, this book began to take shape. My first manuscript was completed in 2014 and my dear wife was so kind to trudge through my attempt at making sense of the art of storytelling. She was called "Miss Spell" in her ad agency days for her wicked proof-reading skills with the eyes of a diamond cutter.

But I didn't publish that first go. It felt to me somewhat naïve. I wanted greater proof that the Story Cycle System™ not only builds purpose-driven brands, but helps its apprentices become more compelling and confident communicators in the process. So I spent the last six years consulting, speaking, coaching, and teaching around the world on the applied science and bewitchery of story-telling in business. I've spent the last 16 months filling this book with real-world anecdotes and revising how you can apply this proven storytelling process to excel through the stories you tell.

Poor Michele. Not only did she lose me for hours/days/weeks in the rewrite, but she gallantly proofed the entire manuscript. Again!

For her love, encouragement, understanding, and gentle (well, sometimes not-so-gentle) advice about certain stories I should perhaps reconsider sharing, I am forever beholden. I couldn't be blessed with a more loving copy-editor-in-CHIEF. To our daughter, Corbin, and sons Parker and Caedon: thank you for the laughs you bring and the stories you share every time we gather. Your individual insights on growing up, building careers, starting your own families, and being your authentic selves are invaluable. You are the mentors, sidekicks, and threshold guardians (and occasional shape shifters) on my journey. You teach me something new each time we talk.

Thank you . . .

To Luis Medina, the most talented creative director I have ever worked with, thank you for challenging me to find novel and daring ways to express my thoughts and creativity.

To Pete Walsh, an extraordinary leadership coach and my Arizona pal who loves life as much as I do, thank you for your continued support and pushing me to new levels of personal and professional success. You have helped me excel through the stories I tell myself.

To Kent Sorsky, for your expert editing and publishing guidance. You've reined me in, clarified my instruction, and sculpted my narrative while preserving my voice.

To my Northwest childhood buddies Paul Herrick, Dan O'Boyle, Mike Martin, Rick Paynter, and A.J. Gollofon. You have instigated some of my favorite escapades and shaped me as the storyteller I am today.

To Dan, Melody, Tom, Steve, Chris, and Mike, my siblings, who from day one have helped me not only find my place in our sprawling family, but in the world.

To my mom, Pat, for instilling in me my love of music and the no-nonsense grit to persevere through thick and through thin. And to my dad, Keith (also known as K.C., Uncle Skeeter, and Chief), who has taken his stories above and beyond. I am eternally grateful for his Norwegian storyteller's sense of humor, his Viking's quest for adventure, and the honest work ethic he endowed in each of us that makes it all work. I am especially thankful for the best piece of advice he ever gave me. I asked him, the day before Michele and I got married, what the secret was to family success?

He said, "Just give them your time and your love."

This happy bit of advice extends beyond family. It's also how I crafted this book.

Thank *you* for choosing it.

Index

ABOUT THE AUTHOR

"Since stories make us human, why not use stories to humanize your brand?"

Park Howell is a 35-year veteran of the branding arts, running his own advertising agency, Park&Co, for 20 of those years in Phoenix, Arizona. He was the professor of storytelling for the Executive Masters of Sustainability Leadership at Arizona State University for five years, helping international executives become more confident and compelling communicators to advance their social initiatives faster.

Park now consults, teaches, coaches, and speaks internationally on the applied science and bewitchery of business storytelling. Leaders and marketers for such organizations as Coca-Cola, United States Air Force, Wynn Resorts, McCormicks, American Express, Hilton, Cummins, and Dell Technologies have learned his narrative frameworks and Story Cycle System™ to craft and tell compelling stories that sell.

He began honing his craft of brand and business storytelling at Washington State University, where he earned degrees in communications and music composition and theory. Park's goal as the world's most industrious storyteller is to help leaders of purpose-driven brands excel through the stories they tell.

CPSIA information can be obtained
at www.ICGtesting.com
Printed in the USA
BVHW071757040221
599249BV00006B/1406